To: Wes &
Friends Indeed. Thanks
for welcoming us to
Georgia -- our new Home.

Lonie Boyd
September 5, 2007

Kentucky Boy—The Top First-Grader

Louie Boyd, 1963.

Kentucky Boy—
The Top First-Grader

Including a Record of the Boyd family from 1807

LOUIS J. BOYD

ISBN: 0-9778715-0-9 (cloth : alk. paper)

Table of Contents

❦ Preface ❧

This is for the Grandchildren . . .
and for their Grandchildren.

The greatest legacy we can leave our children is sweet memories. About memories it has been said: "When a person dies, a whole library closes;" "memories are a paradise from which no one can be evicted;" or "memories are God's gift of roses in winter."

The South is keen on family stories. It is important to be reminded what's important, like memories about people we loved or things that happened to us—things we can laugh about or shed a few tears about. Everyone should look back at some time and reflect on the turning points in life—the highs and the lows. One can never predict ahead the turning points or "God Points," but many are clearly in focus later.

It is indeed a common human characteristic to look back on our ancestors with reverence and awe. Yet, we know that we have not inherited the earth from our Grandparents—we too shall pass, so we are simply borrowing it from our Grandchildren.

Certainly each generation is shaped by its own experience. Being the son of Depression-era parents and sharing my first 18 years with them had a profound effect on me. As a youngster, hard work was the order of the day. We learned early that there was no free lunch and anything gift-wrapped was a rarity. Early in the Great Depression, which lasted from 1929 to 1940, President Franklin Roosevelt declared that one-third of the 124 million Americans were "ill-fed, ill-housed and ill-clothed." The economic conditions and standard of living in rural America during those years were certainly comparable to the "Less Developed Countries" across the world that many Americans learned about following World War II.

So I urge you not to be too disappointed in the lack of adaptation to the modern society by someone who is 40 to 60 years older. Most previous generations have been there, too. My parents had an eighth grade education which was standard for the day. My Grandfather Boyd never had a bank account, never drove a car, never had a telephone, electricity, running water, nor an indoor bathroom. In my early years, especially the teen years, I was ashamed that they didn't adapt to the meager but new world that I was discovering. Yet, maturity has generated a whole new understanding and appreciation for my ancestors who brought forth an environment that I could enjoy so immensely.

History is usually written by the winners, perhaps because they are the survivors. However, I prefer the definition of History as "His Story," which is mainly a recording of happenings and remembrances over the vast portion of a lifetime.

Hopefully, this compilation is not a constant barrage of "Now in my day, all we had to eat was . . ."—or, "we didn't have . . ." Undoubtedly, I was guilty of such when our children were small in the early 1960s and living what seemed to be the affluent life. However, that is far from the purpose of this writing. I feel that life is precious, and in today's uprooted and scattered society memories can help maintain family ties, traditions, and values.

As You Go Along Your Journey:

Develop and nurture a good attitude.

Match that attitude with keen intellect and strong work ethic.

See the good in people and places, while others may see only the bad.

Don't allow wars or depressions to blind you to the deep and abiding goodness of people.

Observe carefully what is going on around you.

Ever be cognizant of the needs of others.

Remember that people come and then they go, but, find and hold that which endures and stands forever to give continuity, direction, identity, and purpose.

Cherish Precious Memories—How They Linger.

❧ Introduction ❧

"History is a block of cement, and some carry it around and are weighted down by it, but others put the block down and stand on it and see farther and can reach higher because of it."

—ALABAMA STATE SENATOR HANK SANDERS,
speaking about the 1960s Civil Rights Movement

Following a halfhearted handshake and an awkward embrace, we said goodbye. As I parted to go into the U.S. Army recruitment station in the basement of the post office in Mayfield, Kentucky, I heard my brother's voice quiver, and I wheeled around to see him crying. I was one scared little country boy heading to the army that morning, at 18 years and 1 month of age. But his crying was quite a shock to me, because I thought, *who am I for him to be so concerned about me?*

Nelson, my older brother by seven years, had been in the Air Force for three years, so he knew much more than I did what I was entering into. I had purposely wanted him to take me to town the morning I would be sworn in and then immediately departing on the train.

I had graduated from high school on Friday night and left for

1

the army on the next Monday morning. Things were happening fast. Three of my high-school buddies, Billy Warmath, Jimmy Morton, and Easton A. Terrell Jr., were being inducted the same day. Nelson picked me up early that Monday morning, because I didn't want Mother and Daddy to embarrass me by creating a scene over my leaving. Even at home Mother had a really hard time bidding farewell to her baby, and Daddy, ever the "men don't cry in public" person, said "Don't forget the Lord." The vast experiences embarked upon that spring day, April 23, 1946, opened up unknown vistas to me and certainly changed my life.

1

The Beginning Years

"May you look back on the past with as much pleasure
as you look forward to the future."

—PAUL DICKSON

On March 14, 1928, a son was born to Mr. and Mrs. Bernice B. Boyd of Route One, Lynn Grove, Kentucky. He—that is, I— was named Louis Jefferson Boyd, after both of my grandfathers. Bernice Boyd, my father, was the only son of Lewis Grey and Hattie Murphy Boyd. Bernice was born on March 25, 1893, near Tri-City, Kentucky, in South Graves County. My mother was the former Ethel Turnbow, daughter of Jeff and Molly Page Turnbow. Ethel was born near Brown's Grove General Store in Southeast Graves County on May 12, 1893. Her father, a brother, and two sisters died from typhoid fever when she was twelve years old.

I was called Louie by my family, and L. J. by others until I was a junior in high school. At that time, Mrs. Eston A. Terrell, my high school teacher, started calling me Louie, and the name was adopted by others. I was the third child, having an older sister, Kathleen, who was twelve years older than me, and a brother, Nelson, who was seven years older. The baby book my mother filled out lists the following information:

> Wednesday, March 14, 1928   5:00 A.M.
> Louis Jefferson Boyd   At Home, Graves County, Kentucky
> *Father:* Bernice Boyd   *Mother:* Ethel Turnbow Boyd
> *Nurses:* Mrs. Jetton and Mrs. Yongue
> *Weight at Birth:* 11¾ lbs; 1 month, 12 lbs; 6 months, 19 lbs; and
>   1 year, 23 lbs.
> *First gifts:* Toilet seat, shoes, blanket, wash rags, Baby Book, rubber
>   sheet, socks, supporters
> *Baby goes bye-bye to:* Mrs. Jetton, Mayfield, Grandfather Boyd,
>   Grandmother Bazzell
> Laughs out loud at 7 weeks at Aunties; 6 months, one tooth; 9
> months, five teeth, 1 year old says "Hi" and crawled to Mother's lard
> jar and was playing in it when she found me. Mother and I also went
> kodaking. The attending physician was Dr. C. H. Jones. (Dr. Jones
> lived at Lynn Grove and was a person I greatly admired. It was a joy
> to me to visit him when I was visiting in Kentucky.)

I do not remember much of my first six years; however, there are a few things that are vivid in my mind. The most prominent of these is when Kathleen (Kakki) got married. I must admit that her wedding day is the only time that I can remember Kakki before she got married. I was six years old then. This has been quite depressing to me at times, because I never realized I had a sister until I was old enough to learn to love her as a sister. She must have played an important part in caring for me as a baby, but I cannot recall a single instance before her wedding day. Consequently, as a youngster, I always felt closer to Nelson, and I can remember many happy occasions that we spent together at home. I remember vividly when Kakki left with Sylvester in the A Model Ford Coupe to get married. We watched them drive down the long driveway from the house, and we waved to them as they passed

Louie Boyd, 1928.

the barn. The most striking thing of this occasion was Mother crying as she went back to her ironing in the living room. I remember her explaining why she was crying, but apparently the explanation didn't register with me, because I saw nothing to cry about.

I do remember one occasion, apparently before Kakki married, when Nelson and I swiped some of her candy from the front sitting room. I recall only the candy and how good it was, but do not remember Kakki's reaction or the punishment she must have given us for doing it.

I remember going to the field once with the family when they were hoeing tobacco. (Kakki must have been there, as it was a family affair.) I played along the fencerow and would anxiously wait for them to hoe a "round" back to where I was. This occasion registers only because it was the time I ate the pie "wif-out the ants off it." Mother took a piece of pie to the field for me and when she unwrapped it, ants were all over it. When she was being so slow in getting the ants off, I announced that I wanted to eat it "wif-out the ants off." My family never let me forget that saying, which is perhaps responsible for my remembering the incident.

Another memory was of Daddy returning from town one evening with some towels he had bought. They were small ones and were called "shaving towels." He didn't have one for me, which made me very mad. I went to the brick hearth and bumped my head soundly and while crying I told them that I was "nevah, nevah gonna shave." (When I got mad, I always went to the brick hearth in front of the old fireplace, got down on my hands and knees, and bumped my head many times. Although I remember doing this only a few times, they tell me that my forehead stayed bruised most of the time.)

I remember the old car shed down by the water well and the old T Model Ford. One Sunday afternoon we were going someplace—to visit Uncle John Boyd near Murray, I believe, but I am not certain of the destination—and I didn't want to go. Daddy and Nelson

Nelson and Louie Boyd with family car, 1929.

were in front and Mother and I were in the back of the open-sided car, and I was crying to stay at home. Daddy told me to get out and stay, so I climbed over the door and headed to the house. Before he had turned the car around, I had decided I didn't want to stay in that empty house alone, so I hopped in the car and went along.

Another trip in the old T Model was over to Grandpa and Grandma Bazzells when they lived over at the Wilkens place across the Lynn Grove highway. Uncle Vernon and Aunt Hattie Young (Mother's stepsister) were with us. Daddy's hat blew off, and Aunt Hattie caught it before it went out the open window in the back. One Sunday when it was raining and the roads were bad, I remember going to Grandpa Bazzell's in the wagon. We put straw in the wagon, covered it with a tarpaulin, and had a wonderful trip. We were real pioneers, and with a wagonload of people, it was indeed a fun trip. When we went over there, Paul (my cousin) and I always had a separate room to play in. I remember when they used to come visit us, too. Grandpa Bazzell had a T Model Ford truck, and to crank it he would jack up a rear wheel and turn it. When it did crank there was a deafening sound. Once after he cranked it he yelled for Daddy to smell the exhaust and see if it was running, and then laughed heartily. Nelson remembers that Grandpa Bazzell drove the topless Model T to California in the 1930s.

One Sunday we drove our Model T up in front of the house and as I was crawling out over the rear door, one of the family closed the front door on my finger. It bled profusely, and today I carry a scar on my right middle finger as a result. The only medication for such an injury was to pour kerosene on it.

I remember when Nelson went to school at Lynn Grove. He would walk to Browns Grove to catch the bus. The students had to pay for their transportation, and they rode the back end of a poorly enclosed flatbed truck. I would wave goodbye to him every morning (when I was up) and would meet him down by the barn in the afternoon.

I had a supposed attack of appendicitis when I was five years

Louie Boyd, 1931.

Louie Boyd, 1932.

old. I stayed in bed during the summer for about three weeks. They talked of taking me to the hospital and that scared me very much. During the day, I lay on Mother and Daddy's bed and was just long enough (arms outstretched) to reach across it. I was quite tall for my age. During that sickness Mother would lift me and move me from her bed to mine. Once, she remarked, "You are too heavy for me to lift," and that was the last time that I remember her lifting me and holding me in her arms. When I would have a fever, I would be dry and thirsty and crave cold water. Mother never believed in giving cold water to a feverish body, so she would dip warm water from the reservoir on the old wood stove and give it to me. It was awful.

I remember Mr. Doran, the pack peddler, when he would come to our house with the pack on his back. He would spread out the black sack on the living room floor to display the items he had for sale, such as Watkins products. Later, modern times arrived and Bill Jordan from Cookesville was the peddler. He had a big, blue, frame structure built on a wagon pulled by a team of horses. The sides of the wagon opened to display the goods. Mother used to give me an egg, and I would trade it for an all-day sucker or a stick of candy. Sometimes it took two eggs to make the trade (when eggs were selling for less than twelve cents per dozen). The day the peddler came was often the highlight of the week, as it gave us contact with other people. Once a stove drummer came to our house in a buggy late in the afternoon and wanted to spend the night. He did spend the night, and I well remember the miniature sample of a wood-burning cookstove that he had. I wanted it so badly. Daddy was in town that day at a school-board meeting and as usual he didn't get home until after dark because he always liked to talk too well. While we were waiting for supper and wondering why Daddy wasn't home, I volunteered that they might have him in jail. It was very embarrassing to Mother and the stove drummer was quite shocked at my statement, and until Daddy arrived he wasn't certain but that he was going to be faced with a drunk.

A few years later, the peddler used a pickup truck rigged as a traveling store. Some summers Billy Kreisler, a classmate of mine, would come once a week with his uncle, peddling merchandise from his father's store in Sedalia. It was a treat to see him.

I remember when Daddy traded the T Model for a 1931 A Model Ford. It was on a Monday, and he had been to town to a school-board meeting again. It was dark when he came in, but we all rushed out to see the new car. He took us happy people for a short ride in it.

The house where I was born was a white frame house that had been built about 1900. It was at the same location where mother had been born (in a different house). The house faced south, toward the livestock barn and car shed. There was a porch across two-thirds of the front. The door opened into a hallway, with the living room on the left and Mother and Daddy's bedroom on the right. At the end of the hallway were the steps to the upstairs with two bedrooms and a storeroom. The hall opened into a large room where we "lived." Actually, it was a "den" with a fireplace, though we didn't even know that we had a modern den. There was a bed in this room, where I slept in the winter, and there was a porch on both sides. On the left (west) side, the porch faced the tobacco barn and the road, which was about 150 yards from the house. The dining room and kitchen were just beyond this room, and they were separated from the rest of the house by a short hallway. The kitchen was a favorite spot to sit by a cozy wood-fired stove on a cold morning. It was my job to keep the wood box filled with stove-wood for cooking.

There was a swing on the front porch and I took many, many imaginary trips in it. I drove the "bus-swing" furiously, making frequent stops to pick up passengers. Once, I found a bantam egg in a nest at the stables and put it in my back pocket to bring it to the house. En route, I plopped down in the swing and had a great mess with the broken egg in my pocket.

The cistern was on the west porch, the one that faced the road.

We caught our drinking water off the roof when it rained by directing the gutter-spout into the cistern. Catching water for use was a ritual every time it rained. Daddy would let the "roof wash off" and then go out in the rain to direct the water into the cistern. People who didn't let their roof wash off before catching their drinking water were considered to be trash.

The front living room, which faced south, was seldom used. I never remember being in there except to steal that candy that Sylvester had brought to Kathleen (chocolate-covered cherries—a magnificent treat!).

The house was really cold in the winter, as I mentioned, and I would sleep in the room with the wood fireplace (the "den"). I always had a serious problem with earache in the winter. In fact, I was in bed with an earache every Christmas until I was 10 or 12 years old. Tobacco smoke was supposed to be soothing for an earache, so my uncle (Jasper Wheeler) would blow cigar smoke in my ears. Every time I went outside in the cold winter Mother would stuff cotton in my ears to protect them. One winter, following a prolonged bout of earache, I lost my hearing in one ear. The next summer we found a wad of cotton in my ear and when it was removed my hearing returned.

I never washed my hair during the winter months. Such irresponsible behavior would have caused a severe cold and greatly aggravated the earache problem.

One winter, a few days before Christmas, I was confined to bed with an earache and that night it started snowing. I really wanted to get out in it. Before Daddy went to bed he pulled off his shoes and went out in the yard and walked barefooted in the snow. I could never understand why his feet didn't freeze. It made such a lasting impression on me.

One cold winter afternoon after Nelson and I got home from school, we were at the house alone while Mother and Daddy were stripping tobacco at the barn. I had gone into the cold kitchen to get something to eat. Nelson locked the door on me and would not let me back in the warm room by the fireplace. In my frustration, I kicked the door real hard and broke out the nice ornamental panel in the bottom of the door. When Mother came to the house, it was a bad time. She just cried and said that we could never have anything nice. That hurt much worse than a severe whipping.

Taking a bath in the winter was a memorable experience. Even though I took a bath only once a week, I really never liked them. Once, while resisting the bath rather strenuously, I asked Mom if I could take two baths at once so I wouldn't have to take one the next week. The weekly bath on Saturday night was a family ritual. The galvanized wash tub would be filled with warm water, and all the family used the same water. The kids were last—*yuck*!

I started at Dulaney School—a one-room school about a mile from our house—in 1934. There were eight grades in the school; I was the only one in the first grade. The teacher was Miss Lucille Galloway. When it came time for my class, I would go to the front of the room and sit on her lap and read to her. I have had great fun over the years telling everyone that I was the top student in my first-grade class. That record still holds. Some of my schoolmates, who were all older than me, were John Earl Adair, Jimmy Woods, James Elbert Walker, and Euple Jetton. Euple lived about 200 yards from our house and James Elbert lived about a half mile. I went by their houses on the way to school and we walked together. Sometimes we walked with Junior Tracy Turnbow whenever he went to school.

It was common for the teacher to let younger students sit at the desk for a while with the older students. Boys never sat with girls and girls never sat with boys. It was a real treat to get to sit with an older boy, and, of course, this enhanced the learning process.

Once, the older boys dared me to smoke at school—it was probably corn silks because nothing else would have been available. Anyway, Miss Lucille found out about it and lectured the whole roomful of kids, saying that the smallest boy in school was smoking. There wasn't any question about whom she was talking.

Dulaney School, the "one-room schoolhouse."

Miss Lucille, the teacher, used to ride a horse about three miles to school, and it was a delight for any of the boys to take her horse to a nearby stable and unsaddle it. Later she drove her brother's A Model Ford to school. Once she spent the night at our home. Her brother and little sister brought her over. I remember Anna Lee Galloway and thought her curls were mighty cute. (Later in life I thought that again for a spell.) When Mother and Daddy went to town, they left me there sometimes at the Galloways', where I had lots of fun playing. Miss Lucille's older brothers, Robert and Raymond, were grown men to me—they teased me and I liked them. I ate parched yellow corn there for the first time. The Galloways had a large family—about eleven children, mostly girls.

Mr. Hickman Baldree, the county superintendent, came to our school, and we sang him a song. We had practiced for three weeks before he came. Mrs. Anice Walker, James Elbert's mother, was our substitute teacher when Miss Lucille was away.

2

At The *Big* School
Goodbye to the One-room School

"Where we love is home—home that our feet may leave,
but not our heart."

—OLIVER WENDELL HOLMES, SR.

The next year, in 1935, history was made in the Graves County schools, as many were consolidated and the big yellow bus transported us to Sedalia. Nelson said, "I'm not going to Sedalia even if the bus backs up to my door," but after three days he loved it and would not go back to Lynn Grove for anything. There he met a little black-headed, bowlegged girl named Sue Wilson. One day at recess I saw my brother swinging so I started toward him. He was swinging with this girl so when he saw me coming he began motioning for me to go back. The closer I came to them the more he turned loose of the swing and motioned for me to go back. As I remember, the recess bell was the only thing that saved him from the little brat brother showing up at such an inopportune time. That afternoon on the school bus I was warned not to tell it at home.

I was in the second grade and Miss Rupayne Turner was my teacher. She was a very good teacher and real kind to all of us. I was in a large class compared to the one at Dulaney, and I hardly knew what to do. Carolyn Boyd, Linda Ray, Phyllis Sue Bradly, and Mayna Sims were students. The latter two were my first girlfriends. I barely could write my name and couldn't spell anyone else's. Becky was in the same grade, and we were in school together from second grade through high school—eleven years.

Much to my disgust, I had to wear long underwear to school in the winter and long brown stockings over the long underwear. The only way to hold up those long stockings was with a garter belt, unless you wore garters—and it sure was tough on a boy to have to wear a garter belt to hold up those ugly long stockings. One morning Mother didn't stand over me with an axe as I got dressed, so I slipped off without my long stockings. All day at school I sat with a foot in each aisle on each side of my desk. I had my long underwear pulled up high and well concealed and my breeches legs pulled up to my knees. I was real proud of those bare legs.

I got sick one day at school and A. J. Turner, Miss Rupayne's brother, took me home in his A Model Ford Coupe. I was so glad to get home that I offered him my piggybank, but he wouldn't take it. Mr. B. J. White was principal, and Mr. Alcock was Nelson's vocational agriculture teacher.

In third grade, Mrs. Juanita Barton was my teacher. She is the one who really taught me to read. That year Mrs. Barton had each student contribute a recipe to a recipe book for Mother's Day. Mine was for potato soup, and the recipe book is still in the family—more than sixty years later.

Klondike, a big collie, was my dog. He and I used to wrestle, and one day he got me down and Daddy came to my rescue as he heard me pleading with Klondike to let me up. James Elbert Walker and I used to play together with our dogs. We made harnesses out of baling twine and hooked the dogs to homemade carts. His dog, Lady, was a real good harness dog, but Klondike never worked.

Daddy was on the county school board for eight years and served as a trustee at Dulaney School before that. In 1935 the

Kentucky School Bus Law was passed, and the forerunner of the modern school bus started. There was no heating or cooling, as the bus was merely a long, enclosed wooden bed on a truck with a long bench on each side and a bench in the center that was shared by two rows of students back to back. The bus was painted yellow. Bus drivers were regular truckers who contracted for the school bus route. They would remove the school bus bed from the truck body during the summer and haul gravel or other goods. Rex Mason was the longtime driver of our bus route.

We lived only seven miles from Sedalia, but the bus went a long, circuitous route totaling forty miles to school. The bus went from our house to Beech Grove Church, then to Boyd's Crossing, on to the Tennessee state line at Boydsville, and then on to Sedalia. I was the first one on the bus each morning and the last one off at night, so I rode eighty miles every day. The gravel roads were very bad in the winter. Occasionally, we got stuck in the mud and had to be pulled out. Practically every day in the winter the bus was running in deep ruts in the road and in low gear.

When I was in second grade, Daddy came home with a letter that the county school superintendent, Mr. Baldree, had received from a second-grader in Carroll, Nebraska. This one-room country school in Nebraska was running a contest to see who could get an answer first to a letter that each student wrote to some distant place. Mr. Baldree sent the letter to me since I was the same age as the writer. I immediately responded to Robert Bodenstadt and he won the contest, but best of all we commenced a pen-pal relationship that still continues. Of course, Mother was instrumental in my maintaining this relationship, and I am so pleased that she pushed me. Bob and I corresponded all through grade school and high school. He was a farm boy, and we wrote about the different crops we grew. Once I sent him a leaf of tobacco to show him what tobacco was like. Bob and I went into the army right after high school, so his mother and my mother corresponded while we were in service. When each of us got married, our wives continued the

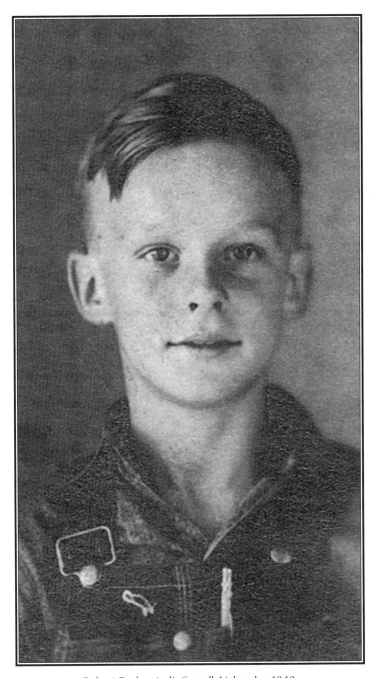

Robert Bodenstadt, Carroll, Nebraska, 1940.

correspondence. Our first face-to-face encounter came in 1966, when our family visited theirs on their farm in Carroll, Nebraska. Later, he and his family visited us in Michigan, and then in 1986, Becky and I visited Bob and Marilyn in Wayne, Nebraska, where they now reside.

When I was in the third grade, it was the year of the big flood of 1937 at Paducah, Kentucky, on the Ohio River. Even though Paducah was thirty-five miles from Sedalia, our school was closed and displaced residents filled our school building. I remember going to the school to take blankets and clothing. Of course, I was happy to be out of school, but the sight of families sleeping on the floors in the rooms and hallways made a deep impression on me.

In the summer of 1937 we started to build a new house. The first job was to arrange temporary living quarters. We separated the kitchen and dining room from the old house, and rolled the structure on logs out in the side yard. This became home to four of us—Mother, Daddy, Nelson, and me—for several months. We then tore down the old house, pulled out nails, and saved all of the lumber. The two-room house leaked really badly. One night it was raining, and Daddy got up to check on us boys in the next bed. He found that water was leaking in on the pillow and running down in my ear. I slept through it all.

After tearing down the house, our next big job was to dig the basement. We used a team of mules and a pond scraper to move the dirt, but the ground was so hard we had to dig it up with a pick and shovel. We did hire an old steel-wheel tractor with a large steel-beam plow to break up the ground, but the steel beam of the plow bent so we returned to the hard, hard labor of pick and shovel. While we were working on digging the basement, Asher Rogers from Texas stopped by to visit. He was one of Mother's relatives by marriage, but I'd never known him before then. When they drove up to our place, he jumped out of the car and started running toward us screaming and waving his arms. I remembered him thereafter and in later years when his family visited in

Birthplace of Ethel Turnbow and homeplace of her father,
Isaac J. Turnbow, and grandfather, John Turnbow.

Kentucky. I thought his daughter, Verna Gail, was right cute and would brag to my local friends about her as my girlfriend. The Texans talked about bluebonnets, which I had never seen, but I thought Verna Gail would look just great standing in a field of bluebonnets.

After the tractor and steel-beam plow failed to solve our problem with the hard ground, Daddy sent me to Mr. John Turnbow's to borrow a foot-adys (like a pick) to break up the dirt. I repeated the name of it, "foot-adys," all the way over there (about a mile), and then when I got there I forgot the name of what I was supposed to borrow. Mr. Turnbow named several tools and asked what work they were doing at home, but nothing helped. It meant another trip.

Pete Barley from near Hickory built the house. By saving lumber from the old house and cutting trees by hand for lumber, we built the five-room brick house with full basement and full upstairs for less than $2,000. The house is still standing and looks exceptionally well more than sixty years later.

Raising tobacco caused a lot of young men to leave the farm. Working in tobacco was terribly hard. It was referred to as the "thirteen-month-a-year" crop. We grew dark-fired tobacco as our main cash crop. In January we would burn the plant bed by piling wood on a selected spot of ground and burn it to sterilize the soil. The soil would be pulverized and the small tobacco seed would be scattered on the ground in February. The plant bed was covered with canvas cloth to protect the young, tender plants from the frost when they came up in the spring. The bed would be thickly covered with thousands of tobacco plants that were six to eight inches tall by early May.

At this time, the fields would be prepared for transplanting the tobacco plants. This was back-breaking work. The field would be plowed and worked up real well, then marked off with a corn drill to lay off rows four feet apart in both directions. At each place where the rows crossed, we would drop a handful of fertilizer, use a hoe to pull up a mound of dirt over it, and pat off the top to create a "hill." After a rain, while the hills were wet, we would pull the plants from the plant bed and set a plant in each hill. You would have to bend over and use a wooden peg to make a small hole four inches deep in the hill. The plant would be inserted in the hole and the peg used to push dirt to the roots of the plant. As the tobacco grew, the hills had to be scraped once or twice to kill the grass and weeds growing around the plants. The four feet of earth between the plants had to be cultivated several times to keep grass from growing and to "stir the soil." The plants also had to be sprayed to kill insects. When the plants got about four feet tall we would "top" them by breaking out the flowering bud that produced the tobacco seeds. This caused the leaves of the plant to fill out and it also caused suckers or "young buds" to grow out between each leaf and the stalk of the plant. These suckers had to be pulled off the plant so the plant nutrients would go into the remaining leaves. Each plant would have twelve to twenty leaves, and suckers would have to be pulled from the plant at least three times over a four- to six-week period. Suckering tobacco was the hardest of all hard work on the farm.

I developed a new method for suckering tobacco because, instead of bending over each plant, I crawled on the ground. This saved the back but it sure was messy getting the tobacco gum all over my face and hands and *really* messy when the ground was muddy.

The plants filled out, finally matured, and were harvested after about 100 days in the field. We harvested them by splitting the stalks from the tops to about eight inches from the ground with a sharp tobacco knife. We then cut the stalks off at the ground and allowed the plant to wilt in the sun. We would hang the wilted, pliable plants over a tobacco stick that was four feet long. We would hang about six plants on one stick. We'd haul the tobacco sticks with the plants on them to the barn by wagon and hang them on tiers in the barn for curing. The leaves of the tobacco would turn yellow, and after two weeks the fire-curing process started.

To fire-cure the tobacco, we would build wood fires on the dirt floor throughout the barn. As the log fires began to burn well, we smothered them with sawdust to create dense smoke. This smoking took place in an enclosed barn for three to four weeks. The smoke put a fine finish on the tobacco leaves so they could be used for snuff or for cigar wrappers. Sometime between October and December, when the tobacco came "in order" (when the tobacco became soft and pliable from high humidity), we took the tobacco down, removed it from the sticks, and piled it in bulks in the barn.

Later, we stripped the tobacco by classing out the leaves according to quality. We pulled off the poorest-quality leaves, usually those that were next to the ground, and sorted them out as lugs; then we pulled off the other leaves that were not top quality and piled them up as seconds. The top-quality leaves we left on the stalk. Later, we stripped these top leaves from the stalk and tied them into hands. Each hand of tobacco would contain six to ten leaves that would be wrapped at the tops of their stems by a carefully folded leaf of tobacco. The lugs and seconds would also be tied into hands and placed in separate bulks. The price for the tobacco was based on quality of the tobacco leaves. The tobacco was usually sold in December or in January. That was why it was called a thirteen-month-a-year crop: many times, the new crop was started before the old crop was sold.

Cutting the tobacco and stripping it were neighborhood events at which farmers swapped work and helped each other out. In the winter it was common to gather at a neighbor's barn at night for a tobacco stripping. It was difficult to keep warm, so some people would move the tobacco into a room in the house—but this was never done in our house, because it was just not proper to bring the dirty tobacco inside. Sometimes neighbors also helped each other set out the tobacco in the spring. Really hard work.

One year, apparently, Becky and her sister, Linda, grew an acre of tobacco to have some money. Becky was so afraid of the tobacco worms that she carried a pair of scissors to cut them rather than touch them.

I remember so clearly a year during the depression. In the late 1930s, Daddy came home from selling the tobacco. Mother and I were in the back yard when he told her that the tobacco had brought only five cents a pound. Mother broke out crying because it was such a little amount of money. The entire crop couldn't bring enough money to pay just for the fertilizer used to grow it, and this was the main money crop for the entire year.

Tobacco was the main cash crop so we got money only once a year. You would work really hard all year and get money all at one time, so it had to last a long time. That was when you would pay interest on borrowed money, pay the bill at the local general merchandise store, and stock up on staples such as flour, meal, and sugar. We were fortunate to have a radio in the mid-1930s. We would always buy new batteries for the radio when we sold the tobacco, and they would last about six months. When the batteries gave out we would have to do without the radio until the next tobacco crop was sold. The families with radios usually had a lot of company, because neighbors without radios would come and listen. Boxing was a most important event. I remember many neighbors gathering at our house one night to hear the Joe Louis–Max Schmelling prize fight for heavyweight champion of the world. This event dominated neighborhood conversation for several weeks.

The less-stable families would spend their money foolishly. Many a tenant-farmer family would buy a junky, used car that would last a few months, and then they would be without transportation until the next tobacco crop was sold. A very few men would go on a big drunk when they took their tobacco to town to sell it. They might stay gone for three days or a week, and their families wouldn't know where they were. When they finally came home, they might have a used car, but usually they were empty-handed with absolutely nothing to show for their year's work. No one knew about alcoholics in those days—such people were just plain drunks. They would come home and become the ever-loving, hard-working family men who would raise another crop of tobacco and repeat the same process next year.

Tobacco was money. I remember one Saturday afternoon we went to town (Mayfield) and Daddy gave me twenty-five cents. The cowboy movie cost ten cents, and I had another fifteen cents to spend. He gave me a stern lecture about spending the money carefully because that quarter was as much money as four tobacco plants would bring when sold. That comparison stayed with me for a lifetime. On another occasion, I had only ten cents—just enough to get in the theater. Shortly after I got inside, the theater began filling with smoke, so I got scared and ran out. It was only the popcorn burning, but I had lost my dime and the chance to see the cowboy movie. My parents never went to the "picture show," but when the Jesse James movie was on, we went. Mother, Daddy and I along with Uncle Vernon and Aunt Hattie went to Mayfield one night to see the show—a big event.

January was moving month for tenant farmers who didn't own their own farms. A tenant family usually would have a team of mules, a wagon, and some farm equipment. The tenants would load up their household goods and other belongings and move into a tenant house or move in the house with the landlord on a new farm to make a crop the next year. If they did well and the landlord was satisfied with his or her share of income from the crop, then that family might stay more than one year. But usually the tenants moved on to different farms every year or so.

Daddy and Mother bought our farm after Kathleen was born, soon after World War I. They bought it from my mother's mother and sister. It was the place where my mother was born, and it was bought on a long-term debt. In the early 1920s, my aunt (Mother's sister) and her husband went to make their fortune in Detroit. They soon ran out of money and asked for the farm money that Daddy and Mother owed them. Daddy borrowed the money from Miss Emma Cobb (later Mrs. Luther Mills), who lived at our house and taught school at Dulaney School. It took twenty-five years to repay this debt. In fact, the farm was not paid for until the latter part of World War II. For many years, after the tobacco was sold, I would go with Daddy to Mr. Luther and Miss Emma's house near Lynn Grove for him to pay the yearly interest on the debt. At my young age, I never knew why we went there, but it was an annual trip.

In the winter of 1938, shortly after we had moved into our new house, we were sitting by the fire when Daddy came in from the stockyard sale barn at Murray. He reached in his big overcoat pocket and pulled out a baby goat and put it on the hearth. Imme-

Birthplace of Louie Boyd. The house was built around 1900 on the site where his mother, Ethel Turnbow, was born.

diately the goat wet on the floor, beginning a long-lasting bad experience. The goat grew fast and I had a lot of fun with it, but somehow he could not stay out of trouble. One Sunday afternoon we came home and he had eaten all of Mother's flowers and broken all the flower pots on the rail around the front porch. The goat had the run of the place except in the house. I made a harness for the goat and hooked him to the homemade cart just like the dog. This was never very successful. Another day we came home and the mules had gotten out of their lot and kicked or pawed the goat. He was pretty well banged up with several broken ribs, but he soon recovered. We finally launched a program of trying to keep the goat corralled. We put him in the fenced woodlot, but he would back up and sail over the fence and gate just like they weren't there. We finally put a chain around his neck and tied a big fence post to him that he had to drag everywhere he went. Shortly after that we found him hanging by the neck, still alive, from the top of the gate. He had tried to jump the gate and made it over himself, but the post didn't, so he was just hanging there. That goat still had several more lives left before we finally gave up on him and had a barbecue supper.

Gedric, Kathleen's first child, was born in February 1937. I was almost ten years older than him so this was quite an event for me, and being the first grandchild, he was pretty special. Just after Gedric was born, Sylvester bought a 1937 gray Plymouth that had been in the flood in Paducah. You could see the water line on the upholstery at the top of the doors.

My fourth-grade teacher was Miss Ada Adair, who later married Leon Farris, who ran the general store at Tri-City. Miss Lucille Galloway, my first-grade teacher, was also my fifth-grade teacher. She had married Johnson Easley, and once while I was in her fifth-grade class, a Rogers boy and I spent the night with them. She rode the bus to school just like the students. Miss Katherine Kesterson was my sixth-grade teacher. She was a splendid teacher. Her sister, Rebecca B., was in our class. At Christmas of 1939 the school at Sedalia burned. We were called while it was burning because Daddy was on the school board, and we went to Sedalia that night to watch it burn. It was a sad time for me. For the rest of the sixth grade and during the next school year, we met in vacated store buildings, churches, and homes in Sedalia.

One day Mother didn't have time to fix lunch, so she gave me a dime to eat at a little restaurant next to the store building where our class was meeting. Openon Ray ran the restaurant. I ordered a hamburger and chocolate milk; that was the first time I ever remember ordering any food of any kind. It was great. The only problem was that the hamburger cost a dime and the drink a nickel, so I had to bring him a nickel the next day.

One day our class was going down the street in Sedalia, returning to the store classroom from recess, and we met Mr. W. P. Barton, an elderly store owner there in Sedalia. We had been studying in school about William Penn, and I knew that Mr. Barton's name was William Penn, so I yelled at him and said, "Hi to William Penn." I thought this was really cute, but it embarrassed Miss Kesterson mightily to think that some kid would have the nerve to address one of his elders in such a crude manner.

In the seventh grade, Miss Lucille Cook was my teacher, and we met in the basement of the Methodist Church. She was a very lax disciplinarian, and she just could not handle our class. The classroom was kind of like a circus all year—certainly not conducive to learning.

The new school building was completed before I started the eighth grade the next year. The new building was really nice. We changed classes in eighth grade just like in high school, so it was a big deal.

As work-stock on the farm we had mare mules. Lots of farmers had horses, but we were mule farmers, and they were wonderful animals. The team of mules became a sacred part of the family. The team was named Jane and Lize. Jane was a lively, but gentle, sleek black animal. Lize was reddish brown and much more lethargic. They made a good team, and Jane was my favorite. When Nelson and I got big enough to work a team, Daddy bought a team of young mules—Lou and Kate. It took special talent and patience to break young mules to the harness and to work. This took a long time. Lou was a high-strung, crazy mule that could never be trusted. She got out of control and ran away several times, but fortunately no one was hurt and no equipment damaged (beyond repair). This new team was quite an investment, and a farmer with four mules was a rarity. The only way Daddy could control Lou when he was breaking her was to cut down on her feed and keep her hungry.

We got our first tractor in 1942. This was quite an event. We sold the young team of mules for $475 and paid $750 for the trac-

Louie Boyd and the family's first tractor, 1942.

tor. It was a one-row Allis-Chalmers tractor on steel wheels. There were no rubber tires on tractors during the war, but two years later Daddy was able to buy rubber tires, so the local blacksmith, Alvie Farris, cut the steel spokes, welded rims on the wheels, and added rubber tires. It was great fun to drive the smooth-riding tractor really fast.

One Saturday I stayed home and worked while Mother and Daddy went to town. It had just rained and the ground was slick. I would drive the tractor real fast in road gear and then lock the left brake and spin around. After the third or fourth time, the tractor started to turn over on the spin. As it tilted, my foot slipped off the clutch, engaging it and causing the tractor to lurch forward and regain its balance on all four wheels. That was the only thing that saved the tractor, and possibly me, from serious injury. I stopped spinning, but I never told anybody about the near accident. I didn't have to tell because the skid marks on the grass left all the evidence needed for a stern lecture.

Jane and Lize survived the tractor and were kept on the farm for light work. Lize developed severe rheumatism and was hardly able to move. Daddy sold Lize to Mr. Sewell Jordan, and I was at home alone one day when Mr. Jordan rode a horse over to get her. He paid me $10 and put a halter on Lize and tried to get her to trot behind him on the horse. Lize was so stiff in her joints that she couldn't trot. After several attempts he got off his horse and picked up a large stick and beat Lize unmercifully. This was a sad day for me as I watched him from the house. I started to get Nelson's .22 rifle and go down there and give him back his $10 and take back old Lize. I didn't do it, but I have wished ever since that I had. After the severe beating Lize did trot, but I could tell she was hurting. They disappeared down the road and this was the last time that I ever saw Lize, who had played a big part in paying for our farm.

Mr. James B. Deweese, the principal and coach at Sedalia, came to our house when I was in the fourth or fifth grade. Daddy came in from the field and sent me to the stables to unharness Jane and put her in her stall. I was too short to reach the horse collar and unhook it at the top. I led Jane up to the elevated floor in the gear room and took off the collar. But I was so mad because I could not stay at the house with the visitors that I put the collar back on and in an irritated voice yelled for help to get the collar off. From that day on I was called "horse collar" by Mr. Deweese.

Mr. Deweese was a controversial principal and a rather successful coach at Sedalia. Daddy lost the election for his third four-year term on the school board. The main issue of the election was whether Mr. Deweese would remain as principal. I remember being at the courthouse in Mayfield while the votes were being counted on election night. Daddy lost by seven votes, and on the way home I asked where we were going to stop to cry. Since Daddy lost the election, Mr. Deweese had to leave as principal. But the outcome was that the forces supporting Mr. Deweese started working with the newly elected school-board members and got Mr. Deweese appointed school superintendent—a post that he held for about twenty-five years. Mr. Deweese got his wife appointed super-intendent while he was away in the army during World War II, and then he resumed the post when he returned.

Mr. Pete Barley, who built our house, was one of the newly elected school-board members in another part of the county when Daddy was defeated. Mr. Coy Andrus, Daddy's cousin, who took over as principal at Sedalia when Mr. Deweese left, was appointed assistant superintendent and was instrumental in running the school system for several years. When I returned from the army and started to college, Mr. Deweese, who was called Baby Deweese, told me, "Old Horse Collar, you'll never make it, but if you do I'll frame your diploma." I delighted over the years in sending him the bill for framing my B.S., M.S., and Ph.D. degrees.

During the drought and depression years of the late 1930s food was not too plentiful. Actually we had sufficient food, but there was no variety. I remember one year when we had nothing but dried black-eyed peas for dinner and supper. We ate dried peas every day during the winter and spring until May or June, when some of the garden vegetables became available. The dried peas were stored in a sack in the top floor of the cellar-house adjacent to the back porch of the main house. The kerosene used in the lamps to light the house at night was also stored in the same room. Yes, someone—but no one knows who—spilled the kerosene on the sack of dried peas. Nothing could be done to get rid of that kerosene taste, so we ate the foul, kerosene-flavored peas every day for the long winter and spring.

The usual practice on the farm was for Mother to cook a big din-ner at noon, and we would come in from the field to eat. Cornbread was a staple every day. After dinner the plates and silverware would be removed and washed. The food would be covered with a tablecloth and left there for a cold supper that night.

One summer Mother started making egg custard pies for des-sert at dinner. One wasn't enough, so she started making two, and then three, so that Daddy, Nelson, and I each had a whole pie for dessert. One of us would save a piece for Mother, but generally each of us would eat a whole pie for dinner. Those were days of hard work on the farm, and it took a lot of energy to keep working.

My first lesson in nutrition came one summer day when working on the farm, though I didn't really understand it until years later. Mother had to be gone that day to take care of Grandpa Boyd, who was sick, so she wasn't home to cook dinner. I asked her to buy some corn flakes since we very seldom had any store-bought food. That was to be a real treat for me, and I was excited about the good food. I ate a huge amount of corn flakes for breakfast and then went to work suckering tobacco. I got really hungry and came in for lunch at 11:00 A.M. I ate several bowls of corn flakes and milk and was completely filled with all I could hold, so I went back out to work. By 3:00 that afternoon I was totally exhausted and so weak that I had to quit work. I simply couldn't understand why I was weak when I had eaten enough to be so full.

Store-bought food was a treasured delicacy. About the only thing we would have from the store was canned salmon. Occasionally, I would spend the night with Billy Kreisler on a school night. His Dad ran the store in Sedalia and his Mom would bring food such as bologna, wieners, and cheese from the store for us to eat. This was marvelous for me. I enjoyed it so much. When Billy would stay with me, I was so ashamed of our plain country food. All we had was home-canned vegetables, home-canned meats, cornbread, and biscuits. But Billy always raved about the food, and I never understood that until several years later.

One winter soon after Daddy got the 1931 A Model Ford, he and Mother drove to Lexington in January for the Farm and Home Demonstration Week at the University of Kentucky. I stayed with Uncle Jap and Aunt Tola. On the way back from Lexington it was extremely cold and the roads were icy. One of the front wheels froze, and it skidded on the ice. Daddy did not know it until a big hole the size of your hand wore in the tire and it went flat. He brought the ruined tire home and I played with it for several years.

Rolling tires was a favorite pastime for boys. The tire would become a special car or truck and you would travel widely. The tire with the big hole in it was a very special vehicle, because I could grip the edge of the hole and spin my tire for a really fast take-off—truly a "scratch off" (in the words of the hot-rod aficionados)!

Another special homemade plaything was a small steel rim about ten inches in diameter. This was something we would find around the farm, and we'd make a wooden T-bar to use in rolling the wheel. You could go slow or real fast. As long as you kept pushing the rim with the T-bar it would keep rolling along. This became our vehicle as we traveled the "world" on the dirt and gravel roads near our house. We would also make "tom-walkers" as stilts and walk for miles on them. Each stilt would consist of a long piece of wood, about two by two inches, and six to ten feet long depending how high off the ground we wanted to be. First, we would nail a triangular piece of wood to the long stilt, to use as a step or stirrup. It would have a leather strap going from the outside of the stirrup at an angle up to the stilt to help hold the foot in the stirrup. The stirrup would be nailed about one to three feet from the bottom of the stilt, again depending upon how high we wanted to be in the air. (This can be restated by saying how far we wanted to fall when we fell off the stilts.)

To start walking, you turned the stirrups inside toward each other then backed up against a building or a tree; you placed the long stilt under each arm next to the body with the top part of the stilt extending behind your arms and up above your shoulders; then you stepped up, placing your feet in the stirrups while leaning against the building. Finally you leaned forward and started walking by lifting each stilt with your hand and moving it forward with your foot to take a step. When you fell—well, you'd try again.

I don't remember a lot about Dulaney School, but I do remember some of the minstrels and plays that were put on by people in the community. (Negro minstrels, in which people would dress as Negroes and act on the stage, were quite common. All such plays were comical and usually demeaning to Negroes.) I remember one play—not a minstrel—in which Ronald Bazzell, Mother's half brother, was in a pasteboard car on stage acting as a race driver. Ronald was quite comical, and the play was really funny. The schoolhouse was an important entertainment center for the community. Sixty-five years later, Nelson told me why the crowd laughed so much at Ronald. He was acting with a crank at the front of the car to "start the motor," but because he was left-handed, he was turning the crank the wrong way.

Also, it was common for many traveling shows to come to the communities and set up for one or two night performances. These shows would come to Browns Grove, a small village consisting of one or two general stores and a blacksmith shop located two miles from our house. The families in the area would come in and pay five or ten cents per person to see the show. The shows would travel in old enclosed trucks or homemade trailers, and were a take-off on traveling carnivals or circuses. Usually the entertainment was fairly clean and family oriented. I remember seeing a sloth hanging upside down on a pole in a cage. To see an animal from another country was indeed fascinating. When I was fourteen or fifteen, I was allowed to go to a show with James Elbert Walker, who drove his Daddy's A Model Ford. When we got there we met Billy Ray Miller, who lived at Browns Grove, and we were cutting up a bit and perhaps a little too loud. Anyway, I got a bad name out of it the next day when the neighbors gathered to cut tobacco on one of the farms. Mr. John Young stuttered, and people could hardly understand him. Apparently he was at the show and saw us because he was telling the neighbors—"That Boyd boy, shoo, he is bad one."

Memories of working on the farm are a lot more pleasant now than the actual events were at the time. It's like writing a dissertation. It's a lot more fun having done it than it is doing it!

One fall, Daddy, Nelson, and I took a wagonload of cane sorghum over to Mr. Vernon Easley's to make molasses. This was an all-day affair. We cut the sorghum by hand and loaded the wagon the day before the trip. Then we left before daylight for the five-mile ride. The cane stalks were ground up and pressed to squeeze out the sugary syrup. This grinding and squeezing was powered by a mule hooked to a long arm extending out from the grinder, and the mule would pull this arm around and around in a circle. When the cane was ground and all the syrup collected, it had to be cooked for five or six hours. The cooking vat was about twelve inches deep and the size of a wagon bed, with a really hot fire under it. Mr. Easley would stir the syrup continuously with a long paddle. My fondest memory of this day was the food that Mother prepared for us. We had cold pork and beans, and we ate them out of the can, which was a real treat for me. We also took corn and hay for the mules to eat. It was after dark when we got home, but we had several gallons of delicious sorghum molasses to enjoy during the winter with hot biscuits and butter.

One August day Daddy, Nelson, and I were headed out immediately after dinner to help a neighbor cut tobacco. We were running a little late and Daddy started the mules off in a trot. I was running along behind the wagon trying to get on while Nelson kept kicking me off. After a few failed attempts to get on the wagon, I picked up a big rock from the road and threw it at Nelson as hard as I could. He ducked and it hit Daddy solidly in the back top of his head. The rock cut a big gash in Daddy's head and knocked him out cold. He fell backwards in the wagon. As he fell back he pulled on the reins to the mules and they stopped. Things were pretty tense for a few minutes, and I was some scared. He regained consciousness soon and went to the house to put some kerosene on the cut on his head. We were soon on our way again, and this time I got on the wagon! I received no punishment but I was indeed mild and meek that afternoon.

I didn't always miss my target, and apparently I used my throwing arm as a means of defense against the big brother. Once, Nelson was giving me a real hard time in the back yard, so I picked up a brick bat and hit him on the knee. It caused a lot of bleeding, and I paid the price for my action, which was a stern lecture.

The outdoor toilet, or privy, on a farm is indeed a memorable place—especially in the cold wintertime. Ours was located fifty yards from the house, down behind the chicken house at the edge of the orchard. We had a wood door that actually fastened, and this was a measure of prestige and class far above those who had only a burlap bag as a privy door. It certainly didn't take long to accomplish nature's call in cold, cold weather. But in the summer one could be more relaxed, and the privy became a library, especially to browse through the public pornography in the Sears and Roebuck catalog. The Sears catalog was the only toilet paper available and was always in the privy. The real live pictures of models advertising ladies' underwear were a pleasant sight to behold. Never had a young country boy seen such a sight.

The man of the house seldom used the privy. This was too feminine. He would go to the stock barn or to a secluded spot outside for nature's call. Even the young males in the family rarely went all the way to the privy for anything other than the most advanced bodily eliminations. We would urinate in the yard or maybe off the back porch if it was cold or if we were scared to go out in the dark at night. But one rule was always observed: we didn't urinate where the urine would seep into the cistern and contaminate the drinking water. Trashy people didn't worry about this important ecological matter and they—male and female—would urinate off the porch right next to the cistern. It was easy to detect who had this habit because no grass or anything else would grow in these frequently used places.

I remember that as an early teenager I was enamored with tree climbing. When I needed to go to the bathroom for a "number two," I would go down in the woods lot by the tobacco barn and locate a tree with level, V-shaped limbs on it. The V shape made a handy toilet seat. It didn't have a flushing mechanism, but green leaves were always available as toilet paper, so it worked quite well.

The "slop jar" was a constant fixture under the bed at night—in summer and winter. Beware to anyone who would use it for anything other than urinating, because you had to take your own pot out and empty it the next morning—which could be a most unpleasant job!

My biggest problem in going to the privy was getting past the old setting hens. I was always scared beyond measure of either a setting hen or a mother hen protecting her chicks. The old setting hen would flog you with her wings, scratch with her claws, and peck you. I avoided them explicitly. Our neighbors, the Hubert Dearings, had geese, and the old gander would chase me. I was *really* afraid of him.

One summer day I was lingering on the hole in the privy, and Nelson slipped behind the privy and reached up under the seat and punched my exposed fanny with a long stick. I thought that old gander had already consumed my private parts so I jumped up and shot out the door as fast as I could with my overalls down around my ankles. Nelson came around the corner of the privy doubling over in laughter.

We grew a few acres of winter wheat most years. It fit into the recommended crop rotations, provided our flour needs, and also enabled us to sell a few bushels of wheat each year. Mr. Jim Woods was the only one in our area who had a wheat binder, and he did custom work for the neighbors. In the early years he pulled the binder with horses, but he was one of the first farmers in the area to get a tractor. He had a Farmall with steel wheels, and it was wonderful to watch it. The wheat binder would cut the wheat and tie the stems with the heads attached into bundles about twenty inches around. Our job was to pick up the bundles and set them upright together in shocks consisting of ten to twelve bundles. Then we would take two bundles and bend the stems in the middle and put them over the top of the shock to form a pointed roof and protect the wheat heads from the rain.

One summer Mr. Jim Woods had many acres of wheat, and Daddy arranged for Nelson and me to help shock all of Mr. Woods' wheat to pay him for cutting ours. We worked every day for about three weeks. Jimmy Woods helped his daddy on the binder, but he had a sister, Bobbie Sue, who was an absolute beauty. She was two or three years older than me, but I really loved to look at her. One day she brought us a bucket of ice water in the field just across from her house. She had on a pair of shorts and a loose halter top. When she leaned over to set down the bucket of water she was well exposed, and how gorgeous! I could have shocked wheat there forever.

After the bundles dried in the shocks for about three weeks, the wheat thrasher would come into the neighborhood. This was a wonderful time of year. I loved working in wheat because I didn't have to work in the tobacco during this time.

Mr. Delmus Bazzell, from Farmington, owned the thrasher, and he and two other people would come around to thrash the wheat. He had a big steel-wheeled tractor to pull the large thrasher from farm to farm, and at each stop the tractor would operate it by a long rubber belt fitted on a pulley on the tractor.

All of the neighborhood would come with their wagons and mules and follow the machinery until all of the wheat was thrashed. The thrasher would set up in a woods lot or near the stock barn on each farm and the neighbors with their wagons would haul the bundles from the field on that farm to the thrasher. One of the employees with the thrasher would cut the binder twine on the bundles placed on the "feeder table" and then feed the wheat stems into the mouth of the thrasher, which would shake out all of the wheat kernels and then blow the straw out the stacker. The straw might be baled for cattle feed or for bedding for livestock. Daddy usually built a large frame, about ten feet high, out of poles from the woods. Then the thrasher would blow the straw onto this frame to form a nice shelter for machinery or for cattle. Also, once a year many of the farmers would replace the straw in their bed mattresses. The new straw would have a pleasant odor and would be real soft for a month or so.

The most memorable of all was the wheat-thrashing dinner. All the women in the neighborhood would come to the farm where the wheat thrasher was and bring in tons of food for dinner. A table thirty to fifty feet long would be arranged under shade trees in the yard and completely laden with all kinds of food. That's why a farm person will frequently refer to a big feast as "enough food for a wheat thrashing." The women would prepare the table and then use tree branches with lots of leaves to keep flies away from the food. As many as thirty men would eat the big dinner. It would take about a week to thrash all the wheat in the neighborhood, so there would be a big dinner like this every day.

Mother, who was born in 1893, had one brother and four sisters. The oldest sister died at six months of age. Later (in August 1905), my grandfather, Isaac Jefferson Turnbow, died, and about two months later Mother's brother and two of her sisters died as well. All of them had typhoid fever. So my grandmother lost her husband and three children in less than two months. She was left with a farm and two daughters—Mother, who was twelve years old, and her sister Nona, who was six years old. Later Grandma married Matthias Bazzell; his wife had died, and he had two sons and three daughters. After they were married Grandpa and Grandma Bazzell had one child, Ronald. So mother had one sister and one half-brother in addition to the stepbrothers and stepsisters. But, as a latecomer on the scene, I viewed everybody as one family. Aunt Nona had a son named Paul Meadows, who was six months younger than me. Ever since I could remember, she and Paul had lived with Grandpa and Grandma Bazzell. When they lived at the Wilkins place across the Lynn Grove Highway toward Protemus is the first I remember of them. Later they moved to Hickory, six miles below Mayfield toward Paducah. I used to love to go to their house to play with Paul, even though he was a terribly spoiled brat who always got his way and was very aggressive in front of his mother and grandparents. I was much quieter and more easygoing and would never even defend myself, especially in front of parents and grandparents. This used to make Daddy so mad because Paul would tackle me and beat me up in front of the elders, and I would never fight back in front of them. When we would leave, Daddy would really rave at Mother and me for letting it happen. I was always much bigger than Paul, and I could easily handle him. When we got away from the parents, it was a much different story.

When we were eight- to fourteen-year-olds, I would spend a week with him and he would spend a week with me every summer. I really enjoyed staying with him because he lived in Hickory, and this was a big town to me. There were two or three stores, a post office, and a train station. Clay pits were nearby. We would pick blackberries and take them door to door in Hickory and sell them for ten cents a gallon. We felt rich. We were never close as teenagers because Paul began to run with a wild crowd. I don't think Paul ever graduated from high school, and if he ever worked I never knew it.

He did go into the army for a couple of years, though. When I was overseas in the army in 1946, Grandma Bazzell wrote me a letter with glowing comments about how great Paul was and offering some rather strong suggestions that I just didn't measure up. After reading the letter three or four times I tore it up, but after more than fifty years I still haven't gotten over it completely. Grandpa and Grandma Bazzell both died in the early 1950s. Aunt Nona moved to Mayfield and continued to work at the Curlee Clothing Factory, where she had been working for many years. When Paul returned from the army, he lived with his mother, and she continued to give him all of her money just like she had when he was a kid. He lived a fast, rough life, and at age twenty-four he was killed late one night about thirty miles from home in an automobile accident. Although there was definitely an accident with

Homeplace of Lewis Gray Boyd.

three people in the car, and the official records list it as the cause of death, there were whisperings that the auto accident was a convenient happening to cover more serious causes.

Daddy had three sisters all younger than he. Aunt Tola was next to Daddy, and she married Jasper Wheeler and lived most of her life farming on Grandpa Boyd's farm. Clarice was next. She had a speech impediment and never moved very fast. Irene was the youngest and the jewel of the family. She went to Murray Normal School and became a teacher. She taught at Hazard, Kentucky, where she contracted tuberculosis and soon came home to die. I remember when she was sick in bed at Grandpa's, but I don't remember the funeral. She never married and was only thirty years old when she died. I remember her as a smart, wonderful person.

Clarice married and had two girls. She was divorced soon after the second child was born, and she came home to live with Grandpa and Grandma Boyd. The young girl, "Baby Sue," never developed properly, and she died at about three years of age. I remember that we were setting tobacco one May afternoon in the new ground on the back of our farm when we saw Uncle Jap walking across the pasture toward us. He walked up and said that Clarice's baby had died. That night we went over to Grandpa Boyd's, and all four of us spent the night there. This was the first time that I could remember that all of us stayed there overnight. Nelson and I slept upstairs in the same room with Grandpa and Grandma. They were already in bed when Nelson and I went up, and we had to get undressed in the dark. I squatted down against the wall to pull off my shoes, and when I did I passed some gas with a loud noise. I immediately started making similar noises with my mouth to cover my great boo-boo. Later Nelson took great delight in telling this on me.

When there was a death in a family, the body would be embalmed at the funeral home then brought back to the house. Friends and neighbors would sit up all night with the body.

As mentioned previously, I remembered so little about Aunt Irene. But in later years I have come to appreciate and admire her so much. She must have had tremendous initiative and determination to go to college when it was so unusual and actually frowned upon for women to do so. All the graduates could do was to teach, and she had the nerve to take the train alone to a teaching position in a distant and very remote rural area in the coal-mining section of eastern Kentucky, in Hazard. This is probably where she contracted tuberculosis, which claimed her life. There was no treatment other than bed rest for the disease in those days. Even when I started traveling Kentucky as an extension dairyman in 1951, Hazard was notoriously rough and a feared place to visit.

Winters were cold in the poorly heated house, and head and chest colds were frequent. The only treatment for colds was Vick's Salve, the application of which was a dreaded happening. Mother would spread a thick coating of Vick's Salve on a flannel cloth, warm the cloth, and then put it on your chest. There is absolutely no worse "icky" feeling than that on you at night, and sometimes you had to wear one during the day under your clothes. There was no way to wash off that smelly salve.

In the winter the bed was always cold even in a room with a fireplace. Those who slept in a room with a fireplace would cover it with ashes at night so it would hold and could be fired up again in the morning, but that was not an issue for Nelson and me. I would go to bed first at night and get a good warm place, and then Nelson would come to bed and say—"You are sissy unless you scoot over and give me your warm place." It was disgraceful for a boy to be called a "sissy." One particularly cold night he came in from a date and tried this trick, and I said, "You will just have to call me sissy tonight—I'm not moving!"

As a youngster I used to have lots of boils, called "risin's" in those days. I had to go to the doctor several times to have them lanced. Dr. C. H. Jones, my birthing doctor, did most of them at Lynn Grove. Once I had a big boil lanced on my rear end and during my short recuperation I drew a picture of me on the table, Daddy holding me down, and Dr. Jones doing the lancing. I was hollering "Oh Doc!" Daddy carried that picture a long time and took great delight in showing it to Dr. Jones and others. Another time, Dr. Jones lanced a boil on my neck (the scar remains), and I said that I wanted to see the drainage. He said, "I'll show you the last quart." In those days people would say that a boil was worth a million dollars to you because it cleared all the impurities from your blood.

One night, when I was about twelve years old, we were attending a school carnival on the school ground at Sedalia. Dr. H. V. Usher, Becky's birthing doctor, was talking to Daddy and saw me with a large boil under my eye. He took us across the road to his office where he proceeded to lance it.

Mondays were always wash day on the farm. This was an outside operation, and the youngsters in the family played a role. It was my job to draw the water from the cistern and fill the big black kettle (fifteen to twenty gallons), then gather wood and build a fire around and under the kettle to heat the water. When the water was hot, Mother would start the daylong procedure. The hot water would be put in a galvanized tub and then warm water in another tub. The kettle was then refilled so more water could be heated. Sunday clothes and underclothes were washed first. Mother would wash them in the hot-water tub using lye soap and a big washboard. The clothes were scrubbed thoroughly on the washboard, wrung out by hand, and then rinsed thoroughly in the warm water. Again the clothes were twisted by hand to wring out the water, and then hung on an outside clothesline to dry. The dirty work clothes from the farm were another matter. They had to be boiled in the kettle of hot water to "loosen the dirt" before they went through the scrubbing and rinsing tubs. Every washwoman had a special stick about 4 feet long to punch down the clothes in the boiling water and to lift them out and transfer them to the scrub tub. Trying to wring out the water from overalls and work clothes was a real hard job. Many housewives took great pride in their clotheslines and in how the clothes were hung on the lines to dry, because the clothes were on public display. Less caring families did not have clotheslines and hung their clothes on bushes or on regular farm fences to dry. Daddy always said he could tell what kind of a housekeeper a housewife was by the way she hung her washing on the line. In the late 1930s, Daddy bought a washing machine that had a hand-operated agitator and a hand-turned wringer. This was a vast improvement over using the scrub board and wringing out the water by hand. Of course, the water still had to be heated in the kettle and the scrub board was still used for stubborn stains and extremely dirty clothes. The newfangled clothes wringer gave rise to the joke about "getting your tit caught in the wringer."

When we moved out of the old house in preparation for tearing it down and building the new house in 1936, we stored our furniture (other than what was in the two rooms we lived in) in the tobacco barn and other outbuildings. One piece of furniture relegated to the chicken house was an old pump organ with keyboard, pedals, and elaborate woodwork. No one played the organ, so it never made it into the new house. Chickens roosted on it for several years and it finally rotted and was discarded. That organ would be a treasured antique today.

The brooder house was next to the chicken house, and it was fixed up every spring for a new batch of baby chicks. The commercial hatchery was one of the early technical developments in rural areas. The chicks would be mail ordered. Mr. Monroe ran a hatchery in Mayfield, and we would buy 100 to 200 chicks at three days of age every year. We would get them in late February or early March so they would be about six weeks old when spring arrived and the weather was warm enough for their survival—thus the common term "a spring chicken."

A new batch of chickens meant a lot of hard work. The brooder house had to be cleaned out and fresh dirt brought in for the floor. The furnace in the middle of the house had to be rebuilt with bricks that were held together with mud and clay from the farm. It was necessary to have a fire in the furnace day and night for the chicks.

Springtime meant fried chicken, because it is the only time during the year that you would have young chickens. Many mornings Mother would get up early to kill a chicken and fry it for breakfast. That, with biscuits and milk gravy, was indeed a delicacy. She would wring the neck of the chicken by holding its head and rotating the chicken around like turning a hand crank until the head snapped off. The headless chicken still had plenty of life for a while and would run around the yard wildly until it died. Thus the expression "like a chicken with its head cut off."

The chicken would then be immersed in scalding water and the feathers plucked from the body. The innards would be dressed out, and then the dressed chicken would be washed and cleaned thoroughly and cut up ready for frying. Since there was no refrigeration, this process had to be repeated every time you wanted fried chicken.

Hog killing during the cold winter was another means of providing food for the family. This was a big, all-day job and very much a neighborhood event. Most families would kill two to four hogs each year and preserve the meat to last all year.

The hogs would be fattened up to weigh 250 to 300 pounds. The first step in hog killing was to dig a trench about ten feet long, three feet wide, and two feet deep for the scalding vat. The metal scalding vat would be positioned over the trench and filled with water from the pond. A fire would be built under the vat to heat the water to boiling. The hog would be shot in the head with a .22 rifle, and the throat cut for a complete bleed-out from the jugulars. The hog was then dumped into the vat and turned repeatedly with chains, which were manned on each side of the vat. After about ten minutes, the hog would be removed from the vat and the hair would be scraped with a sharp knife from the scalded skin.

The hog would then be hung by its hind legs on a tree limb or scaffold and gutted. The carcass would be cut into two halves; the bones would be chopped with an axe. The half-carcass would be placed on a table to be cut up and trimmed. All of these activities required intense, specialized manual labor, including the lifting. The carcass would be cut into hams, shoulders, ribs, sides of bacon, and tenderloins. The blankets of white fat on the white meat would be trimmed off and heated in the wash kettle to be melted into lard. The chunks of fat would shrink into tiny, crusty morsels as the grease was cooked out. Those morsels were called "cracklings" and were really good to eat. The melted fat would be poured into five-gallon cans, and when cooled, would harden into white lard. This was used in cooking throughout the year. The trimmings with a great deal of fat on them would be ground into sausage and stored in cloth sacks about thirty inches long and three inches in diameter. The hams, shoulders, and sides of bacon would be placed in a wooden salt box and covered with salt to cure. Later they would be smoked along with the sausage and would remain hanging in the smokehouse. Some of the sausage and tenderloin would be cooked and canned in jars, to be preserved for eating in the summer. Hog killing required cold weather so the meat would not spoil before it was cured with the salt. Some of the lard each year would be used to make lye soap, another process that utilized the big black wash kettle.

Hog killing was a great neighborhood gathering that would meet at each house until everyone had "killed hogs." The men would work together with the heavy jobs, and the women would work on the lighter chores.

Making hominy was another all-day family event. Carefully selected ears of white corn would be shelled and the kernels soaked in water until they were about three times their normal size. Then the swollen kernels would be cooked all day in the big black kettle. After the corn was cooked, lye (acid) would be added to the kettle to remove the husks from the kernels. After the husks were removed, wood ashes from the fire under the kettle would be added to the kettle to neutralize the acid lye, making it safe to eat and bleaching the white kernels. After many, many washings the beautiful white kernels of corn would be canned and eaten throughout the year. This is a favorite rural food. In the Deep South, the white kernels are ground up into grits.

Corn in its many forms played a big role in feeding rural people. I used to add water to regular corn meal and heat it on the wood-burning stove, add a little sugar, and then eat the mixture as mush. Others would fry this mixture in lard and eat the browned flapjack with molasses. Country people who didn't have popcorn would parch kernels of regular corn over the open fire and eat the parched corn. The only time I ever ate any parched corn was at the Galloways' when I was visiting with my first-grade teacher, Miss Lucille, and her large family near Cookesville and Farmington.

The country road and the rural mail carrier were the links to the world. As a youngster I was hopeful and excited to see company coming—anybody. From the bedroom-living area with the fireplace we could see only the road right in front of our house. We could not see when someone was coming down the road through our woods, so I always watched our mules in their lot by the stables. When they pricked up their ears and looked, we always knew someone was coming—maybe to our house.

The mailman, Mr. Joel Crawford, from Lynn Grove, would bring the mail by horse and buggy until the mid-1930s and even after that in the wintertime because the roads were impassable by car. Many times he would get stuck in the mud after he started using his A Model Ford on his route. Whenever he was stuck anywhere in our area he would always come to our house to get us to pull him out of the mud with a team of mules. Once, Nelson went out and harnessed the mules and went down the road to pull him out. The mailman paid him three cents—the price of a stamp—for his efforts.

Road-work day was an annual event for all the neighbors. In fact, rural people would get credit on their taxes for their work to help maintain the road. The road grader would come to the neighborhood and everyone would get their shovels and work on the ruts and ditches. The magistrate or someone hired by him to work the big iron road grader would pull it into the neighborhood with a pair of mules, and then someone in the neighborhood would have to provide another team of mules because it always took four mules (two teams) to pull the grader when grading. Daddy always had to provide a team of mules, and it was a traumatic experience because the man in charge would always ride one of his mules and whip our mules, which were hitched out in front of his team. We didn't treat our mules that way, and it really hurt me to see our mules popped with that horsewhip, leaving large welts on their rumps. Pulling the road grader was really hard work, and he was always using the whip to try to get our mules to pull more of the load.

It was a common practice to go barefooted all summer. In early spring, your feet were quite tender, but soon the soles of your feet got tough like the sole of a shoe and you could easily run down the gravel road with no problems. Every home had a foot tub to wash your feet at night before going to bed. We would wear shoes for church on Sunday, but with difficulty, and put shoes on in the fall when school started. Some students who didn't have shoes came to school barefooted. I remember one family whose members had webbed feet (the toes were not separated), and their bare feet in school created quite a spectacle.

Most of the summer I would also go without a shirt. We would really get dirty working on the farm. It was most difficult to try to keep clean, so we rigged a "modern" shower down by the well behind the car shed. We put a ten-gallon milk can up on a scaffold and put a small hose on it. Every morning we would fill the can with water, which would become heated from the sun during the day. At night each man in the family (Daddy, Nelson, and I) would have a warm shower outside. Beware to anyone who used more than his share of the ten gallons of warm water. Even with the shower, though, it was still difficult to keep our skin clean when going without a shirt.

I was always fascinated with country roads, which were the only roads I knew existed. I would spend a lot of time alone drawing a map of the neighborhood roads and challenging my memory by identifying all the houses along the roads. The road led to great adventure. While working alone in the fields, I would watch carefully to see the mailman or rare person who came along. Periodically, I would see Ernest Turnbow, a red-headed young man, walking toward his home in our neighborhood. He was a "hobo" who would ride the freight trains, even though the nearest railroad was fourteen miles away. That was his only education. Later in life he had a nice family and became an accomplished artist in Louisville, Kentucky.

When I was eleven or twelve years old, I was having to help

Daddy harrow tobacco. We used a one-row, spike-toothed harrow that looked like an inverted V about three feet long, with sharp spikes attached to the frame about every six inches on each side of the V. The mule pulled the harrow, which had handles so it could be controlled by the person driving the mule. The harrow would scratch the soil to kill the grass and weeds. This was called "bustin' middles" and was always done once or twice each year between the tobacco rows and corn rows. I was feeling sick at my stomach on that hot summer day and feeling really sorry for myself. Every time I would go around I would stop at the end of the row at the turn and lie down on the ground. Daddy would yell to get me up and keep me working. After I had stopped to lie down three or four times, Daddy stopped harrowing and jerked me up and took me to the house and made me take a big dose of Epsom salts dissolved in warm water. Then I got to quit working for the day, and after the Epsom salts I was indeed sick—or at least I thought I was.

Once, I was certainly sick, but this was self-induced. I decided it was time to start smoking after watching neighbors "roll their own" cigarettes using newspapers and home-grown tobacco. One afternoon I started out to get the cows to bring them into the live-stock barn for milking about an hour earlier than usual. I got some newspaper and matches and went through the tobacco barn and found some old dry tobacco that had been on one of the log beams of the barn for several years. I proceeded through the woods on to the pasture and sat down on the bank of the pond. I tore the paper carefully to the proper size and creased it to hold the tobacco, which was crumbled up into small pieces. I rolled the cigarette, licked the paper to seal it, and then twisted the end—a real artist. All the smoking neighbors would have been proud of me. I lighted up and began to smoke. The cigarette lasted about fifteen minutes, and I was having great fun. Soon the water in the pond began to swirl, though, and I had to grab the pond bank to keep from falling in the water. I got very sick and finally had to call Nelson to come get the cows and of course had to tell him what I had done.

My brother, Nelson, graduated from high school at Sedalia in 1939 and started to Murray to college that fall. He lived in the dormitory but would come home every weekend—by hitchhiking. He started on the National Youth Administration (NYA) program, which provided work for college students to help pay their way in college. He worked on the college farm and washed dishes in the dorm.

When I was eleven years old, I rode the milk truck to Murray one Saturday morning and walked over to the dorm to meet Nelson. He was living with six or seven guys in a suite all sharing the same bathroom. This country boy was really out of place with those big guys in their modern dorm. I had to go to the bathroom and had never before been around an indoor toilet. I didn't know to raise the toilet seat so I splattered it good. Soon a loud voice yelled, "Who pissed on the toilet seat?" I sat numb, cowering in the living room, and have not opened my mouth to admit doing it until now. Later, Nelson lived in a rental room in the home of Mr. Hamp Brooks (and wife Margarerite), who was the Vocational Ag teacher at Murray. Also, he rented a room for a year from Dr. Hicks, who lived on Olive Street. Dr. Hicks owned a plantation in Georgia and tried to get Nelson to come to Georgia and run the plantation. Nelson did go once with Dr. Hicks to look over the plantation, but the war was looming, and Nelson never became a plantation owner.

As mentioned earlier, in the summer I would go to Hickory to spend a week with my cousin, Paul Meadows. His mother, Aunt Nona, was divorced, and she and Paul lived with Grandpa and Grandma Bazzell. This was a fun time because Paul didn't have to work and this got me out of work at home. We spent a lot of time at the store and playing. They lived near the railroad track, which was a source of much fun. One of us would hold the handle of a knife in his mouth and touch the blade to the rail to determine whether a train was coming. Also, we would lay a penny on the rail to see how the train would mash it flat and elongate the piece of copper.

Our cousin, Donald Bazzell, would visit each summer with his parents from La Porte, Indiana. So all three of us would spend a couple of days together.

As an early teenager, I thought Daddy was really old and out of touch, and that he did some really dumb things. My Uncle Vernon, who married Mother's stepsister, always told me how sorry Daddy was as a farmer. And, of course, I frequently told Daddy what Uncle Vernon said and how much I agreed with him.

In later years, it became abundantly clear to me that my uncle had never had anything—never owned a home nor any land—and that he was a very mediocre farmer. His son was frequently in trouble and spending his dad's money. My aunt divorced my uncle when she was fifty-five, and he kind of withered away as a poor, lonely man. He lived for the moment—never sought knowledge and never had any vision of the future. Daddy was a person with vision—it was me who took a while to remove my blinders.

Uncle Vernon and Aunt Hattie indeed had a hard time. Once they took their little 6-year-old grandson along with them while they visited the cemetery at Antioch Church. The child was climbing on the monuments when one fell on him and he was killed.

Uncle Vernon was great to me, even loaning me his car to go on a date when Daddy wouldn't let me have our car. One of Uncle Vernon's relatives lived near us, and he, too, was a haphazard farmer—not too swift with initiative. We drove up to Uncle Vernon's one day and no one was home, so, as a twelve-year-old, I announced that they had probably gone to that trial at the courthouse. My very shocked parents wanted to know what trial and I told them what my older playmate, James Elbert, had told me. It seemed that an eighteen-year-old girl who lived near Cookesville was walking home one day from the store at Brown's Grove when our neighbor was plowing corn in the field along a deserted stretch of the road. He apparently enticed or forced the girl into the corn field and later charges were filed. This story—the fact that I knew about what had happened—really shocked my parents. I had never heard the word "rape," and it was not used then when James Elbert described it to me. My parents never discussed anything about sex with me at any age. It was simply an unmentionable subject. I always wondered how James Elbert learned about this happening.

A usual winter evening scene would be to see Mother churning milk by the fire to make butter and good buttermilk. Her legs would be covered with red splotches all winter where she would sit by the open fire and let her legs "bake" in the heat.

One Christmas after the new house was built, we were sitting in the front bedroom by the fireplace. The rest of the house was real cold, with no heat. Mother made sandwiches and brought them in by the fire. Otherwise, we'd have to go to the cold kitchen to eat supper. What a thrilling treat to have the cold pimento cheese sandwiches and cold milk for supper in front of the fire! Uncle Jap and Aunt Tola Wheeler had come to visit that evening.

My first experience with blacks was with Aunt Tola. There were no blacks in our neighborhood, and I was never around any. The only time I saw any was when we would go to Grandpa Boyd's and see them pass by on the highway. No doubt I was taught subtly to fear them, because I was really scared of them. Aunt Tola lived next door to Grandpa's, and one day she and I were hunting guinea nests in a field near the highway. I was holding their bird dog on a leash and he was sniffing for nests. A Negro man passed by in a wagon on the highway near to us. I got so scared that I turned the dog loose and he ran away. My aunt laughed so hard, but I was far from amused. The Negro man on the wagon was amused at my behavior, and I can still see his pearly white teeth shining as he smiled.

Just before Nelson left for the army, he was dating heavily and out late at nights. One day we were sitting in the swing on the front

L. G. and Hattie Boyd, fiftieth anniversary in 1942.
Son Bernice, granddaughter Kathleen, and great-grandson Cedric.

porch and he was cleaning his long fingernails, which were real important to him with his fascination with the girls. But, at my age, they didn't mean anything to me—it was much more fun to bite my nails into the quick. Nelson was so sleepy so he asked me to finish cleaning his fingernails with his knife while he took a nap. While he slept, I dressed up his nails by cutting notches all across in all of them. I thought this was really unique and attractive, but when he awoke he didn't appreciate my handiwork. I was indeed punished by him.

In my early teens, I had warts all over my hands. At one time I counted 47 warts on both hands and I was so ashamed of them, especially in front of the girls. Of course, there were all kinds of comments about playing with toad frogs as it was common knowledge that frog urine caused warts. There were all kinds of old wives' tales on how to get rid of warts. I tried many of them, such

The tobacco barn at Boyd home farm as it appeared in 1996.

as kissing a redheaded girl and stealing a dishrag and burying it in a rotten stump in the woods. None worked, but during my sixteenth summer, just before school started, I got Dr. Jones at Lynn Grove to burn the warts off with an electric needle. It worked beautifully, and I was happy with my smooth hands and ready to start holding hands with the girls.

3

A Few Things That Were Common on the Farm

Feather beds   The feathers from ducks kept on the farm were used for pillows and feather beds. The feathers would be packed tightly into a muslin "bag" about twelve inches high and the width and length of a bed. The feather beds were used especially in the winter because you could sink down into the feather mattress and keep good and warm. They were removed from the bed in the summer because they were too hot. That was a problem at our house, because Nelson liked the feather bed and wanted to sleep on it all the time. I didn't like it in the summer, and to show my displeasure I would sleep under the feather bed next to the hard mattress while he slept on the feather bed on his side of the bed. Of course, it was much hotter under the feather bed than on it, but I could assert my independence best by fighting the feather bed.

Straw mattresses   The less well-to-do farmers could not afford feather beds and used straw mattresses. They were not nearly as soft and they soon became lumpy and hard. Holes would form in the straw where you lay on the mattress, and there was no way to revive the straw except to replace it, and that happened only once a year, at wheat-thrashing time. The great advantage of the feather bed was that it could be fluffed up and made fresh and soft every day. Mothers were artists in reviving the feather bed to look new every morning.

Quilting parties Most winters, the woman of the house would make a quilt. Scraps of material from old aprons and dresses and other items of clothing would be cut into small pieces and sewn together by hand in various designs and patterns.

The next step was to clear a room of furniture and hang frames from the ceiling. The wood frames would be the size of the quilt to be quilted. The bottom of the quilt would be a solid piece of cotton fabric similar to a bed sheet. It would be attached to the four sides of the frames, a layer of cotton batting would be placed on top of the fabric, and then the pieced quilt top would be placed on top of the batting.

The neighborhood women would gather with their needles and thread with just a little gossip thrown in to spend the afternoon stitching the top to the bottom around each piece of the fabric. Periodically the quilted part on each side would be rolled onto the frame so the women could continue the quilting until they met in the middle and the quilting was completed. At night or during the day when no quilting was being done, the frame would be lifted to the ceiling out of the way, especially in the room where there was a fireplace or bed.

The quilting party was a jolly time for the neighborhood women, similar to a hog killing or tobacco stripping. The kids would play under the quilt while the women worked, and the refreshments usually served were cake and sour pickles—at least in our neighborhood.

The homemade quilt was a work of art, and women would take great pride in their creations. It was common practice to give a quilt to newlyweds for a house-warming, and other special events. Aunt Tola Wheeler gave us a Double Wedding Ring Quilt that she had made especially for Becky and me when we were married.

Water bucket and dipper A water bucket with a single dipper was used by the entire family. The water bucket was kept on the

Nelson and Louie Boyd with parents, 1943.

porch in the summer and in the kitchen in the winter to keep the water from freezing. Everyone, including visitors, drank from the same dipper. Many farmers used a gourd dipper as they could not afford to buy a metal one. When neighbors were working together in the fields, all would drink from the same dipper or from the same glass jug if the family water bucket was not brought to the field. This was not fun when the tobacco juice and lips from all of the men in the neighborhood were all over the dipper.

A story I heard for years after leaving the farm was about the city visitor to the farm family. The father drew a fresh bucket of water from the cistern and offered the well-used dipper full of water to the visitor. The reluctant visitor could see the dirty-faced kids gathered around and the tobacco juice running out each corner of the father's mouth, but he finally decided to drink from the dipper by placing his lips next to the handle of the dipper and tilting it backwards. The father said, "That shore is strange—you're the only person I have ever seen who drinks from the dipper the same way I do."

4

The War Years
1941 to 1945

"If mothers were in charge of International Relations
for each country they would say in unison,
'No more wars, stop the killing.'"

—LJB

The war—World War II was "the war" for my generation—
started December 7, 1941, with the surprise Japanese attack
on Pearl Harbor, and ended in August 1945. But eighteen-year-
olds were still being drafted until October 1946, so the "war" continued beyond 1945 for me since I was eighteen on March 14 of
that year.

World War II years were a tough, stressful time for U.S. families,
especially in rural America. Sunday, December 7, 1941, is burned
indelibly in my mind. We were visiting my sister, Kathleen, and her
family at Midway, near Hazel, Kentucky. They didn't have a radio
so we hadn't heard any news that afternoon. We started home
about 3:30 P.M. in our 1931 A Model Ford to go through Murray,
so we could drop off Nelson at the college dorm. When we got on
the highway at Midway, Nelson picked up a college hitchhiker, and
he told us that the Japanese had attacked Pearl Harbor. I was thir-

teen years old and didn't see much problem with the news, but Mother started worrying and grieving, which never ceased until long after the war was over. She knew Nelson, at age twenty, would have to go off to war. The next day the entire junior high and high school classes at Sedalia gathered in the library to hear on the radio President Franklin D. Roosevelt declare war on Japan.

Nelson joined the navy and got a college deferment so he could attend classes until he graduated; then he entered the navy and later the Air Force. Before he graduated from college, he had to have an appendectomy. As he lay in the Murray hospital so very sick, he was real thirsty and kept asking Mother if they had any water in the navy. He went into service in 1943. The day he left for service was such a sad day. We took him to the train in Mayfield, and I thought Mother created such a scene—she was so heartbroken, I can remember hearing her grieving every night. She seldom slept and almost jeopardized her health. During the next few months, Daddy got her a job in Mayfield through Mr. Deweese, the county school superintendent. She worked at a nursery school in Mayfield, where she kept young children during the day for working mothers. She enjoyed those children so much, giving them lots of TLC, and it was a lifesaver for her emotionally. It was indeed a new experience for a fifty-year-old woman to drive fourteen miles every day to work in town at her first job off the farm.

Before I left for the army I had been to only one place outside the state of Kentucky, and that was Starkville, Mississippi, when Nelson was stationed there during the war. I remember only two trips to Starkville, which were long, long trips in those days. The most memorable one was when Nelson and Sue got married, on May 13, 1944. (An interesting sequel is that Becky and I took Nelson and Sue on a surprise trip for their fiftieth wedding anniversary. On May 13, 1994, we had reservations at the Hotel Starkville where Nelson and Sue had spent their honeymoon fifty years earlier. We also went out to get some of the good ice cream at Mississippi State University, which I fondly remembered from 1944.)

Nelson and Louie Boyd, Starkville, Mississippi, 1944.

I also made two trips to Louisville, Kentucky, when I was a teen-ager. At age fifteen, I attended the Kentucky Boys State program for one week at the Kentucky Military Institute in Louisville. This was a training program in government, whereby we campaigned for offices, held elections, and ran sham local and state govern-ment offices for a week. Mr. Doyle Hutchinson, manager of the Double Cola Bottling Plant in Mayfield, was in charge of the Graves County delegates to Boys State. There was a last-minute can-cellation, so Mr. James B. (Baby) Deweese, county school super-intendent, arranged with Mr. Hutchinson for me to go on this trip. The other delegate from Graves County was Jack Vincent, whose parents owned and operated Vincent's Clothing Store in Mayfield. Daddy took me to Mayfield and I rode with the Vincents to Padu-cah to catch a bus loaded with delegates from Western Kentucky. Jack Vincent was two years older than me, and I was indeed the timid, embarrassed country boy so out of place with these sophis-ticated city people. But I had a great time at Boys State, and it was a tremendous experience for me.

My other trip to Louisville was on the train with Mr. T.C. Arnett, the principal and vocational-agriculture teacher at Sedalia High School, as a member of the Future Farmers of America (FFA) dairy-cattle judging team. The three-member team was composed of Jimmy Morton, James Leach, and me. Yes, we won the Kentucky State contest in 1944. But there was little or no recognition for this achievement, since there was no national contest held that year due to the massive war effort in the United States. The state con-test was held at the State Fair Grounds at the fabulous Churchill Downs—home of the Kentucky Derby. We slept in barracks on the fairgrounds and the toilet was a good distance away, in the infield of Churchill Downs. I well remember a late-night fast trip through the tunnel to the toilet with a good case of food poisoning.

I went to Bowling Green during the Christmas holidays at age seventeen. Billy Warmath and I rode the bus there to drive back our favorite teacher, Mrs. Velma Cloys, who was visiting her parents there with her new baby. Mrs. Cloys' husband, from Farmington, was in service and she did not want to drive back alone with the baby.

Aside from these trips to Mississippi, Louisville (225 miles), and Bowling Green (125 miles), the farthest I had ever been from home was 40 miles. Those were the rare trips to Bob Noble Park in Paducah, where I also saw the awesome Ohio River, and a couple of family trips to Columbus State Park on the Mighty Mississippi River.

At the beginning of the war, rural America was still struggling to recover from the serious economic Depression years of the early and mid-1930s. The Rural Electric Association (REA) was a government program that brought electricity to the farms of America in the late 1930s. But to get electricity, every farm owner between you and the main power line had to give an easement for the electric line to go across his property. One of our neighbors would never give the easement, so we had to wait until after his death in late 1946 to get electricity. So I left a real country home in April 1946, then returned in July 1947 to a "modern" home with electricity and an indoor bathroom!

In our part of the country everybody was totally consumed in the war effort. The draft age had been lowered to eighteen, and the young men went off to fight the terrible war on foreign land. Everyone else sacrificed and joined in the war effort in every way possible. Food, gasoline, rubber tires, and hundreds of products needed for the war effort were rationed. We used ration stamps for our allocation of gas, sugar, and many other products. No automobiles were made from 1941 till 1946. All manufacturing plants were engaged in building army equipment. Sylvester, Kathleen's husband, bought a 1941 Ford car for $700 before the war started, and he sold it two years later for $2,000. Soldiers were paid $21 per month, but money was also becoming available to people back home because of the defense plants and other jobs available to assist the war effort. Even clothing was not available to civil-

Louie Boyd, 1944.

ians. There was no elastic, so tie-strings were used to hold up underwear. This caused some embarrassment for the ladies because if the string came untied, the underwear fell off—even while walking down the street. Pantyhose had not been invented and did not come on the market for another twenty-five years.

In our high school, basketball was big and the only sport for boys. There were no sports for girls. We couldn't get rubber-soled basketball shoes so we had to play in leather-soled shoes. They were very dangerous as we could not stand up—we were always sliding all over. I had no school clothes for my sophomore year in high school and could buy only one pair of pants. I wore the same pair of pants every day for the whole school year. It was a wild pair with a weird, brown-gravy speckled color, and I was terribly embarrassed about them. I was fifteen years old and beginning to notice that girls were different, and I wanted them to notice me for some reason other than the fact that I was wearing the same pants every day. For two years in high school, I was the School Boy Patrol on the bus. At each stop I would get off the bus to stop cars and escort younger students across the road.

Tractors were beginning to come on the scene to help with food production for the war effort. We could get tractor fuel and some rationed gasoline for farming. And it was not unusual for some of the "farming" gasoline to find its way into car gas tanks, even though the farm gas had an additive that could gum up a car's engine. When I started running around with my friends who could get their family cars, we would carry a can of gas in the trunk just in case we ran out. Sometimes, when the car motor was warmed up, we would pour in tractor fuel. This really was tough on the car because the blue smoke rolled from the exhaust, and if the motor got cold it would not start unless we poured gasoline in the carburetor.

In the summer of 1943 a defense plant was being built at Viola, north of Mayfield about twenty miles from our house. Daddy got a job there as a carpenter making almost $20 a day—a fabulous salary. Mother was still working, and this left me as a fifteen-year-old home alone to tend five acres of tobacco and harvest the crops. We did have a neighbor, Mr. Ira Hill, to help me some. But I really worked hard and learned to hate working in tobacco more than ever.

One tobacco incident is still clear. When the tobacco plants were almost mature, and it was a fine crop, Mr. Sam Motheral, who married the sister of Nelson's wife, Sue, came to measure the tobacco ground. Each farmer had a specific base (acreage) for growing tobacco, and the central agency would come to the farm each year to make sure the crop did not exceed the base acreage. We had a tenth of an acre too much, and Sam told me that I needed to cut down two rows of tobacco around an enclosed area in the center of the tobacco patch. Sam left and did not stay to supervise the compliance. In most such cases the farmer might conveniently forget to cut down the tenth-acre of plants, or if he did cut some plants he would rightly select the areas of the field where the worst, most straggly plants were growing. But not me—as soon as Sam left I ran to the house and got the hoe and rushed out to cut down two rows of the finest plants in the entire field. I was real happy to cut them down because it meant I didn't have to pull suckers from those plants anymore. But when Daddy got home that night and saw those beautiful tobacco plants lying on the ground, he was some mad. And I got a right stern lecture, first of all for cutting the best plants instead of the poor-quality plants, and second, with a strong hint that I should not have cut any plants at all.

As much as I hated tobacco I still succumbed to the teenage fad of smoking. It was the manly thing to do, but I always slipped around to smoke—never in front of Mother and Daddy. One night after milking the cows Mother and I were straining the milk into the ten-gallon can at the water tank/milk cooler and she smelled tobacco on me and asked if I had been smoking. I said yes, and she lectured me good—not so much for the smoking but for spending money on cigarettes (Avalon cigarettes cost ten cents per pack) when I should be buying stamps and bonds to support the war effort. She said those soldiers would be dying over there and my brother might be one of them. It made an impression on me but I didn't stop my secretive smoking. After all, I had to be one of the guys and do my part to impress the girls.

The war was financed with war bonds and war stamps. Much effort was put forth for citizens to buy bonds. It was the patriotic thing to do. The smallest-denomination bond was $18.75, which could be cashed in for $25 after ten years. But war stamps could be bought for twenty-five cents each. The common practice was to buy stamps regularly in small quantities and paste them in a book.

When the book was full, with $18.75 in stamps, it could be traded in for a war bond. Farm kids had very little money, but they were admonished to save what they had to buy war bonds. In the summer of 1944, we set aside one acre of tobacco and raised it for Nelson while he was in service. When it was sold, the money went into his savings account.

Tobacco was the chief cash crop in our part of the country, and a farmer could make more money from an acre of land in tobacco than from any other crop. Yet it meant there was money only once each year, and that was usually around Christmas. Farmers were always on the lookout for other cash crops that would bring in more money and at different times during the year. In the early 1940s during the war, green wrap tomatoes surfaced as the new crop—good money. My chief interest was that they were easier work than that blasted tobacco I hated so much.

A tomato-marketing cooperative was set up at Murray, so we set out an acre of tomatoes. They were a cinch and easier work than tobacco. The tomatoes were picked green and taken to the marketing shed at Murray. There they were graded and individually wrapped in paper and boxed for shipping to New York. The tomatoes ripened en route and arrived as hard, red, green-picked tomatoes ready for the consumer. The new venture went great. We received $965 that year from our single acre of tomatoes. So the next year we planted even more—and as so often happened in farming, there was no market. The New York market was lost, and we received $33 from more than two acres of them. The tomatoes rotted in the field, a lot of work and expense for only $33 income. Then back to tobacco as the sole cash crop.

At ages fourteen and fifteen I was doing a lot of work on the farm but didn't have any money. Our neighbor, James Elbert Walker, was older than me and he was allowed to drive his Daddy's car—a 1931 A Model Ford. I was allowed to ride with him to church functions, like Baptist Training Union on Sunday night. One night our Sunday school class was having a picnic, and I really wanted to go. The big stumbling block was that it was going to cost fifty cents for the picnic, and I didn't have it and knew that I couldn't get it from my parents. I worried about my dilemma for three or four days and about mid-afternoon on the day of the picnic the scrap-iron man came through, buying scrap iron. I had collected a pile of scrap iron for the war effort, and this man paid me $1.50 for the pile. I was one happy camper because I now had money and was able to go to the church-class picnic.

The scrap-iron man was Clarence Jackson, who lived over on the Lynn Grove Highway at the Graves County–Calloway County line. He had a truck and did a lot of hauling. We called him Smooth Mouth Jackson because he had no teeth. He was also our ice man in the summer. He delivered ice two days a week. He would bring us 100 pounds of ice each time but by the time he got to our house on many hot days the ice block on the open truck would be more like sixty to seventy-five pounds. But that ice box on the back porch was a wonderful modern convenience. We could keep milk and food cold and also had ice for everybody's tea.

A few months later, when the tobacco crop was sold in the winter, I didn't get any money from the crop. I registered a pretty serious complaint because every Sunday night on our way to church James Elbert would stop at the country store at Brown's Grove and buy a Coke and a candy bar for ten cents. And I needed money for this important weekly activity. In response to my complaint, and mostly at Mother's urging, Daddy gave me $10 for my year's work in the tobacco crop. What a wonderful gift, and how rich I felt. The next Sunday night I made quite a production of presenting the ten-dollar bill to pay for my Coke and candy. I got back a ton of money ($9.90) and I was absolutely wealthy—felt just like a millionaire.

The $10 from the tobacco crop was soon gone, and as I was getting older there was an increasing need for more money. So I struck a deal with Daddy to get up every morning and milk six cows before going to school in order to get a monthly allowance. I

Louie Boyd and parents.

had been milking at night for a long time without any payment, but I had not helped with the early morning milking before leaving for school. This was a cold, miserable chore, but it provided some badly needed money.

The summer I was fourteen Mother and Daddy bought me a new bicycle. It had been ordered and they brought it home when they went to Mayfield on Saturday afternoon. I stayed home and worked on the farm, but I well remember when they got home with the shiny black-and-white bicycle—my first and only.

The same summer, I went to town with Mother and Daddy and stayed there to spend the night with Mother's Uncle Frank Page. He was quite old and lived alone in town and worked as night watchman at a used-car lot. We were going to Grandma Bazzell's at Hickory the next day for Sunday dinner, so this provided a good opportunity for me to sit up all night with Uncle Frank, and then they would pick me up on their way to Hickory the next morning. The used-car lot was next door to a drive-in barbecue restaurant, so I really enjoyed the "city eating." I stayed awake all night, which was more of a struggle than I'd imagined. Early Sunday morning Uncle Frank went to his room to go to bed, and I was left on the bench to wait a few hours to be picked up. When the family hadn't come to pick me up by 11:00 A.M., I became concerned and started walking and hitchhiking home. Meanwhile, the family came by and I wasn't there so they went on to Hickory. Later that afternoon Nelson drove back to Mayfield (about six miles from Hickory) twice to look for me. It took me about four hours to get home—a distance of fourteen miles. I got three rides while hitchhiking, and one was with our school-bus driver, who was driving a milk truck during the summer. Then I had to walk from the highway which was about four miles. When I got home, I was real hungry and sleepy and it was hot. So I put on my bathing suit and lay down on a cot in the shady yard. Uncle Jap and Aunt Tola came over and woke me up to learn that no one else was home. I was so sleepy and quite mad to be awakened, and I was not very nice. But just as

I was awakened, in my ill-humored stupor, a neighbor, Charles Butterworth, came riding up on his yellow bicycle. So I revived my strength, got in a good mood and changed clothes and took off with him for a long bike ride while my Uncle and Aunt were still there in the yard. Later when the family got home they assumed that I was around someplace because my bicycle was gone.

Charles D. lived about a mile away, and he and I spent a lot of time on the bicycles. For ten cents we could spend an entire Saturday afternoon at Browns Grove, Howard's Store, or Darnell's Store, nursing a large Double Cola with a bag of peanuts in it. Or for the same cost we could have an RC Cola and a Moon Pie—a really special treat.

One Saturday afternoon, I went with his folks to Murray. Charles and I were really uptown and got our first introduction to tipping, by going into the Bluebird Café to order a Coke. The people in the booth before us had left some money on the table, so we picked it up and kept it. Knowing nothing about leaving tips, we just assumed the money was ours, since we found it. We drooled over our Coke for a long time, then left. The only trouble was that when we went back about two hours later, the first thing the waitress said was that she knew we'd taken her money from the table earlier. Great acquaintance with tipping—something we didn't know about at Brown's Grove or Howard's Store.

5

Church Attendance

"Count reminiscences like money."

—CARL SANDBURG

Church was not a memorable activity until the beginning of my teenage years. We went to church a lot in earlier years but weren't regularly involved in Sunday school. We would go to take Grandpa Boyd to Beech Grove Cumberland Presbyterian Church some Sundays. That church had preaching only one Sunday a month. Grandma Boyd was a member of Bell City Baptist Church, so we also took her to church several times on different Sundays. Grandpa Boyd died in 1948 at age eighty-one (almost eighty-two), and he never owned or drove a car. When we would take either of them to church it meant a big Sunday dinner and an afternoon spent sitting on their front porch—about five miles from our home. Their newspaper did have the funnies in color, so I enjoyed reading the funny paper—Maggie and Jiggs, Little Orphan Annie, and the Bumsteads. We never got a Sunday paper at home, so no funnies. As a youngster I was the court jester, standing on my head and performing antics in the front yard for the audience on the porch.

Attending revival meetings was an expected practice. Sometimes, the summer meetings would be held in a brush arbor, which was a frame built out of poles with leafy tree limbs piled on top. All sides were open so it was cooler for night meetings. It was lighted with lanterns and people would sit on wooden benches. It was customary to go to the revival meeting each year at the churches in the community. We would go every year to the Burnetts Chapel Methodist Church, where many of our neighbors attended.

Our church was Salem Baptist Church at Lynn Grove. When we did go there, irregularly, for Sunday school, my teacher was Mr. Gordon Crouch. When we first started back one summer, I had been promoted to Mr. Gordon's class and each Sunday the kids would report a number to him. I soon joined in and learned that a high number got a lot of oohs and ahhs but I really didn't know what I was reporting. Later I learned that the numbers were for the number of chapters in the Bible that you had read the preceding week.

When I was fourteen, the preacher holding the revival came home with us from the morning service and stayed until the night service. After dinner (at noon), he lay on a quilt in the yard. That afternoon he talked with me about becoming a Christian and joining the church. He (Brother J. R. Guess) and I went down behind the tobacco barn, where he prayed for me. That night I joined the church and later was baptized in a pond nearby.

Church became much more important when I discovered girls. I could watch a girlfriend in the choir and also could always go to church on Sunday nights with an older boy—James Elbert. But I couldn't go anywhere else with him in the car. On Sunday mornings I would sit with James Key, a redhead. I would make a noise and everybody would look toward us—he would get real red-faced and I would sit calmly so everybody would think he'd made the noise.

6

Many New Beginnings
Army, College, Marriage (1946 to 1948)

"Happiness is the thing that humans pursue for its own sake;
everything else we do is aimed at achieving happiness."

—ARISTOTLE

Climbing on that train with other new army recruits in May-field was a frightening experience. To act as big as I thought I was, I took a pack of cigarettes with me as a continuation of that grown-up, secretive vice started in high school. In my saddened state and disgust over leaving, I threw the half-pack of cigarettes out the train window and never smoked another one. (After my discharge from the army, I did smoke cigars and a pipe for several years. I had a self-imposed limitation, smoking only twice per day, and all smoking ceased when I was about fifty years of age.) We changed trains in Louisville and proceeded on to Camp Atta-bury near Indianapolis, Indiana, for induction. As we were wait-ing in line in our birthday suits for vaccinations, a guy behind us kept yelling up to the ones being vaccinated to watch out for the square needle. It was Carl Howard from Cuba, whom I knew and had played basketball against in high school. When he got to the needle, he fainted and keeled over. We were amused and smiley.

There were scads of forms and physical exams. The soldier administering one of the sessions told us that we had to fill out the forms but that they weren't important and that it didn't matter what we did—we just had to be sure to sign our names. So on my second day in the army and facing my first-ever testing outside the classroom, I took him literally and didn't take the forms seriously at all.

It didn't take me long to learn that I had made a big mistake and that I would suffer the consequences for it. One of the forms was an IQ test, and I didn't do well at all on it. I didn't even know what an IQ was, or that there was such a test. I learned that induction records stick with you like glue throughout the army and for a long time afterward. I spent time on several occasions trying to convince superiors and assignment officials that I was a notch or two above my near-imbecile rating on the IQ test, and that I was capable of doing something worthwhile in the army if given a chance. My first lessons learned in the army were not to take tests lightly, and that I should have worked harder and taken high school more seriously.

From Camp Attabury, Indiana, I was assigned to Fort Knox, Kentucky, for basic training in field artillery. I was placed in a company with all the guys from the Bronx in New York. Most of these guys had been in the army for six months already but had not yet taken basic training. Upon being drafted they were immediately assigned to help with the discharging of the veterans returning from Europe. Thus, they already knew how to goof off and hide when work was to be done. As the sole southern boy, with an easy name to pronounce among the masses of unpronounceable names from the Bronx, I caught lots of work details.

My second lesson came within a couple of weeks while I was on K.P. I was assigned to scrub food trays with a G.I. brush at 6:00 A.M. and the corporal told us that if we really worked hard we would get to change jobs at noon. I really worked my tail off while noticing that several others goofed off quite a bit on their jobs. At lunch, I sat down exhausted to eat and await a new assignment.

Private Louis Boyd.

Others were reassigned, but the corporal looked at me and said, "You've been goofing off, so get back to washing trays!" About 4:00 P.M. I finally figured out that this was the only way he could get a good job done, and on time. Dumb ole me!

Another lesson on volunteering came when the sergeant asked who had a driver's license. I proudly raised my hand, thinking I might get a job driving a jeep or a truck. But the assignment was pushing a wheelbarrow!

I rode the train home several weekends while I was at Fort Knox. The train was the primary means of travel, and the Illinois Central ran from Louisville through Fort Knox to Mayfield. The trains were always crowded and usually the soldiers would stand

Louie Boyd and Gedric Paschall.

in the aisles for part of the ride. I remember a few of these trips. Once, I was sitting on the arm of a seat on a crowded train. I raised my arm to turn around and my sleeve caught the long hat-pin in the hat of the lady sitting in the seat. The hat was ripped off along with some mussed-up hair, and the lady didn't think it was very funny. (Soldiers weren't held in high esteem by some of the prim and proper old ladies.)

One Sunday I went with Mother and Daddy to Grandma and Grandpa Bazzell's at Hickory. Afterward they took me back to Mayfield to catch the train back to camp. Grandpa's house was near the railroad track, so as my train passed by I stood in the doorway to wave my tie to all of them standing in the yard watching for me. Another visit home, I was really taken with the multicolored shoestrings popular with the Bobby-soxers at the time. So I bought a pair and put them in my army shoes. On the train I noticed that a captain kept eyeing me but nothing was said. As I got off the train at Fort Knox he was standing there waiting—called me to attention and chewed me royally for being out of uniform. When he spit me out, I removed those shoestrings, threw them away, and ran about two miles to my barrack.

The last lesson came on a trip to Mayfield when I was sitting beside a beautiful young lady with a baby. I was trying my best to get really friendly with this girl, and because of my weakness for the motherly instinct, I was working through the baby to make time with the mother. While I was working feverishly and feeling so proud of my progress, a sergeant came over and invited the girl to go have a drink, and said the private here would be glad to baby-sit for her. So they took off to the club car while I baby-sat. A valuable lesson.

Basic training began at Fort Knox the last of April, and I'd been in the army only two or three weeks as of Mother's Day. But spending that day alone in a vast army camp I'll never forget. I was so homesick—it must have been the worst day of my life. My mother meant a lot to me that day!

We completed basic training and had a two-week furlough before heading overseas. I had to report to Camp Kilmer, New Jersey, but I didn't know where I was going. I waited there a week for orders and went into New York City for the first time. It was quite an experience to see Times Square and the big buildings. The first TV I ever saw was a six-inch screen on display in a show window at Times Square (June 1946). We stayed all night in the big city, but I got sleepy and slept in a phone booth for two or three hours.

Camp Kilmer was the port of disembarkation for the European Theater, so when we arrived we were issued all woolen clothes, including long-johns and a heavy wool overcoat. There were still troop ships in the Atlantic Ocean from the European fighting, and they were needed in the Pacific to transport troops from Japan and the Pacific Islands. So they loaded 3,000 of us on a 1,500-capacity ship and sent us, in our woolens, through the Panama Canal to Manila, Philippine Islands. The ship was the *Pomona Victory*. We slept in hammocks strung between two posts, eight deep. I was in the sixth hammock near the top, and getting in and out of it was quite a feat.

We left New York late one afternoon and steamed out under the Brooklyn Bridge and by the Statue of Liberty—two meaningful and marvelous sights for me. It was a proud moment. I had heard so many stories about sea-sickness that I just sat on the deck for several hours waiting to get sick. I ate supper and still waited but never got sick. Yet, there were many opportunities. The chow hall had stand-up tables so you could hold on with one hand and eat with the other. The chow hall was next door to the head (the toilet). While eating, many guys would get sick and run for the toilet, but not all would make it there before vomiting. Yes, the chow hall usually had a strong odor, and the walkway along the hall would be slimy and slick. At other times, the toilets would get stopped up and water (and other contents) would be eight or ten inches deep in the hallway. As the ship would rock, the water from the toilet would slosh up over the door frame and flood the chow hall.

We had plenty of saltwater because it was used for mopping, flushing, and bathing. Washing your hair in salt water was different. Going through the Panama Canal was wonderful—a sight I'll never forget. After two weeks, we stopped in San Francisco for refueling. We were allowed off the ship but held in a securely fenced enclosure, where we had a great USO show. The overnight stop meant we could stretch our sea legs briefly and also have a freshwater bath.

We were on the water for thirty days. I saw my first whale in the Pacific Ocean. As the whale surfaced, it looked just like the top of a 1937 black Ford car. That was a monstrous fish to me.

We arrived in Manila in late July 1946, just after the Philippine Islands received their independence (on July 4). It was the rainy season, and we were dumped at a replacement depot, where we slept in tents on folding cots. My tent was on an incline and one morning when I got up my shoes and other items had washed down from under my cot to the end of the tent.

A very special, really lucky break came my way in a few days. Why? Because high school during the war years had left much to be desired. I'd never heard the words "chemistry," "physics," "biology," or "calculus." Certainly a lot of my deficiencies were my own fault, but I really didn't learn much outside of English. Even though we'd had some great teachers there, the war years were extremely difficult. For example, we had seven different teachers in our algebra class one year—the last one being the local Methodist minister. I did learn that he got angry and shoved you down in your seat if you threw someone's book out the window! Anyway, I didn't have a very good background and, as mentioned earlier, the day I was inducted into the army I wasn't in much of a mood to do competency testing. My first realization of what an IQ was and how poorly I had done on the army induction test came just three months later when I arrived in Manila. Fortunately, my record showed that I'd had typing in high school. Many veterans of World War II were returning to the United States from the Pacific area, and the army needed replacements badly in the Headquarters Commandant's Office (for all of the Western Pacific), so, because of the typing I was interviewed by the personnel officer. He was a tall, skinny soldier wearing glasses and a pleasant, kind facial expression. There I learned that the induction test had been testing IQ, and that I'd rated *low*. So despite my typing ability (or inability), I had to convince the interviewer that I really was above the moronic category in intelligence. I apparently convinced him and was assigned to the Morning Reports Section at the Headquarters Office for all the Armed Forces in the Western Pacific. Otherwise, I would have been assigned to the infantry, out in the mud and rice paddies like the other country bumpkins I was with. It was a choice assignment for me and had an important influence on my career and what I ended up doing in life. It was so meaningful that I have told this story many times since 1946!

My assignment to Philippine University at Dilamon near Manila was a great experience. I really didn't have to type (actually, I couldn't very well) because there were Philippino girls employed as secretaries. I was assigned as supervisor of a section—the Morning Reports Section, as I mentioned previously. Most of the soldiers in the Headquarters Office were going home, and the unit was left wide open for promotions. Three days after arrival I was promoted to PFC (private first class); ten days later, to corporal; three months later, to sergeant; and four months later, to staff sergeant. I was eligible for promotion to technical sergeant, but I wanted to come home instead.

There is a most interesting sequel to the army story. In the army I kept a little black book with my personal stuff, and I still have it more than fifty years later. I wrote down the names and home addresses (in 1946) of several army buddies I was either with in basic training at Fort Knox or served with at Philippine University. Throughout the years I kept regular contact with Mortimer Cohen in Long Island, New York, and had some contact with Ed Hammett in St. Louis after 1985. In January 1995, Ed Ham-

Sergeant Louis Boyd
(age 18).

mett was in Atlanta and came over to Athens for a short visit. I dusted off my old army photo album and also found my little black book. He and I had a fun-filled day reminiscing and laughing. There were thirty names and old home addresses in the little black book. He and I resolved to find some of these army buddies. During the ensuing twelve months we located fifteen of the thirty people. One of these veterans turned out to be the tall, skinny, be-speckled, kind-faced soldier who interviewed me in 1946 and gave me the office assignment! He is Henry G. Stratmann of Dupo, Illinois. I didn't remember writing his name and address in my book, and it never occurred to me throughout the years that I had it. But when I located him and talked on the phone with him fifty years later about where he'd been stationed and what he'd done in

Manila, it became abundantly clear to me that he was the one who "saved my life" with the office assignment.

We arrived in the Philippines in time for the monsoon season. Life at the American Forces Western Pacific (AFWESPAC) Headquarters was relaxed and easy after the war was over. The Morning Reports Section maintained a daily report accounting for all service personnel at every base in the Western Pacific. As chief, I was responsible for the Morning Reports Section, but the secretaries and others working in the section knew how to compile the reports, and they kept the section going in good shape.

I looked forward to mail and kept in contact with Mother and Daddy back home. I soon learned that surface mail arrived in two weeks and airmail arrived in one week. So I would write two letters every two weeks, sending one by airmail and the other by surface mail so the folks could hear from me every week.

We lived in barracks with outside latrines and cold showers. The mess hall and USO Hall were just across the street from my barracks. We walked about two blocks to the Headquarters Office Building. We were about ten miles out of Manila, so there was not much to do at camp. Regular meals, lots of sleep, and little activity contributed to much lethargy—I gained thirty pounds before I knew what was happening.

A *New York Times* reporter visited our base and wrote a series of scathing articles about the lax and flabby soldiers having it so easy. After that the army cracked down, and we all had to meet roll call every morning and march to work. Even our barracks sergeant didn't know how to count cadence. This strict discipline didn't last very long, however, and the laxity took over again.

The chapel was about a block away and I went some at first, but I began to go much more often after I met the substitute organist— Beverly Platt, who lived on the base with her parents. Her father was Lt. Colonel Platt, who was the associate commander of the base. Beverly was an eighteen-year-old tall, blonde, beautiful girl from Minnesota. They had moved to Manila from Manhattan,

Kansas, where Colonel Platt had been with the ROTC at Kansas State University.

Beverly and I became fast friends and dated regularly for about ten months. They lived in a nice, separate, barracks-type home on the base. Beverly and I would use her daddy's Jeep to go to Manila to the movies. We went to the beach and other trips arranged by the chapel or the USO. The most memorable trips for me were to Lake Taal, to the road where the Bataan March was held, to the American Graveyard in Manila, and to a lepersarium (the first and only one I have ever seen). The patients wasting away would rise up in bed and beg for candy, which we took to them. Another trip was a boat trip to Corregidor, the island experiencing such devastation during the war. Also, Beverly and her parents were at the r&r camp at Camp John Hay in Bagiou, a mountain resort in the northern part of the Luzon Island, the same week I was there in June 1947. This was the first time I ever played golf. The "greens" were made of sand and had to be smoothed out after each putt.

Following my return from Bagiou, I was headed home. I was a staff sergeant and could have flown, like most of my buddies—the orders for returning to the states originated in our office, so most of the section chiefs cut their own orders for air transport. But I loved the water and was in no hurry to get home, so I elected the slow boat. With my rank I got "first-class" accommodations on the troop ship, and no duties. When we got to California I had forty-five days of sea duty in the Atlantic and Pacific, which was more than many navy men had in service.

Lieutenant Norton in our office brought Beverly to the dock at Manila to see our ship off. As the ship, the *General Morton,* was ready to leave, there were 3,000 soldiers leaning over the rail high above the dock. I could see Beverly, but she couldn't see me until a tall buddy, Irv Deibert, put me on his shoulders and hoisted me well above the other soldiers. She spotted me and we waved goodbye on the Manila dock—that was the last time I ever saw her. (Fifty-one years later, Ed Hammett from Florida and I found Irv Deibert living

Beverly Platt and Louie Boyd, Manila, the Philippines.

Louie Boyd on a water buffalo in Manila, the Philippines.

in Asheville, North Carolina. Becky and I had dinner with Irv and his wife, Barbara, in Franklin, North Carolina, on May 26, 1998. It was a splendid evening as the first meeting since we left California in July 1947.)

On the ship returning home, I saw a country boy from West Virginia whom I had met on the crowded troop ship going over to Manila a year earlier. On the way to Manila, he'd been a homesick, meek, dejected country boy who had tried to get out of service to take care of his widowed mother. He had applied for a military exemption to run the farm, but to no avail, and even after being drafted and sent overseas, he had still been trying to get out. We talked a lot on the ship going over, and he asked me to pray for him to be able to go back to the farm to take care of his mother. I don't even know his name and didn't enter it in my little black book, but I remember what a changed person he was a year later. He was cursing every breath and gambling every day—a different outcome than you like to read about in such chance encounters.

Arriving in the good ole U.S. of A. was wonderful—just to have ice cream, fresh milk, and hamburgers. We no longer had to pour black coffee over our cereal in place of the awful powdered milk. As we approached the Golden Gate Bridge, I was certain that the smoke stack would hit it—but no, the ship slid right under it with plenty of room to spare. We were assigned to Camp Stoneman to await further orders. We waited there for two or three weeks with nothing to do. The war was over and they didn't need the soldiers. I was staying alone in a private room (the barracks-leader room) in an empty barracks. One weekend I went out to Yuba City, California, to visit Uncle Leon Bazzell and took Irv Deibert with me. Uncle Leon's wife, Faye, had a daughter our age, so one of her friends and the three of us went swimming in the Feather River near their house.

We continued to wait at Stoneman with nothing to do, so to ease my frustration I called my brother, Nelson, and told him to get me home. Grandma Boyd had had a stroke a few months earlier while I was in Manila, so Nelson went to Dr. Usher in Sedalia, who contacted the Red Cross and arranged an emergency furlough for me. Two days later, I left Camp Stoneman. Before I left camp my orders came through for me to report to Ft. Sill, Oklahoma but my furlough had already been approved.

I told my friend Irv Deibert about my emergency furlough, and the next time I saw him—fifty-one years later in Franklin, North

Carolina—I learned about his attempt to get out. His father was a physician in New Jersey, so Irv tried my method of getting a furlough, but his father refused to help him. Thus, Irv was later assigned to an army base in Washington State and had to serve several more months before being discharged. This was not a good experience for him and actually caused a little friction between him and his father.

Once I was furloughed, I went first to Uncle Leon's, about 100 miles from San Francisco and stayed three or four days. He took me to an Air Force Base near San Francisco, and I started hitchhiking home by plane. I got on a military cargo plane immediately to Denver, but once there, I was told that there wouldn't be a plane going east for at least two weeks. So I went to the Greyhound Bus station and started riding to Mayfield, Kentucky. It took me three or four days to get home, but I didn't care because I was free and having a big time riding across country—and there were lots of girls traveling by bus in those days.

I had two more weeks before I had to report to Fort Knox to finish out my enlistment. I arrived in Mayfield early one morning and went out to Nelson's house on South 16th Street. He and Sue were at work, so I took a wonderful bath, changed clothes, and headed out to the farm. I stopped by the Parks-Belk store in Mayfield to see Becky Conner—and from that brief meeting came another great development in my life.

I called the folks to tell them I was home and then started hitchhiking the fourteen miles out of Mayfield. But Daddy had started toward town in the pickup truck to pick me up. I caught a ride with one of our former school-bus drivers and just beyond Sedalia we met Daddy and were able to flag him down. So I returned to a great homecoming in a house with electricity, running water, and an indoor bathroom—all new additions since I'd left home a year earlier.

When I reported in at Fort Knox, it was the same story—they didn't know what to do with me. Again I lay around waiting with nothing to do. I had too much rank to pick up cigarette butts or do K.P. duty, so I just waited. I hitchhiked home two or three weekends. The army's solution for what to do with me came after a month, when they discharged me, and I headed home with an honorable discharge.

When I'd been inducted in the army, the base pay was $75 per month. With the promotion and overseas pay I'd been making $125 per month and sending $100 of that home to put in a savings account. At the time of discharge, I had $1,800 in the bank and felt rich. I could have bought a new Oldsmobile for that amount. After the war, all auto plants had switched from making military equipment back to making automobiles for eager consumers. Car prices had gone from $500 in 1940 to almost $2,000 in 1947. New cars were scarce, and the prewar cars were wearing out. Still, I resisted my own urge and the encouragement from others to buy a car, and kept my money in the savings account.

When I stopped by the store in Mayfield to see Becky, I asked her to go out that night to catch me up on all our classmates and friends. She and I had been classmates for eleven years, and we had double-dated for more than a year before I left for the army. That night I kissed her for the first time, but I told her it certainly wasn't the first time I had wanted to do so. We had three or four more dates before I had to report to Fort Knox. Daddy had sold the car and bought a pickup truck while I was in the service—so we dated in a pickup truck many, many years before pickups became popular for teenagers and adults.

Before leaving for the army I'd taken Charles Butterworth, my neighbor, with Jimmy Morton and me to the Conners'. Jimmy and Becky had been dating then, and Charles had asked Becky's sister Linda to go with him that night. She did, and that began a long-term relationship. When I got home from the army, Charles and Linda were still dating, and when I began to date Becky we all went out together on occasion.

I had no idea what I would do when I got discharged. I had just

Becky Conner, 1945.

assumed that I would go to college at Murray for a year or so, but plans were indefinite. Since I was discharged early, I got home in late August in time for the fall term at college. I helped Daddy some on the farm and also helped Mr. Butterworth cut tobacco one day. Charles had gone to Murray State for a year, and he was transferring to the University of Kentucky in Lexington to get his degree in agricultural education. He was going to Lexington to find a place to live that fall, so I decided to go with him. We started out hitchhiking one morning from his house near Lynn Grove. We got to Louisville about 10:00 P.M. and marched into the Brown Hotel, the most elite in town, and asked for a room. They did not have a room but they rented us the bridal suite for $5—a good deal. The next day we moved on to Lexington.

I was quite impressed with my first trip to Lexington and decided to go to school there. I got admitted and we started looking for a room. In 1947, veterans were literally swarming to the colleges to take advantage of the G.I. Bill of Rights. Although getting admitted to college was simple, housing was very scarce. We looked at some rat-holes and finally rented one—a single room all the way across town from the university but only one block from the bus line. What an experience in that old house that fall, when Charles and I had to sleep in the same bed and share the bathroom with Mrs. McAfee and her two grown children, Ann and Tommy. To get to the cold bathroom we had to go through Tommy's bedroom every night after he went to bed, and every morning before he got up. The setup wasn't very conducive to studying.

When our mission was accomplished and we'd hitchhiked back from Lexington, Becky and Linda were planning a trip to Nashville over the Labor Day weekend and they had gotten permission from their parents to invite Charles and me to go along. They were going to visit their great-Uncle and Aunt, Jonah and Alta Cobb, whom my parents knew. The Cobbs had a daughter named Rebecca Jane who had just gotten married and lived in a little house behind her parents' home. So Charles and I stayed in the little house with Dan,

Rebecca Jane's husband, and the girls stayed in the parents' house. We rode the Southeastern Stages bus to and from Nashville. We took an airplane ride (Becky's first) and also drove the girls' great-Uncle's pickup truck around to see the sights of Music City. Their home was near Shelby Park.

In mid-September, Charles and I moved to Lexington in a ten-year-old, heavily loaded Willys car with Glenn Sims from Cuba. I went home several weekends that fall. Traveling the 300 miles and taking a chemistry class did not mix very well. I had a chemistry test every Friday afternoon, and many weekends I left school early on Friday to get home and then headed back to Lexington on Sunday, either riding with someone who had a car or hitchhiking. The next semester I had the opportunity to take freshman chemistry again.

The biggest event of my first semester in Lexington was that the famous racehorse, Man O' War, died and his funeral attracted a huge crowd. Early in 1948 I hitchhiked to Frankfort for the Governor's Inauguration and another occasion to visit the state House of Representatives. The Speaker of the House was Adrian Doran from Graves County and he introduced me to the assembly.

One semester living with the McAfees on Rand Avenue was enough. After Christmas we moved to Forest Park, where Glenn Sims lived—much nearer the university. Again, a single room and one bed sharing the bathroom with Glenn and an older couple as the owners. The second semester went quite well. The New Year of 1948 was a leap year, and marriage plans were being made. Becky and I became engaged at 12:01 A.M. on Sunday, February 29, 1948—a date that has been on Sunday twice since that time (in 1976), and the "second anniversary" of our engagement was in 2004. We were to get married after school was out in June, but we didn't worry about announcing a date. Charles and Linda were also getting married after school was out. Charles's parents were helping with their arrangements by purchasing a trailer for them to live in. This materialized in mid-April. Becky and I didn't want a double wedding, which we thought might be suggested, so one night while "studying" I suggested to Charles that they go ahead and get married to take advantage of his new home. I urged him strongly, so he picked up the phone and called the Conners. The family was having supper, and when Charles asked Linda she started crying and turned him over to her daddy. It worked, as they were married right after her graduation from Sedalia High School on the night of May 6, 1948. Becky and I then finalized our plans and set the date for June 12.

I helped Charles and Linda get settled in their new home in Palmer's Trailer Court on South Broadway in Lexington. There was a golf course behind the court. More than fifty years later the golf course is still there, and the trailer court is the site of the Campbell House Hotel. In late May 1948, Becky came to Lexington to apply for a job as secretary in the English department. I had learned from Mrs. Dan Hutson, who was from Murray and who was teaching in the UK English department, that this job would be coming available in the fall, and she had arranged for Becky to apply. This was the first time Becky had ever traveled alone, so I met her bus in Louisville, and we rode the bus on to Lexington. She stayed with Linda and Charles and rode the bus back home. No decision was to be made on the job until September, when school started. One Saturday morning, just before school was out, I walked over to the trailer to help Charles work up the small yard around his trailer and sow bluegrass. On the way, I stopped at a corner grocery and bought a packet of mustard seed. That afternoon, as he was sowing bluegrass seed, I ambled around discretely dropping mustard seed in the finely pulverized soil. The next week Charles and Linda went to western Kentucky for school vacation, and I moved back home to get ready for the wedding.

The only preparation for our wedding was to reserve the church—Lebanon Church of Christ (Becky's church) in Sedalia, Kentucky—borrow some potted plants as flowers, and arrange for a minister. We were married on Saturday morning, June 12,

Louie and Becky, June 12, 1948.

Becky and Louie, just married.

1948. Brother Benton Carmen from Mayfield married us. Only the two families and some of our classmates attended. Becky's close friend and neighbor, Molly Doran, was the maid of honor, and my brother, Nelson, was the best man. After the ceremony I noticed the minister going to his car, so I asked Nelson to go pay him. He didn't have any money so I gave him my billfold and Nelson paid the minister $5.

Both families went to the Conners' for lunch. That afternoon

Mr. and Mrs. Conner took us to Mayfield, where we caught a train at 4:00 P.M. to Memphis for our honeymoon. Carolyn Boyd and other of our classmates were at the train depot to shower us with rice as we boarded the train. As we arrived at the William Len Hotel, we were very careful so they wouldn't know we were newly-weds, but the falling rice during registration let everybody know. The second day there we lost the key to the hotel room—a disturbing happening. We were assured that no one else could get in when the door was locked from the inside, and we were given a new key. The next day, the original key fell out of the cuff of my trousers as I took them off the hanger.

Two days later, Mrs. Conner called to tell us that the English department at the University of Kentucky had called and wanted Becky to come for an interview as quickly as possible. So we cut short the honeymoon and went back home to get ready to go to Lexington.

Linda and Charles were moving a lot of things to Lexington as they went back, so Mr. Conner let us take his new 1948 Plymouth to move their things. On the way to Lexington, we spent the night in a motel at Horse Cave, Kentucky, and made our first visit to Mammoth Cave.

As we arrived at the Butterworths' trailer, Charles was eager to see his bluegrass lawn. There was very little bluegrass, but there *was* a fine crop of something growing tall. He couldn't figure out what it was and I didn't tell him; but since I did tell the folks back home about it, it didn't take him long to find out that I was responsible for the fine crop of turnips in his yard.

After the interview, Becky and I drove back to Mayfield for the summer. She got the job in the English department, so we were anxious to move to Lexington in the fall. We lived in Mayfield for two months before moving to Lexington so Becky could continue working. Housing was extremely scarce everywhere. The only place we could find to rent in Mayfield was one room in a large house just one block from the town square. We shared the bathroom with six other renters on the second floor. We had a hot plate in the room but no refrigerator. I went looking for work and found a job at the Double Cola plant for $20 per week. I worked for Mr. Doyle Hutchinson, who had arranged my trip to Boys State six years earlier. We didn't have a car, so Becky's parents or mine would come get us on Saturday and we would go home for the weekend. One night, while we were sweltering in the hot room, Becky's parents stopped by to visit. Becky was ironing and had on a pair of shorts. Her Daddy lectured her good and told her to change clothes.

During the spring term in Lexington, I had been looking desperately for an apartment for the fall. Many others were seeking a place to live and the residents renting their rooms were very choosy. One day I saw an ad in the paper for an apartment to rent but no address listed, only a phone number. I called but the lady would not tell me the location because she did not want to rent to a married couple. So I went to a phone booth in one of the campus dorms and searched the phone book till I found the phone number and location of the renter. It was located on the east side of town, just off Richmond Road. I rode the bus out and convinced the lady to rent to us as newlyweds starting in September. The house was a block and a half from the bus line where you transferred downtown to get on a bus to the university—most inconvenient, but a place to live. I left Lexington for home happy and ready to get married.

In early August, I wrote the lady a letter telling her when we would arrive, as Becky was to start her new job on September 1. The lady promptly wrote back and said that she had decided that she would not rent the room where we were to share the kitchen and bathroom with her. But, she said we could stay there for a week while we found another apartment. I was very much disappointed with this news.

So the last weekend of August we packed our worldly possessions in two small suitcases and one pasteboard box and boarded the bus for Lexington. We took a taxi to our new place and moved in. Perhaps it could have been worse as we waited for Becky to start her new job and for me to find an apartment, but at the time we didn't think so. Anyway, a new era was dawning for me at twenty years of age—it was my second year of college and our first year of married life. Without the excellent army experience and the subsequent G.I. Bill, I would never have been at the University of Kentucky in Lexington. It is possible that I would have gone to Murray State College for a year and then taught veterans. In 1946, immediately after the war, the on-farm training for returning veterans was a big program, and one could teach in that program with only one year of college. After all, teaching agriculture was the only nonfarm job I knew about in the agricultural field. Otherwise, I would probably have gotten married and headed to Detroit for one of those "good jobs" in a factory where you could make $5 a day. This is why leaving the farm for the army in 1946 and my fortuitous return in 1947 have been so meaningful to me.

The World War II veterans returning home and entering college in the late 1940s became the parents of the Baby Boomers. They were also known as the first generation to educate *two* generations—themselves and their children.

7

Moving to the Big City

"The great cities rest upon our broad and fertile plains.
Burn down your cities and leave your farms, and your cities
will spring up again as if by magic, but destroy our farms
and the grass will grow in the streets of every city in the Nation."

—WILLIAM JENNINGS BRYAN

Becky was excited about the move but quite apprehensive. She had never been away from home except for a year at college in Murray—and that had been just twenty miles from home. She was also very nervous about the new job at a big university.

On September 1, 1948, we got up early in our one room, used the shared bath, gulped a bowl of cereal in the shared kitchen, and headed out to Becky's new job. She was to be paid a wonderful salary of $135 per month, so we were most eager for a good start on the job. We walked to the bus line and rode the bus downtown on Richmond Road to Main Street, then changed to the Rosemont bus out to the university. Then we walked a block to McVey Hall to the English department. We were excited but quite nervous and scared. Becky was to start out working for the head of the department—Dr. Herman E. Spivey. Compounding the problem was that

100

he was writing a textbook, and on the very first day he started dictating the book to her—she had not taken dictation in more than a year. She heard many unfamiliar words in that textbook.

I had a most challenging job also, and that was to find a place to live. There were no such things as student apartment buildings in town, and there was a two-year waiting list for married veteran housing. The limited number of rental rooms in private homes was never advertised, because the landlords would not rent to minorities or married students, and they wanted to charge more than the wartime Office of Price Administration (OPA) would allow. So most rentals were handled privately and unofficially. I checked every possible source anyway—newspapers, housing offices, bulletin boards, and individuals, and finally began walking the streets knocking on doors and asking if anyone knew of a place for rent.

The first three days were especially rough for Becky—she was the farthest she'd ever been from home, we had no place to live, and she was really struggling with a stressful, nerve-wracking job that she didn't feel qualified to handle. Every day was the same story—we'd ride the bus to campus for her to work and for me to walk all day. Her nerves and my shoes were wearing out.

Then we got the bright idea of running an ad in the paper seeking an apartment. Becky got permission to list her office number for calls, so we wrote a great description of a wonderful couple looking for a place to live. But we got no calls, and I was getting desperate. Things weren't going too well with the old lady where we were living. So on Friday morning I found an unfurnished apartment in a dirty old house near the football stadium. I was ready to take the apartment and trying to decide how we could round up some used furniture, since we had nothing at all. But it was lunchtime, and I went to Becky's office to meet her for lunch. Before I could reluctantly tell her about the cruddy place I was about to rent, she excitedly told me she had gotten a call in response to our ad in the paper. So we skipped lunch to ride the bus out South Limestone to find the apartment. What a lovely area—a beautiful, clean, tree-lined street. There was no separate entrance (we had to go through the family living room to get to the upstairs steps), but there was a gorgeous, clean, well-furnished apartment upstairs over the living quarters of a nice family. There was a small living room, large kitchen, large bedroom, and large bath. We convinced the family to rent to us. The price was $60 per month, and the man called me aside to whisper that this was above the OPA price. I assured him there was no problem. Oh, how fortunate we were— we were really being smiled upon.

The next day, on Saturday, we called a taxi and moved all of our worldly possessions (those two suitcases and the pasteboard box) into our new home at 138 University Avenue. The owners were Mr. and Mrs. Marksbury, whose daughter, Gayle, and Gayle's ten-year-old daughter were living with them. This was a wonderful place—our home for two years. It was a mile from school, and we walked that distance four times a day. Becky had 90 minutes for lunch, so I always arranged my classes so we could walk home each day for our meal of cheese, crackers, and soup.

I didn't buy any clothes when I first got home from the army. I had several pairs of army khakis and woolen pants and two Eisenhower jackets. I had the wool jackets and pants dyed and wore old army clothes during my undergraduate days. I did buy a suit in February 1948, which I wore when we became engaged, and then bought a new one for our wedding. I had several pairs of G.I. underwear—size thirty-six boxer shorts that were much too big, but that I tied up and wore anyway for the next two or three years. For our wedding, Mother, being extra thoughtful, bought me a new pair of white shorts—or so I thought. As I opened and unfolded the package on my wedding day they turned out to be knee-length tight underwear. So back to the green army-issue shorts for the wedding.

In addition to Becky's salary of $135 per month I received $120 a month from the G.I. Bill, plus tuition and books each quarter. We were living well when we got married. Becky had $400 and

I had $1,800 in a savings account. When we arrived in Lexington we still had the $1,800, so we started saving for a car.

The fall quarter started, the apartment was nice, Becky became more comfortable in her new work, and we were indeed enjoying life. I had extra time between classes, so I got a job working in the horticulture greenhouse on campus for 25¢ per hour.

My college friend Floyd Ellis, from Bowling Green, had gotten married, and we were close friends with Floyd and Sarah. Charles and Linda Butterworth lived in Lexington for a year, so we spent time with them, as well as with Ralph and Margie Taylor from Farmington, Kentucky; Tommy and Sue Murdock from Murray, Kentucky; Dale and Carolyn Lester from Mayfield; and Charles and Robbie Lassiter from Murray. The Taylors had a car, so the Butterworths and Boyds went lots of places with the Taylors. The car was a coupe with one bench seat in front and, behind it, a bit of space (but no seat). Four could fit in the front seat while Charles and I squeezed in on the floor in the back. We visited lots of big horse farms in the Lexington area. In those days you could drive onto any of the horse farms and walk through the barns. At Calumet Farm we could walk through and see big-name horses like Citation and Coaltown. On Saturday nights we could go out to a Chinese place where we could eat chicken chow mein for a dollar each.

On election night in November 1948, I lay awake most of the night listening to the election returns on the radio. This was the year of the big upset when Truman beat Dewey for president. The media were predicting a big win for Dewey, and many newspapers, including the *Chicago Tribune*, printed a giant headline declaring Dewey as winner. But it didn't happen.

The next morning, as we started walking to school, I had some discomfort in the lower abdomen. After one block we got on the bus instead of walking the rest of the way. I went on to the campus infirmary, and late that afternoon a surgeon came in and diagnosed appendicitis. They called Becky, and the surgeon took us in his car to Good Samaritan Hospital for surgery. Of course, I was

Louie and Becky, first anniversary.

concerned about the cost, but the surgeon, Dr. Sprague, laughed and said, "I don't charge students much—I make it up on the big horse-farm owners around Lexington." (That was satisfactory until we got the bill, which was for the full charge of $150. We paid it in small amounts over an extended period.)

Upon arrival at the hospital, Becky called Ralph Taylor, who, as mentioned earlier, had a car (and lived near the hospital). She spent the night with Ralph and Margie. Before I was fully anesthetized I remember talking to the doctor about the election and also telling him that his wife would be mad at me for making him late for supper. Little did I know that she was accustomed to such emergencies. The next morning I was moved back out to the campus infirmary to recuperate at no cost. Nelson brought Mother and Daddy to see me over the weekend. They gave us $100, which was the only financial support we ever received for my college education. (Of course, there were always other kinds of support over the years—like on every trip home, when Mother would load us down with food!)

In the spring of 1949 I took a dairy course and signed up for a two-week travel course in June. Charles Lassiter went too; we were with forty or so other students led by Dr. D. M. Seath, head of the dairy section at the University of Kentucky. The trip meant that I was away from home on our first anniversary. I had hidden a gift in the closet, and on our anniversary I called Becky. It was a great gift, I thought—a set of cookware—which we used for more than 50 years.

It was an exciting trip for me. Artificial insemination of dairy cattle was just getting a strong start in 1949, and we visited bull studs where bull semen was collected and processed. We also visited Ohio State University, Michigan State University, University of Wisconsin, and University of Minnesota, as well as dairy plants, cheese plants, and large dairy herds. At Michigan State we met Dr. Shorty Huffman, who showed us a cow with a window in her stomach. We also met Mr. Fred Pabst at Pabst Holsteins, owned by

Pabst Brewery in Wisconsin; Mr. Bill Knox, editor of *Hoard's Dairyman Magazine* at the Hoard's Dairy Farm in Wisconsin, and Dr. W. E. Petersen at the University of Minnesota, who authored the dairy textbook I used in class. This was big-time for me. We attended the annual meeting of the American Dairy Science Association (ADSA) in St. Paul, at the University of Minnesota, and heard many scientists present their research papers. This trip motivated me to major in dairy science. During the next year I worked some at the dairy-processing plant managed by Mr. Emmett Dozier, and also milked cows at the dairy farm managed by Mr. Garland Bastin.

Charles Butterworth graduated in the spring of 1949, and he and Linda moved from Lexington as he began teaching vocational agriculture. Nelson and Sue lived in Lexington during the fall semester 1949 while he took courses so he could be certified to teach agriculture. Harold and Wanda Ford, from Sedalia, were also living in Lexington, where Harold was working on a master's degree in dairy science. The six of us spent a lot of time together that fall. Sue and Wanda were pregnant, so Sue moved back to Mayfield at Christmas and Nelson moved into a room in the home of a Mrs. Derrickson, just across the street from where Becky and I lived on University Avenue. He had to stay until the end of January to finish out the semester. Harold and Wanda moved at Christmas to Frankfort, where he was appointed assistant commissioner of agriculture for Kentucky. The Fords' first girl, Karen, was born in early January 1950, so on the following Saturday Nelson, Becky, and I drove over to Frankfort to see the new baby. When we got back to Lexington we found they'd been calling all afternoon to tell Nelson his son Greg had been born. He raced off for Mayfield immediately.

Basketball was king in Kentucky (and still is!), and in the late 1940s Adolph Rupp's "Fabulous Five" were famous. We tried to see as many games as possible and always listened to the others on the radio. One national tournament game from Madison Square

Garden in New York was especially exciting. Jim Line was one of the reserve players. His girlfriend lived next door to us, so we thought we knew all the players personally. Paul "Bear" Bryant was the football coach at the University of Kentucky in the late forties and just beginning to achieve success. He had a real successful season and participated in a postseason Bowl Game. That year the UK athletic supporters gave a new Cadillac to Rupp and an engraved gold watch to Bear Bryant. Shortly, The Bear left Kentucky for Texas and later moved to Alabama. In the unbelievable scandal of the century, point-shaving charges were made against Kentucky basketball players who had taken bribes to reduce point spreads. I was so disappointed and hurt—I just couldn't believe it had happened.

After we had been in our neat apartment for about a year my name came up for a unit in the veterans housing in Cooperstown. We really weren't ready to move, but we didn't want to give up this rare opportunity to get university housing. At the same time, Dale and Carolyn Lester's first baby was born, and they were being kicked out of their apartment. Carolyn and the baby had to move back to Mayfield just a few weeks before Dale graduated. So to enable her to stay in Lexington, I let them move into our veteran's unit under my name. It didn't take long for the new baby to attract the attention of the authorities, so I was called in to Dean A. D. Kirwin's office for a strong reprimand. The Lesters were kicked out of the unit, and my name was removed from the waiting list.

The spring of 1950 was a big time for us. The Korean War was heating up, and it appeared that I might have to go back into service. Also, we decided to buy our first car. New cars after World War II were still very scarce and usually required a long wait. But my sister's husband, Sylvester, thought he could find us a car. So one weekend in April I went to Murray, and he took me around to several car dealers. By paying cash I was able to purchase a 1950 Chevrolet in Paris, Tennessee, and had it delivered through the same dealer's garage in Murray. It was a two-door sedan that cost

Becky and our first car.

$1,650. When all taxes, license, and everything was paid I had to borrow enough money from Nelson to buy gas to drive back to Lexington.

By going to school full time, I was to graduate in the summer of 1950. So we decided that I would go on for a master's degree. This meant we needed cheaper housing, so I tucked my tail and went to see Dean Kirwin, humbly requesting to get back on the waiting list for veterans housing. This effort succeeded, and, as many veterans were graduating by 1950, the housing crunch was less serious.

In June 1950 Becky and I went with Charles and Robbie Lassiter to attend the ADSA meetings at Cornell University in Ithaca, New York. A friend, Aurel Hardison from Sedalia, and his wife Frances lived in Ithaca, where he was working on a Ph.D. They were out of town so we stayed in their apartment to save money. It was a great trip through the Catskill Mountains, and we stopped in New Jersey to see a Rotolacter—a merry-go-round arrangement onto which a cow would move to be milked while it made one revolution around. Quite modern, but an invention that never caught on.

I graduated with a B.S. in August and started the master's degree in the fall semester. I got a graduate assistantship paying $900 per year. I was doing my M.S. with Dr. Seath as my major professor, but I worked for Dr. Elliott in his nutrition laboratory for my assistantship. We got a unit in veterans housing shortly after school started that fall. We had one side of a prefab duplex unit left over from the war. Our side was about eight feet wide and twenty-four feet long, and included the living room, dining room, kitchen, bedroom, study room, and bathroom. The couch folded down for the bed, and there was a two-eye hotplate. The room was separated from the adjacent apartment by a thin "pasteboard" wall.

We wanted to repaint our new mansion before moving in, so I went over between classes every day all week and finally got the cabinets painted. This pace was much too slow for Becky, so she went over one Friday night to paint while I studied. She was back in two hours and had finished painting the rest of the room and bathroom. The next morning I found several strips that hadn't been painted, as the roller had seemed to cover the area so quickly in the poorly lighted room. This provided a rich source of teasing over the years.

We adjusted to the one-room living rather easily. In November,

Louie Boyd, B.S. degree, 1950.

Becky's uncle and aunt, Buford and Geneva Byrd from Detroit, stopped in Lexington and Becky prepared a marvelous Thanksgiving dinner on the hotplate with its ten-inch oven.

Our unit was only fifty feet from a big field on the Experiment Station Farm. That winter there was a big snow which drifted across the front of our house up to the roof. We and the couple next door could not get out of our houses. We opened up the small vent in the roof of the bathroom to stick my head out and yell for help. Our first snowbound experience.

We went home in our new car for Christmas in 1950. The meals were not too appetizing to Becky so after we returned to Lexington and started the new year it soon became abundantly clear that Becky was pregnant. That started a long period of really being sick. For her, morning sickness lasted all day for more than four months. For breakfast, lunch, and supper, she would start to eat, rush to toss her cookies, and then come back to force-feed herself as much as possible. A friend, Tommy Murdock, had a class with our next-door neighbor, Bernie. One day Bernie was telling the class how thin the walls were in the veterans housing and said that he knew his neighbor was pregnant before her husband knew it, as he could hear her vomiting. She continued working for three months but lost sixteen pounds. None of the medications prevented the nausea. At home, she slept most of the time, but the old rolling, lumpy, fold-down couch was not too comfortable.

The sickness finally subsided before the intense heat of summer. Becky quit working in May. I was pushing for August graduation, and Becky typed several versions of my thesis before the days of Xerox—only messy carbon paper. Mother and Daddy came up in August for my graduation with the M.S. degree. Our friends Levi and Jerry Oliver from Princeton lived around the corner from us, and they were not home so Mother and Daddy slept there. The Olivers were rich residents, so they had an actual bed crowded into the one room. The next morning when I went down to get Mother and Daddy for breakfast, I found that the bed had fallen, and that they'd slept all night with the head high and the foot of the bed on the floor.

We were indeed enmeshed in the postwar generation—veterans going to school, wives working, and jointly creating the Baby Boomer generation. The veterans housing at the University of Kentucky was located on the research land used by the College of Agriculture. Dean Thomas Poe Cooper was quoted as saying, "The land was never as fertile or productive as it was when the veterans were living on it." The University of Kentucky awarded PHT degrees to working wives—Put Hubby Through—and Becky earned her degree there.

❧ **8** ❧

New Job and New Family

"As the children heard many times, especially when we were trying
to get everybody up in the morning—'This is a time to make tracks
in the sand, as there are miles to go and mountains to climb.'"

—LJB

A fortunate event for me was that I was being hired in a temporary position to do statewide extension-specialist work
there in the dairy department. Mr. Glynn Williamson, who held
the position, was being recalled as an army reservist for the Korean
War. I was replacing him, which meant I did not have to look for
a job or move out of university housing. So at age twenty-three I
was hired at $4,000 per year. I still remember that first talk I gave
to county agents and dairymen—I was some nervous. I started to
work on September 2, since the September 1 was on Labor Day.

Our first baby was overdue, but she was born on September 11.
I was scheduled to work at the state fair in Louisville that day, but
Becky was in labor early in the morning, so we rushed off to Good
Samaritan Hospital and waited twelve hours for delivery.

We were so excited over the birth of Beverly Charlotte. As I was
a new employee in dairy, we sent announcements about the birth

of a new "bawler." Becky was placed in a room with another new mother. In talking with her the next night I learned that she had not seen her baby and did not know whether she had a boy or girl. I rushed out to find a nurse to give her a piece of my mind for being so lax—only to learn that Becky's roommate was an unmarried mother who had given up her baby for adoption. Another new experience for Becky and me.

The next day after Beve was born I went back to work at the state fair in Louisville, which was the tenth day on my new job. In fact, I always kidded Becky and Beve about being so inconsiderate in timing as to cause me to miss a day of work while waiting all day at the hospital. This was long before anyone had ever heard of maternity or family leave, even for women—and certainly not for men.

The one child meant a one-bedroom unit in Cooperstown, the veterans housing—a unit almost twice as big as the one we were in. We had a separate bedroom with a full bed and room for a baby bed—a big step up from our previous home. I moved from Hobbs Court to Hilltop Avenue while Becky was in the hospital. Our unit was adjacent to the university observatory and veterans housing office, so we had a large bluegrass lawn in the back of our house. It was a wonderful place for our new family.

My work as field agent in dairying involved extensive travel, as I was subject to go over the entire state working with the 4-H dairy program, county agents, dairy farmers, breed associations, and artificial-insemination associations, as well as judging dairy shows. Frequently, I would leave home on Monday and return late Friday. Neither of us knew anything about taking care of a baby, but Becky missed having me to share my ignorance. Polio was rampant in the early 1950s, and was the most frightening possibility for children and young mothers.

One night when I came home, the house was all dark, which was much different from what I had become so accustomed to—a nice cozy home with supper ready, and being greeted so lovingly by

Beverly at eight months.

my family. I opened the door and the baby was crying, so I rushed in. Becky was in bed with stomach cramps and diarrhea—she just knew it was polio. She had been to a party that day at one of the departmental wives' homes to show off our daughter. I asked what she had eaten, and she said nothing, except that she'd drunk some sweet cider! I laughed because I had eaten enough green apples on the farm to know what had caused the problem. She got so mad at me that she got out of bed and fixed supper.

The first Christmas we loaded up and went home with our three-month-old. We took the bassinet and everything else imaginable. Becky's folks, the Conners, had just moved from the farm to Murray so we went to their new home. Mr. Conner had purchased the Allis-Chalmers tractor dealership in Murray and was starting into business.

When Beve was one year old we became eligible for a two-bedroom home. It was still in a barracks-type building, but was a separate unit all our own.

My work was going well. I was enjoying it and gaining valuable experience working with so many wonderful people. One was Jack Caldwell from Burlington, Kentucky (near Cincinnati); he was secretary of the Kentucky Brown Swiss Breeders Association. He was a dairy farmer, and I traveled a lot with him to meetings. He took minutes at meetings, typed them up, and handled his own correspondence—even though he was blind. One night he was staying in the motel room with Fred Idste, the national executive secretary of the Brown Swiss Breeders Association. Jack always waited until others were finished in the bathroom before he went in to get ready for bed. The next morning at breakfast, Fred told Jack that he'd left the light on the previous night when he went to bed—Jack, of course, being blind, never knew it was on. At meals we would order for Jack and tell him where on the plate each food item was—according to the numbers on a clock—and he could do really well eating. New walk-through milking parlors were just being built on dairy farms, so my real challenge was to lead Jack through a new milking parlor and describe how it operated while he was "looking" at it by sound and feel.

After I'd considered other opportunities, it soon became apparent that I wanted to stay in academic work and be located at a university. However, extension work with much travel was not conducive to having a happy young wife and raising a family. There were so many veterans in colleges after the war, and many were getting Ph.D.s. So it was obvious that, if I wanted to be in academic work, I had to have a Ph.D. I knew that I wanted to specialize in animal reproduction, so in the fall of 1952, I began considering where I wanted to do graduate work. The really good programs were at Illinois, Cornell, and Penn State. I wanted Illinois, but I tried Penn State first because one of my former UK professors (Durward Olds, a veterinarian) was going to Illinois for his Ph.D., and I didn't think I wanted to go there and be compared with him all the time. However, the department head at Penn State would not commit to a graduate assistantship for me, so I quickly turned to Illinois.

At Christmas 1952, we were in Murray visiting family, and I took a trip to Illinois with Charles and Linda, who were living at Chrisman, Illinois. The next morning Charles took me about ninety miles to Champaign-Urbana before daylight so he could be back at work by 8:00 A.M. I visited the University of Illinois, the dairy department, and Dr. Glenn Salisbury, then caught a bus back to Mayfield, Kentucky, that night. It was a wonderful visit that set me off big-time for Illinois. I got an assistantship and began making plans to go back to school in the fall of 1953.

When I was hired at the University of Kentucky at $4,000 per year, I was told that my salary would be increased the next July. The university salaries at Kentucky were very low at the time because state law mandated that no state employee could make more money than the governor, whose salary was $5,000. My salary wasn't raised, so after July 1, I asked about it, and it was raised to $4,600 in September 1952. (This was the first and *only* time I ever asked for a salary increase throughout my entire career.) In addition to my salary I was paid 6¢ per mile for travel and $6.50 per diem, which covered lodging and meals. In most of the small towns I could get a room in a hotel or tourist home for $2 and could eat quite well on $4.50 per day. We were paying only $30 per month for rent, so we saved all of my expense-reimbursement money for the two years I worked. That was what enabled us to go back to school.

In June 1953, we traveled with the Lassiters in our car to ADSA in Madison, Wisconsin. We'd left Beve at Linda's, back in Illinois.

Louie, Becky, and Beve, ready to move to Illinois.

The night we got back to Linda's, Beve slept with us and she was really hot all night. The next day she was feverish on the way to Lexington, so we were anxious to get her to her doctor. At 8:00 that evening we called him at a bridge party, and he didn't want to come to the house. But I insisted, saying we had deprived her of medical attention for thirty-six hours. He left the party, came to our veterans housing unit, shook his head, and told us to give her aspirin. So much for another polio attack.

In late August, 1953, I loaded our belongings into a small, open U-Haul trailer ready to head to Illinois. We got up in our empty house the next morning to get an early start, only to find the car battery dead. Hooking the trailer lights to the car's tail lights had shorted out the battery. I finally got a jump-start and we headed out of Lexington, through Louisville, and west across Indiana. We stopped at Ernie Pyle Roadside Park, confident that the battery would have charged up during that long drive. But no, it had not, and we had no jumper cables. Finally a young couple stopped, and they were willing to pull me to get the car started but they had no chain. I got a small rope from Beve's swing stored in the trailer, and tied to his car. He had to pull the car and trailer up a small incline. After much spinning of wheels he finally got us moving, but after a few feet, when I tried to crank the car by releasing the clutch, the rope broke. We started rolling backward gently, so I put the car in reverse and released the clutch. Fortunately, the motor started just as the car jack-knifed into the trailer. No damage except for the rope swing, and we moved on to Chrisman, Illinois, stopping overnight at the Butterworths'. The next day I got the battery charged up, and we left the trailer and Beve at Linda's while we looked for a place to live in Champaign-Urbana. We found the housing shortage there even worse than it had been in Lexington five years earlier. With so few choices, we rented a place that day, cleaned it from stem to stern, and moved in the next day.

The Champaign–Urbana Years
1953 to 1956

"A man can fail many times but he isn't a failure
until he begins to blame somebody else."

—JOHN BURROUGHS

The house in which we rented our apartment was at a super location on South Sixth Street in Champaign—just across the street from the Newman Foundation and the basketball field house. That was the end of its assets. It was an upstairs apartment in an old, weather-boarded house with a back entrance. It consisted of two rooms, a small kitchen with a table, a small hallway, and a bathroom. The only source of heat was an open grate in the floor, and the renters downstairs were supposed to fire the basement furnace to provide the heat to come up through the grate to heat our apartment. And there was no sink and no running water in the kitchen. The only source of water for cooking and washing dishes was from the bathroom tap, and we had to flush the dirty dishwater through the commode. Heat was a problem even in late August, but not for lack of it. Our first purchase was a Sears window fan to pull air through the apartment.

The rent was $115 per month, and I was to be making only

$135 per month. We had saved $3,800 in Lexington, but we hadn't planned to use as much of our savings for living expenses each month. After three months, when the landlord came to collect rent, Becky gave a convincing sob story about our low income and told him he could be reported for the high rent on an apartment with poor heat and no water in the kitchen. It worked, because he lowered the rent to $90 per month.

I started to work the first of September. I walked the four or five blocks to the university but later got a used bicycle. Many of the faculty were on vacation, as the fall term didn't start until late September, so I had no duties for about three weeks. I had purchased a beginning French book before leaving Lexington, so I jumped into self-study and soon began translating some scientific articles. I could not find out from anyone what I had to do to pass the French exam; since a person had three chances to pass it, I decided to take the exam and fail the first time just to learn what I was expected to do. I took the exam at the end of September. A few days after classes started, Dr. Salisbury, the department head, called me and said I had passed the exam. I was shocked and kept asking who he was because I thought someone was playing a big joke on me. I was some happy—in just one month I had already cleared one of the five big hurdles for the graduate degree (French, German, prelims, dissertation, and finals). Classes started with difficulty, however, and I was soon trying to figure out what I had gotten myself into. But I did survive the first term.

I kept busy day and night during the fall term, but Becky ventured out and made a big hit with her southern accent. In mid-December Becky's grandfather, Mr. Jeff Byrd, died, and we went over to the Butterworths' and all went to Mayfield in their car. Becky and Linda and the two children, Beve and Chris, stayed in Mayfield while Charles and I went back to Illinois, and they would stay there until each of us drove home for Christmas. Just before Christmas I rode the bus to downtown Champaign one night to shop. It was really the first time I had been downtown, so I got lost and had to ask where I was and what bus to take to get back home.

We survived the winter, although we would often yell downstairs through the open grate for more heat. Occasionally the couple would go out of town for the weekend, and I would have to go through their house to the basement to fire the furnace. We got along real well with the couple. The husband was a barber with a shop nearby. They had a little girl about Beve's age, and then they had twin girls while we were living there. Our only source of phone contact was through their phone.

My nephew, Gedric Paschall, had a severe case of polio during the summer and fall of 1953. While he was in hospitals in Murray and Nashville I wrote him three or four times each week.

Well before spring—which was much later than we two Kentuckians would ever have imagined—it was most evident that Beve was going to have a brother or a sister. Becky was again nauseated for the first three or four months, but not as bad as previously and she didn't lose a lot of weight, even though she spent a miserably hot summer in that upstairs apartment.

I started out working in Dr. VanDemark's laboratory for my assistantship and soon switched to him (from Dr. Salisbury) as my major professor. He and Dr. Salisbury had published a book, many research papers together, and were highly regarded in the reproductive physiology area. I got along real well with Vandy and developed great respect and admiration for him. I started working with dairy bulls and soon became "the bull man" in the department. I would go out to the barn with a helper and collect semen from the bulls in an artificial vagina and bring the semen into the lab for all the researchers who were working on sperm metabolism in different diluters, temperatures, freezing media, and handling practices. Artificial insemination of dairy cows was just getting started in a big way, and frozen semen had just been discovered in England.

During the "pregnant" summer of 1954, I took my hardest course—biochemistry, which was the tough, weeding-out course for graduate students. The class met at 8:00 A.M., five days a week. So I would ride my bike to campus at 5:00 A.M., get a car from the motor pool, go to the bull barn to collect semen, bring it back to the lab, go home for a bath and breakfast, and be in class before 8:00. Usually the graduate students would go back to the building at night to study and work. This started a work habit for me that plagued me throughout my working career.

Well, the summer passed and with the second child on the way our name came up for veterans housing in Stadium Terrace. It would be farther from campus but much cheaper, with more room and more conveniences. The baby was overdue, and we busied ourselves looking for furniture, as the units were unfurnished. One day we found an estate sale advertised, and we really made a haul there. We bought a solid oak table and chairs, bedroom furniture, and almost everything we needed. A man from California was clearing his mother's house, and he gave us a lot of things. After a hard day of shopping, Becky prepared a big supper, but she wasn't hungry. While Beve and I ate she began having frequent hard labor pains, so we jumped up and took Beve over to Durward and Gert Olds's house and then headed to the hospital. In a short time Beda Janine was born on October 7, 1954. I took Beve over to Linda's in Chrisman the next morning and came back to school and to get everything moved into our new mansion. The dirty dishes stayed on the table for three days.

Becky had a spinal block for the delivery, which resulted in excruciating headaches. She was unable to sit up or even feed herself for four or five days. Finally I took her and the baby to a new home; it was the second time I had moved while Becky was in the hospital with a new baby. Stadium Terrace was a large area with rows and rows of tarpaper-covered barracks. It looked like a huge army camp, with each barrack building divided into three apartments.

We had an end unit with two bedrooms, a living room–dining room combination, and a small kitchen and bath. This was indeed living, compared to where we were before.

Becky's mother, Mama Conner, came up for a few days and the Butterworths' brought Beve back to see her new baby sister and home. Becky soon shaped things up into a homey nest, and we enjoyed living there. We went to Kentucky for Christmas. In early January, Tommy and Sue Murdock stopped by from the University of Wisconsin to spend the night. It was bitterly cold. They had some slides they wanted to show, so we loaded into the car to go to the campus to use the slide projector. When we returned, fire trucks were in our neighborhood with much commotion. Sure enough, it was our unit. In our haste to leave, Becky had left a pan of bottle nipples boiling on the stove. Our next-door neighbor had smelled the burning and broke the glass in the door to get in. No serious damage was done, but it was a cold house for company to sleep in, and it took days to clean up the smoke and soot.

School settled into a busy, rapid pace, as I was working on German with a private tutor and going strong with my dissertation research. I was pursuing a study on the effect of poor management (stress) on sperm production and also the effect of frequency of ejaculation on sperm production. I took over one bull that had semen collected three times a week for a year, and I was continuing that schedule to see how long semen production would last. In other words, could we exhaust the supply? I was the one who became exhausted, because the bull was collected three times a week for four years with no harmful effect on sperm production.

Of course, I took a lot of kidding about my work, but the most notorious happening occurred one morning as a young bull mounted the dummy cow. I was too slow with the artificial vagina, and the bull sprayed the semen in my eye. It caused quite a stir trying to explain to the nurses and doctors at the campus infirmary what had happened.

Grandma Boyd died in February 1955, and I rode the train home

Two now—Beve and Beda living in old army barracks in Champaign, Illinois.

for the funeral. Mother and Daddy came up to visit that spring, and all of us went over to LaPorte, Indiana, to visit mother's step-brother, Harry Bazzell, and his wife, Mabel. I had just passed my German exam, and I was feeling relaxed.

The VanDemarks would usually have the graduate students out for Thanksgiving and once or twice in the summer. The Van-Demark children were a little older than ours, but they all had a great time together. We would go out often on Sunday nights to watch that new invention called television. The Ed Sullivan and

Jackie Gleason shows were the rage, and we enjoyed them. Also, Becky and I were asked to join the departmental faculty bridge club. This was a big treat for us, and we greatly enjoyed it and developed some close friendships. Becky actually hosted the club once and had all the faculty, who had nice homes, come in to our little barracks apartment to play bridge—and they loved it.

The big hurdle in the summer of 1955 was the fearsome, all-important prelim. Three of us graduate students were scheduled on the same day, and I was the first one to face the grilling professors. Naturally, I was nervous and didn't get off to a good start, so in the final windup the committee expressed displeasure and was going to require me to come back for another try later. I was truly disappointed and went home crushed because I had seen graduate students wash out at that level and just leave without anything to show for their efforts. I finally gathered enough courage to go back to the building, and late that afternoon after the other two prelims, the committee called me in and passed me with no questions or stipulations. I never asked any questions about how well the others did, or what happened. I just kept on working.

With my coursework completed, I spent full time on research and started on my dissertation in the spring of 1956. In June, I attended the ADSA meeting in Connecticut. I was very much interested in looking for a job, and there were some available. I had applied for a research position at U.S. Department of Agriculture in Beltsville and for a faculty position at Georgia and Tennessee. I was invited for interviews at Tennessee and Georgia, so I arranged to visit each place on the same trip in July.

I went to Knoxville first and had a great visit. While the department head, Professor Wylie, and I were sitting at the airport awaiting my departure flight, he got a call from the dean offering me the job at $6,800. This was impressive. At Georgia I was also offered the job, at $6,500. I went to Tennessee, but for more reasons than the $300 difference in salary. During the Georgia interview the dean had confused me with another applicant for the position, and

Headed to Tennessee with all worldly possessions.

it was so obvious to me during the dean's interview that there was a strained relationship between the department head and the dean. So it took me sixteen more years to get to the University of Georgia.

I got back to Illinois with great enthusiasm for my new job and a sense of urgency to complete my dissertation and final exams. Becky and the two girls were going home on the train for a few days, and I had grandiose plans for concentrating on the dissertation and getting a lot accomplished. But with them gone, I simply couldn't get with it until they returned. Even though Becky had typed my M.S. thesis numerous times, including the "perfect" final copy, I hired someone to type the dissertation. By mid-August all requirements were completed in good order, and I started preparing for a move. When I'd been in Knoxville for the interview I had looked at a neat little house that was near the ag campus and next door to a private kindergarten. After I accepted the job, I rented this house by phone, and we were ready to move, free of all worries.

It was too late for the summer graduation ceremony, so the degree was not awarded until December 1956, and I had no desire to return for the graduation exercise.

Once again, we pulled a trailer behind the little car because we could not afford a moving van. By this time all the other graduating students were leaving town, and I could not find a rental trailer within many miles of Champaign. So I ended up buying a big trailer from my neighbor, who had built it and had it parked by the house. It was larger than what I would have rented but was still too small to carry everything. After eight years and two children, we had accumulated a lot of things to take—the treasures being a sewing machine and a $100 refrigerator. There was no room for the wonderful, solid oak table and chairs or for any of our living-room furniture. But it really didn't matter because we were going to be "rich" with this new job, and we could afford to buy all new furniture—so I thought!

My good neighbor helped pack the trailer and the next morning we pulled out for Murray, Kentucky. We were going to spend the weekend with our parents and then go on to Knoxville on Labor Day. The trailer was actually bigger than the little pea-green 1950 Chevrolet with the rear bumper almost dragging the ground, but it followed along beautifully on the 300-mile trip. Despite the fact that the car pulled the trailer real well to Murray, I began worrying about the rest of the trip. I was concerned that the little car could not pull the trailer through the mountains in Tennessee. This was before interstate highways, and I had never been on the road between Nashville and Knoxville, so I really didn't know what to expect. I learned in later years to "never climb the hill until you get to it," but my concerns and uncertainties weakened my resolve to tackle the mountains. Another "ideal" plan surfaced easily.

Becky's sister Shirley and her husband, Bernice Wilferd, were moving to Lexington so he could go to UK for a term and take practice-teaching to become a vocational agriculture teacher. He was taking all their belongings to Lexington on the Saturday before Labor Day, and then coming back to move the family later. He was using Mr. Conner's three-quarter-ton truck, which had a heavy-duty, high truck bed with oversized tires. My great idea was to hitch the trailer behind this powerful truck and pull it to Lexington with Bernice to unload the Wilferds' belongings; then we would haul the trailer south to Knoxville to leave Becky's and my belongings, and then drive back to Murray, all in two days. Becky and I would then drive safely to Knoxville on Labor Day, as planned, with our trailer already delivered there.

Bernice and I loaded the truck and hooked the trailer behind it; the trailer tongue sat much higher than it had on the bumper of my car. We were ready for the big trip. Both families were staying at the Conners'. Bernice and I got up at 4:00 A.M. on Saturday to head out during a hard rainstorm. I was indeed reluctant to get out of the warm bed and brave the storm. Yet, he and I were excited just like the twenty-two- and twenty-eight-year old kids that we were. I was driving, and the trip was going well until we got out of town. When I would get up to twenty-five or thirty miles an hour, the trailer would weave back and forth, and every time I would try to go any faster it would weave so much that the tires would rub against the trailer. We had gone about twenty miles and had just crossed the Tennessee River Bridge when both trailer tires blew out. It was still dark and still raining. I located a nearby driveway, pulled the trailer in, and woke up the household to ask if I could leave the trailer there—with all our possessions. We unhooked the trailer, Bernice took me back to Murray (where I crawled back in bed), and he restarted his trip to Lexington alone.

I had a busy Saturday trying to find a trucker to move me on to Knoxville. My sister's husband, Sylvester, knew someone with a small truck who had moved some people, so we went to his house, and he agreed to pick up the contents and take them to Knoxville. It was going to cost almost as much as a moving van all the way from Illinois, but my choices were limited at that point. He and I unloaded everything from the trailer onto the truck on Saturday afternoon, came back to Murray, and headed out early Sunday morning. We got to Knoxville, unloaded into the house, and headed back toward Murray. It was late, so we stopped for some sleep in Crossville, Tennessee, then continued on back to Murray on Labor Day. The next day—one day late—the family and I headed to our new place to live. The little car handled the mountains great, and I am confident it would have pulled the trailer without a problem. The empty trailer stayed in the driveway "betwixt the rivers" in Kentucky lake land for several days, until Mr. Conner sent one of his mechanics with some tires to pick it up. He finally sold the trailer for only $25 less than I had paid for it.

10

A Volunteer in Tennessee
1956 to 1962

"We never know the love of a parent until we become parents ourselves."

—HENRY WARD BEECHER

"Mr. Boyd, what does a raindrop look like?"

—DANNY BERRY

We arrived in Knoxville with our two girls—a five-year-old and a two-year-old—all excited to see the little Green House. It had two bedrooms and a living room, dining room, kitchen, back porch, and outside open garage. Of course, the first job was to put up a clothesline, which was what Becky always wanted immediately after each move. This became a great joke over the years and usually one was put up, but sometimes it was inside the house. About all we had to do to get settled in was to get the beds set up, because there was no stove, living room furniture, or dining room furniture. We ate off a card table—our first piece of furniture as a wedding present from Little Mother (Becky's Grandmother Byrd).

We were happy to be in our first real home. Even though we

were renting, it was a separate house, and we had it all by ourselves. It was located at the corner of 22nd and Lake Streets, just one block off West Cumberland. We were happy to see young children in the neighborhood, and we had great neighbors. A private kindergarten was next door, and we were only one block from a grocery, the railroad, and the park.

We became great friends with Jean and Jim Gardner. They had just adopted a son the same age as Beda, so Jean came a-calling as soon as she saw the new kids in the neighborhood. (We kept in contact over the years, and they came to our fiftieth wedding anniversary forty-two years later.) Beve started to kindergarten just next door, and there was a young girl, Sue, nearby who became our excellent babysitter.

Although I was real anxious to get started on my new job, I had a few days to build a nest for the family before my appointment started. My first stop was at the bank to see what I would have to do to borrow money for furniture. We had never borrowed any money, and I just wanted to know how many co-signers were needed and what I had to get lined up. What a shock—I walked out with $1,000 and felt like a millionaire. I could not believe what I had just done and was so proud to become a recognized member of the community. We went on a shopping spree and bought a double-oven stove, dining room table and chairs, a large three-piece sectional couch, and end tables.

I was ready to get to the office and get ready for school to start. My appointment was in teaching and research; I was an assistant professor in teaching, but because of my research and publications I was an associate professor in research. I had a real nice office in McCord Hall, the university building named for a former Tennessee governor. There was a good view of the Tennessee River with its backwater from Watts Bar Dam—the first of many Tennessee Valley Authority dams along the river that extended to Kentucky Lake Dam, which we knew so well in western Kentucky.

My research duties were well defined, as I was responsible for the dairy-cattle breeding project with Jersey cattle at two branch stations in the state. One was located at the West Tennessee Branch Experiment Station in Jackson, which was almost 400 miles from Knoxville, and the other was at the Lewisburg Station just south of Nashville. The latter was a long-time U.S. Department of Agriculture dairy station that was now operated jointly by USDA and the University of Tennessee. The station was run by a five-person committee with two from USDA and two from the University of Tennessee, plus the station superintendent. I served in this capacity, along with the University of Tennessee dean for research who had hired me. It was a fine experience working with Dr. John A. Ewing, the research dean. The Dairy Cattle Breeding Project was a regional project, with contributing projects from each of the thirteen southern states. I was also involved in other research projects at other branch stations and with the University of Tennessee dairy farm and laboratories on campus. The research meant regular visits to the branch stations, which took a lot of time because of the travel involved.

The teaching was less defined, and I had no idea of the time required for all the student activities. I was by far the youngest faculty member in the department. I approached my teaching with great enthusiasm, and students, faculty, deans, and others converged on me to get involved in all kinds of student activities. The first week on campus, the executive secretary of FarmHouse Fraternity in Memphis was holding a meeting on campus to see whether we could organize an FH club, which would grow into a fraternity chapter. I had been initiated as an associate member of FH at Kentucky in 1953. The executive secretary had been alerted that I was at the University of Tennessee, so he called and asked me to attend the meeting. After one week, I had been roped into a big job. During the first three years, I served as advisor to the Dairy Club, FarmHouse Club, Ag Club, and *Tennessee Farmer* (a student publication), and chaired many departmental and college committees. It was routine for me to be back on campus two or three nights a week during the school year for student meetings. I thoroughly enjoyed the students and their activities. In April 1957, at my first of the annual University of Tennessee Ag Roundups, I won the mule-harnessing contest for members of the UT faculty. I got a good start in teaching but naturally placed more emphasis on it than on my research. I would go to Lewisburg and Jackson five or six times a year; this was usually a one-week trip if I went to both places to do some work. There was a research assistant at each location who was in charge of the research work.

We really enjoyed our first home—the little Green House. Well, 1957 was another summer of pregnancy—the third one. Becky had only one maternity dress—a tan-yellow summer seersucker. She looked gorgeous. I said often and still say that she was never more beautiful than when she was pregnant.

Garth Winston was born on August 15, 1957, at Baptist Hospital in Knoxville. I took the girls to Frank and Fannie Clement's as we headed to the hospital. The Clements were new friends—he was assistant basketball coach. Soon afterward, Fannie was in the hospital delivering a new son. We kept up with them over the years when he was basketball coach at Columbus College in Georgia and later with the hunting preserve at Callaway Gardens, Georgia.

During the wait for delivery I experienced the longest hours of my life. After Becky had been in labor about four hours, Dr. Shouse came out to tell me that he had broken the amniotic sac and that the water was all bloody and discolored; he said he didn't know what that meant, but that he would keep me informed. I was really some scared, and probably no one ever prayed any more than me in that Baptist Hospital. He didn't reappear for another four hours, and that was to tell me that we had a big, fine boy.

I picked up the girls late that night and took them home. The babysitter, Susan Elder, kept the girls during the day while Becky and Garth were in the hospital. I stayed home for a week after they came home and had my first experience at housekeeping and child care.

The third one—Garth at ten days of age.

The street where we lived was used by the state police to give the tests for driver's licenses. The two officers spent a lot of time waiting under the shade trees in our yard and became great buddies with Beverly and Beda. They really gave me a hard time that week when I was out hanging diapers on the line.

The two-bedroom, one-bath house was small for a family of four, and even smaller when a new one was added. We had paid off the furniture debt in less than a year, so we started looking for another house—maybe our first home to purchase.

Beda was a dedicated thumb-sucker, which meant we had an every-night ordeal with her clutching her blanket and sucking a thumb. We had tried to break this pattern but to no avail. She finally said that when the new baby was born (when she was three years old) she would give up her baby bed and her blanket and quit sucking her thumb. And without any prompting, she did just that on the day we brought Garth home from the hospital.

The second week after the new baby was home, school was

starting and lots of activity was taking place. Nelson and Sue brought Mother and Daddy to see the new baby. Shortly after arriving they got a call that my sister Kathleen had given birth to her fifth child (Kendred), so they left for Kentucky to see another new grandchild.

During my first year at the University of Tennessee, they were to hire a new scientist at Oak Ridge to work with the isotopes. I had recommended Ray Cragle, a graduate-student colleague at Illinois, and he was hired; he was moving to the University of Tennessee on September 1, 1957. We told Ray and his wife, Phyl, they could stay with us till they got a house if Phyl would do the cooking and whatnot. So Ray, Phyl, and daughter Donna, who was between Beve's and Beda's ages, moved in. Ray started to work in Oak Ridge and was house hunting; I was working; and Phyl was running the house. She took Beve to her first day of school at Fort Sanders School.

That fall was the beginning of the U.S. Space Program. Alan Sheppard made his first ride in space. I had a class starting just after the liftoff, so I took a radio to class to listen to the short ride, splash-down, and recovery. This was during the Cold War with Russia, with lots of talk about Sputnik and fierce competition between the United States and Russia in science education and space travel.

House hunting got real serious in the fall of 1957. We found a beautiful three-bedroom, two-bath house with full basement in Sequoyah Hills next to the school and one block from a little shopping area. We wanted the house—the price was $14,500, and my salary was $7,200. I met with the realtor and lender to check on a loan and payments. We had to have a ten-percent down-payment, and with my salary we could not be approved for the loan if there was any record that I owed any other money besides the mortgage. Of course, I figured out the monthly payment over the twenty-five years, and found out that we would be paying $45,000 for the $14,500 house, and that concerned me. Later I learned that after

I left the meeting the loan officer told the realtor that Mr. Boyd would not be buying that house. He said that he had never seen anyone who figured out the total cost go ahead and buy the house. But we got Daddy to borrow the $1,500 for us in his name at the Bank at Farmington, Kentucky. By noon on the date of closing (set for 2:00 P.M.), the certified letter with the check had not arrived—so I went looking for the postman. Fortunately, he had the letter with the check, so we closed on our very first house at the terrific bargain of $14,250.

We moved in early December. We loaded our little two-door 1950 Chevrolet and went to Kentucky for Christmas. "Becky" forgot to take the Christmas presents, but we did take two girls and a baby brother.

Beve started to the new school after Christmas. She could walk a block to school without crossing a street. The house and location were wonderful, and we owned an extra lot beside the house. Eventually a branch library was built on the school property nearest to our house. Since we didn't have air conditioning, the girls could spend many hot summer afternoons reading and browsing in the air-conditioned library.

I was anxious to get a garden going at our new home, but one lick with the hoe at the brick-like, hard red clay changed my mind. I got the bright idea to have one of my dairy-farmer friends to bring me a big truckload of fresh cow manure. It lay in the backyard all winter and smelled terrible. My neighbors were not real happy. With the internal heat from composting, the straw caught fire; I poured gallons of water on it but it smoked for days. The next spring I chiseled the ground and mixed in the manure. After two or three years, the soil was soft as sand and an ideal garden spot.

Well, guess what—a couple of months after we moved it was obvious that there was another summer pregnancy. We were trying to fill the larger house. This was not a real fun time for Becky— with one girl at home all day, a boy still in diapers, and Becky having morning sickness for four months. But one more time for the

Four children in seven years (1951–1958).

seersucker maternity dress. Again on many occasions I've told Becky that she was never more beautiful than when she was pregnant. And I really meant it; she was simply gorgeous.

In November, I called Jean Gardner to come at about 11:00 P.M. to stay with the children. Early the next morning, a daughter, Bettina Gayle, was born at the University Hospital. I came home and took Beda and Garth to Phyl's in Oak Ridge. Beve was in school so Jean Gardner helped with her.

The clothesline was in the basement. With two in diapers, Becky issued a strong request for a new machine called a clothes dryer. Sears had one advertised for $88. It operated on 110 instead of 220 current. It was obviously a sales come-on, but that's what I wanted. The sales clerk would not sell it to me, saying the 110 current would never work. I insisted on seeing the manager, and he came back to sell me the dryer.

When I got it home, the directions showed how to switch one wire to change it from 110 to 220. The 220 wiring was already in

Beda, Garth, and Beve surround their little sister, Bettina—nine months of age.

the basement for a dryer so I tried it. While I was holding the top of the dryer up, it slipped out of my hand and ripped apart all of the electrical wiring in the machine. Fortunately, it was all color coded, so I got the colors back together and then tied in the 220 wiring. Then I got a long broom handle to punch the "on" button—it worked great and continued to do so for fifteen years.

The basement was unfinished with no heat in it, but it was a good place for the kids to play—they could even ride their tricycles. We enjoyed the new house. One night when I was out of town Becky heard something flying up and down the hallway into our bedroom. As the protector of her brood, she found a bat had come down the chimney. She spent a long time chasing it and finally trapped it in my felt hat, which later became the "bat hat."

The first Thanksgiving with four children—about two weeks after Tina was born—I agreed to buy the turkey. We had invited Cecil Carmen, the herdsman at the University of Tennessee Dairy, and his wife, Lorena, over for Thanksgiving dinner, and it was to be a big day. As per usual for me, I had stayed at work until 6:30 in the evening on Wednesday and was going to pick up the turkey on my way home. It was cold and raining, and I went to six groceries but could not find a turkey anyplace—they were all sold out. I ended up going to Cass Walker Grocery in "Shantytown" and buying two fat, greasy hens to bake. I wasn't very popular at home that night, and was even less so the next morning when I decided to wash the kitchen ceiling while Becky was trying to prepare the dinner for company. But we had a splendid Thanksgiving dinner.

We did not go to Kentucky for Christmas in 1958 right after Tina was born, but we did go the following year. And with four children in the little car, we were no more crowded than we were that first Christmas in 1951 with only one child.

Knoxville was not a particularly great place to live—hot and humid in the summer and cold and rainy all winter. But it was a good place for us. Many of our friends were in their family businesses and enjoyed lake houses, boats, and many luxuries we never knew. Despite the fact we were outsiders, we survived and have maintained many great friends there. One interesting angle is that forty-seven years after we moved from Knoxville we went back to a Georgia-Tennessee football game and got together with our former bridge club. Eight couples all with original spouses got together for a reception and dinner—a real fun time.

The most significant happening in Knoxville was the resolution to our religious life. Becky had been raised in the Church of Christ and I had been raised Baptist. In western Kentucky, those two were extreme opposites. But that didn't keep us apart. We were married in Becky's church by a Church of Christ minister who was a good

The old-hat gang at Mama Boyd's—Karen Paschall, Beve,
Mary Paschall, Beda, and Greg Boyd.

friend of my family—Brother Benton Carmen. In Lexington we
went to the Church of Christ some and to the Baptist church some,
but we were not active anyplace. If there was a problem, we were
denying it.

When we moved to Illinois, we attended the Church of Christ
mainly because the minister, Brother Pat Hardeman, was from
Sedalia and we knew him. But, again, we were inactive and non-
committal. It was easy to become engrossed in school and not
worry about anything else. I was becoming much more convinced
about what I didn't want in a church than what I did want, and I
believe Becky was also, but we never discussed it at that stage.

When we moved to Knoxville with a five-year-old and a two-
year-old, we knew that something had to be done. We wanted the
children to be in Sunday school, and we wanted to be active in a
church and to enjoy being a part of the total community. What we
didn't know was how difficult this would be, and that there would
soon be two more children in the family.

In our generation and heritage, family did matter a great deal in religious choices and actions. Especially between the Church of Christ and the Baptist church, there was no common ground, and families encountered serious splits. We tried going to each church in Knoxville, with the same results as at other places. We both made an honest effort to get involved in the Church of Christ for a while, but it just wasn't in my inner being to believe and practice what I was hearing.

I was so in hopes of finding a church that would be right for both of us and for our family—a church that was not mine nor hers, but *ours*. We tried the Christian Church, hoping that would be it, but it wasn't and we knew it immediately. By this time we were stymied. We had four children and no church—no place we were happy.

Family does matter, as stated earlier, but for me it really didn't. Having left home at eighteen, I felt self-sufficient and free to do what I wanted, but it was much more difficult for Becky. She was greatly concerned about what her family would say or do if she changed churches. In fact, she was so concerned that it caused her intense emotional distress and essentially a nervous breakdown. Religious-family uncertainties, along with four children under seven years of age, puts a terrific strain on the body's defenses and sense of well-being.

Mr. and Mrs. Conner stopped by our house on their way back from Florida when Becky was having a tough time. After a sleepless night, once I had left for work, she went in their bedroom and talked with them about her concerns. Her daddy told her that he would change churches immediately if he didn't think his was the right one for him. This helped her some. Yet, we still struggled trying to find the right place. We were branching out some in our searching. There was a Presbyterian church just one block for our house, but it wasn't the one, either.

One Sunday morning she had all four kids dressed beautifully—we got in the car and headed out, not knowing where we were going. We were headed toward downtown but didn't know where. For three years we had bypassed and avoided a gigantic Presbyterian church high on a hill on Kingston Pike near where we lived. It was just too intimidating for country folks like us. As we approached that church on this particular Sunday, Becky said, "Why don't we try it." I had to stop quickly to turn in to the driveway, and I am glad that I did. From the moment we parked in the lot we were comfortable and knew immediately this was the place. After three or four Sundays the minister, Dr. Joe Copeland (who later became president of Maryville College), came to visit us. It was a wonderful visit. We went through an inquirer's class and soon joined the church in 1959. The church had a counseling pastor from Athens, Georgia, who was extremely helpful to us.

I was appointed to the board of the Presbyterian Center at the University of Tennessee—during a period of troubling times in the early 1960s. Also, I served on the Pastor Search Committee after Dr. Copeland went to Maryville. Dr. Herman Spivey—remember him? He was the head of the English department at the University of Kentucky, and was the man Becky had started working for when we got married. He had come as the vice president of the University of Tennessee and he was in the church we joined. He and I went to Ohio one weekend to hear and interview a minister.

Becky and I had a nice yard with an extra lot. There were two apple trees and a real large Japanese cherry tree that was the envy of Knoxville when in bloom in the spring. There were lots of shrubs along the two streets on the corner lot, and every summer holiday, like July 4 and Labor Day, it was trimming time. I was most unpopular with the entire family on those days because I kept the children busy hauling the trimmings to the trash pile. There was a little hill from back to front on the two lots, and that was where Beve learned to ride a bicycle. I would get her started downhill, and she would crash into the shrubs, screaming at the top of her voice.

One summer evening I was mowing the extra lot when it started raining. I went inside, and when we finished supper on the screened back porch I went back to my mowing. The grass was wet and kept choking up the mower. I was scraping my foot along the edge of the mower frame to remove the grass and, yes, my foot slipped under the frame. I went down and was yelling for Becky to "come here." She was washing dishes in the kitchen and yelling back that it was just as close for me to come in there! Finally, I got her attention, and she took me to the doctor's office, where we learned that a third of the right big toe had been cut off along with the end of a shoe. Dr. Rule cleaned and bandaged the toe, which had not bled at all—during the night, however, it did bleed freely. I took a lot of razzing for six or eight weeks while wearing one toe-less shoe.

Someone gave the kids a baby chick for Easter, so I rigged up a cage in the backyard. After several weeks, the chicken appeared to be full grown, so we agreed to have a chicken dinner. Becky did the neck-wringing and scalding to remove the feathers. The body of the chicken was no larger around than my wrist. All of us took some of the cooked chicken and chewed it up, but I don't think any of us ever swallowed a bite. The big chicken dinner wasn't successful.

We had wonderful neighbors, including the Berrys, Beamans, Coffmans, and Simcoxes. Mrs. Simcox was quite elderly, and her bachelor son, Burton, lived with her. Burton had invented a plastic air-vent for planes and sold it to the military before World War II. Clarence Beaman was the realtor who sold us the house and also handled the subsequent sale. Naomi, the mother of five little Beamans, was Swedish, and we later visited her parents in Stockholm while our family was traveling there. Cindy Coffman was a playmate for our girls, and I always called her Cindy, and then would "cough" and say "man." She always expected that greeting. Dan Berry (who always kidded me about not being able to get a good fire going in the fireplace) was head of the Knoxville Better Business Bureau. Dan and Mimi's twelve-year-old son had been blind from birth. Once I stopped there to visit, and as I started home it began raining. I halted at the door and commented that those rain drops were big. Danny said, "Mr. Boyd, what does a raindrop look like?" I'm still stammering with no answer, but forty-five years later Danny is an accomplished Presbyterian minister in a church in Mississippi. Another of our fine neighboring families was the D'Armonds—they lived on a large "estate" across the street. They had a swimming pool, and Becky and the kids spent many summer afternoons there. Penny, the daughter, babysat for us a lot.

In the late 1950s we still had only one car—the "old" 1950 Chevrolet that had been our first car. It had served us well, bringing four children home from the hospital. Even though the city bus stopped at our front door and ran within one block of my work, I still drove to work every day. Becky needed some relief, so we got a woman named Dollie to come one day a week so Becky could get out. She kept the car on that day. Dollie was a wonderful and sweet older black lady—but was she strict with the kids! She would get a switch after them, and they didn't like that very well.

In the late 1950s, we were probably the only family in Knoxville who did not have a TV. But in 1960 we made some progress, purchasing our first TV and also buying a new car—a 1960 Chevrolet for $2,200. Since we couldn't afford to have two cars, I sold the little green car to Doug Stamper, one of the dairy graduate students, for $165. Shortly thereafter he had some trouble with it, and I gave him back $50.

With the new car we were taking our first family trip other than to visit our families back in Kentucky or to attend a national scientific meeting. We were going to Florida over the Fourth of July to visit Becky's sister Linda. We left on Thursday and stayed that night with Kentucky friends, the Ammermans, in Gainesville, Florida. Early the next morning, nine-year-old Beve asked Bea Ammerman, "Is it always this hot in Florida?" We went on to Orlando for our first visit to Florida since Linda and Charles had moved there in 1956—the same time we moved to Tennessee. The next day we all (four Butterworths and six Boyds) went to Daytona Beach to spend the night (a splurge!) and to play on the beach for two days. Of course, with our unfamiliarity with the beach and our ignorance of sunburn, sharks, and killer tides, we were a nervous wreck with four kids from two to nine years old. We could not find a motel anyplace in the area, so after a full day we drove back to Orlando—arriving about midnight, exhausted, sunburned, and really sandy. The next day we headed back toward Knoxville, stopping at Sea World and a few other attractions. We spent the night in Tifton, Georgia, and went on home the next day, ending a five-day Fourth of July trip—not necessarily a vacation. One big purchase we made was to buy five watermelons for a dollar for Becky, and we actually had room in the trunk for them.

Gedric was in Knoxville that fall (1960) to start a master's degree in business. He lived on campus but came out to the house frequently. That Christmas we drove to Murray together, and Becky with a couple of the children rode with him. During the trip I noticed when I stopped that he would run up close behind us and stop suddenly. Later he told me that the brake lights were not working and apparently hadn't been for some time, but I hadn't known it.

The dairy barn was on Alcoa Highway, just across the Tennessee River from my office. I was at the barn a lot with my teaching and research. Also, Becky and the herdsman's wife, Lorena Carmen, were good friends, and they visited a lot. We would go out on the farm as a family in the fall to gather hickory nuts and walnuts. Also, a favorite trip two or three times each year would be to go to the Smoky Mountains. We would go out Chapman Highway through Sevierville and Pigeon Forge to Gatlinburg, then up the mountain until we saw a "bear jam"—traffic stopping to look at a bear. Then we would turn around and come back through Gatlinburg and return to Knoxville through Maryville. This road ran along a mountain stream, and frequently we would take along a big bag of popcorn. We'd stop for a rest and climb out on a big rock in the stream and sit there to eat our popcorn.

We also spent a lot of time with the Cragles. Ray was an Explorer Scout leader and camped frequently in the Smokies. Occasionally he would take Donna, Beve, Beda, and me along on day hikes. Once he led us around Chimney Rock with a real narrow ledge and a sheer drop of several hundred feet. He and Donna were skipping along going around the rock, and I was following with a firm grip on Beda with one hand and Beve with the other hand. My back was up against the rock wall as I inched around on the ledge. Soon we got around to a beautiful, flat, grassy spot where we stopped for a picnic lunch. I could not eat for worrying about going back around the rock on the narrow ledge. Finally Ray told me we didn't have to go on the ledge but could return on the grassy knoll—then I enjoyed lunch.

We attended many student functions. Once the Dairy Club was having a softball game at the dairy farm, and I tried to act like one of the students—after all, I was only twenty-nine or thirty. I caught a fly ball to center field and immediately threw the ball to second base because that was the only player I could reach with my throw. Well, we made a double play, and I was a hero and didn't ever know what I was doing. (But I didn't tell them that.)

One summer we had a watermelon feast for the graduate students at our house. Several were there, and we were storing the rinds in a wooden bushel basket. One of my graduate students, Lane Parkinson, had just gotten a new car, and he was real proud of it. As darkness was approaching and he and his girlfriend were getting ready to leave, I put the basketful of watermelon rinds in the backseat of his car. Others knew about it, and we thought it was a big joke. Well, when I got to the office the next morning the basket of rinds was sitting in the middle of my desk. I took them outside and never a word was said about the watermelon rinds.

The dairy building where I had my office had a little lunchroom based on the dairy products from the creamery next door. Mabel ran the lunchroom, and she was a delightful person. Many faculty members ate lunch there and had coffee and ice-cream breaks during the day. Fifty years later, Mabel's is still operating as a tribute to her.

In the mid-fifties, many international students were coming to this country to go to school. The University of Tennessee had an agreement with Pakistan for students to be trained in agriculture. Once, a new group of "Indian students" had just arrived and an incident happened while one was going through the cafeteria line in Mabel's. He would not accept the piece of bread that Mabel was giving him. There was a language barrier, and she made several attempts to serve a slice of bread. It turned out that she was using the same tongs to pick up the bread that she had used to pick up a hot dog for the previous person. And he would not accept the bread from the tongs that had touched the meat.

Internally, I reacted very strongly to this incident, and over the years I learned a most valuable lesson from it. My immediate thought was, *we are the greatest,* as that's what I'd learned as an eighteen-year-old in the Philippines. We won the war, our way is absolutely the best in the world, the "ignorant" ones from underdeveloped countries are coming to the United States to be educated, so they should adopt our ways and not try to hold on to their inferior ways. I actually believed that. But over the years I learned how wrong I was. As I traveled and worked in Asia, West Africa, South America, and other less developed countries, it was obvious we didn't have all the answers. Those little underprivileged kids in Africa could speak two or three languages, and I could speak only English. And I had no right to expect them to speak my language in their country, but there and here in my country that was the only way we could communicate. Also, I realized how happy our family was, the year we lived in England, to get together with other American families to celebrate Thanksgiving.

Another significant happening during our residency in Knoxville was the chartering of the University of Tennessee FarmHouse chapter. From week one I worked long and hard on this fraternity organization. It took three years to get students interested, to rent

D. Howard "Daddy" Doane, founder of FarmHouse Fraternity. Photo at Colorado Conclave, 1962.

a house, and to assemble furniture. I spent an enormous amount of time as chief advisor, working at the house, keeping students in line, and doing damage control. I organized an FH alumni chapter even before we had an official student chapter—only a student club. Mr. Skidmore, president of Security Mills in Knoxville, was the most illustrious FH alum in the area, and it was a tremendous experience working with him. Becky and I chaperoned many parties at the fraternity, with such loud music. When we would get home late, the sound of the drums would resound in our heads and bodies for hours. It was a real red-letter day when the national board assembled to charter the fraternity. It was a three-day event, including the chartering ceremony, football game (in which the University of Tennessee beat Auburn), banquet, and dance, capped off with a church service on Sunday. Despite the extended effort to organize the fraternity there is very little legacy to document it. A long-time University of Tennessee professor of ag economics, Professor Willard Ranney, had wanted an FH chapter at the University of Tennessee for many years. He was not a FH member, but he was always so impressed with FH alum Dr. Acker-man, president of the Farm Foundation, that he wanted that high-type student organization available to University of Tennessee students. So at every opportunity it was appropriate to focus attention and credit to Professor Ranney as the motivator and organizer of the University of Tennessee chapter. I was elected to the international board of FarmHouse Fraternity in 1960 for a four-year term. I conducted an inspection at the North Carolina state chapter and completed the last two years of my term at Michigan State.

As mentioned previously, I was much impressed with Dr. John A. Ewing, the senior vice dean who had hired me at the University of Tennessee. He was very smart, with great management skills. He was running the college for the older dean, and it was commonly understood that Dr. Ewing would be the next dean. But after a year or so, it was suddenly announced that an unknown extension specialist in agronomy was the new dean. He was not known by the college faculty and had no administrative experience, but he was the college roommate of the president of the Tennessee Farm Bureau, who was also on the board of trustees for the University of Tennessee and was the person "in charge" of Tennessee agriculture, including the ag college. Dr. Ewing was appointed director of the Agricultural Experiment Station, and I was still working directly with him, but communication among senior college administrators was not good.

About three years later it was announced without any prior notice that Professor Wylie was retiring and that a new department head had been appointed from another state. No one in the department knew anything about it even though he had been secretly brought to campus for an interview with the dean. Again, the new appointee was a college classmate of the dean. This was a time in the early 1960s when faculty rights and student rights were coming on strong, but some of the old political machines were still in control on some campuses, especially in the South.

The new department head arrived, and the first thing he did

Tina, Garth, Beve, and Beda, 1962.

was to bump me from the five-person team responsible for operating the Dairy Experiment Station in Lewisburg. I still had the research project, but had no input on what was done or how it was done. If I had been a part of the "in" political crowd, I'm not sure what I would have done, but since I wasn't, it was easy to decide to get out of Dodge. It is most difficult to work enthusiastically for people you don't respect, and whose actions and motives always make you suspicious. So when I was contacted about the position at Michigan State, it was easy to have a definite interest in the job.

We really didn't want to move from Knoxville. We ticked off numerous reasons why we didn't want to leave—great house, good location for school and library, wonderful friends, wonderful church, proximity to family, and good weather (compared to Michigan's)—but all of the strong positives for staying were for the wrong reasons. We knew that for my work productivity and enjoyment I needed to make a change. So, just after Santa Claus left on Christmas morning 1962, we packed toys and everything else in sight. The Bekins Movers were coming the next morning. The van was packed on the twenty-sixth, and we spent the night with the Cragles in Oak Ridge and left early the next morning for East Lansing, Michigan. The van driver had promised that he was driving straight through and would be there by the time we arrived. As we got on the main road just outside Oak Ridge before daylight on the twenty-seventh, we saw the van parked on the side of the road where he had stopped for the night.

I conked out early in the afternoon with a bad headache, but Becky took over and drove us safely into unfamiliar territory while I slept in the back seat. It was indeed an adventurous trip for the family.

We arrived that night in East Lansing with four children and were staying with friends—the Lassiters—at whose home we waited four more days for the van to arrive. It turned out that the van driver had just gotten married at Christmas, and he went through Ohio to see his bride. What could I say? The good part was that a friend in our church in Knoxville was the Bekins agent, and he told me to pay him for the move whenever I felt like it. This was a tremendous relief for me, because it was unheard of in those days for a moving van to unload without cash payment in advance. We remember well New Year's Day 1963, unloading and getting settled in a new home—completely covered with snow!

Before getting along with the Michigan story I must digress back to the summer of 1962. We had been invited to go to the Upper Peninsula of Michigan for a week at Lake Superior with the Lassiters. This was to be our first family vacation, since the Florida trip two years earlier had not really been a vacation. We were so excited and had such big plans for a fun-filled week on the beach at Lake Superior. Becky packed swimsuits and shorts.

We drove to East Lansing, and the next day we loaded in the Lassiters' station wagon—four adults, six children, plus luggage and supplies for a week—and headed to the Upper Peninsula. At a bathroom stop in Gaylord, Becky had blood in her urine, so we sidetracked to a doctor's office to get medication for a bladder infection. Then we crossed the Mighty Mackinac Bridge and entered a beautiful new country, soon arriving at AuTrain on the shore of Lake Superior. I should have known we were in trouble weather-wise, when, upon arrival at the cabin on August 18, I saw green peas in the garden. In Tennessee they had ripened and disappeared in May.

That first night there was a cold "winter" storm. The cabin was close to the lake, and I could hear the waves lashing the banks and just knew we would be washed away. Becky had packed only one pair of long pants for each of us, so we wore those all week, and all ten of us spent the week hovered around a pot-bellied stove. Little did we southerners know that the summer water temperature of Lake Superior was 55° Fahrenheit, or that the cold weather was normal for the Upper Peninsula.

One afternoon, Dr. Clint Meadows, a faculty member at Michigan State, came over and joined our group around the stove. Long afterward, I realized I had been interviewed and hadn't even known it. Two months later I was invited for an interview at Michigan State. It went real well, and the highlight was that I was interviewed by President John Hannah. Even though I was being considered for a lowly associate professor position in agriculture, Mr. Hannah spent an hour with me. He was signing diplomas of MSU graduates while we talked. (He personally signed every diploma presented during his twenty-five years as president of MSU.) At the time, Mr. Hannah was the chief organizer of the new Agency for International Development (AID) in the State Department, and he took a call from the secretary of state while I was in his office. I was greatly impressed, because I already looked upon Mr. Hannah as the most outstanding president of any land-grant university in the country.

Another funny incident, which was a minor highlight, was my interview with Dean Tom Cowden. He was rather gruff, and as soon as we were introduced and alone he never said a word—just sat there. Fortunately for me, a faculty friend at Tennessee had asked me to say hello to Dean Cowden. So with that entree I initiated a conversation that developed into a pleasant interview. Later, when I was offered the position with a $1,500 increase in salary, the move was mine to make.

11

Way Up North in Michigan
1963 to 1970

"Do not let what you cannot do interfere with what you can do."

—COACH JOHN WOODEN

T he dawning of the new year in 1963 found me at the sink, unpacking and washing dishes. The rest of the family was snugly in bed in our new home. The previous morning I had gotten a call early from the van driver telling me where he was having breakfast. I went there and bought his breakfast along with those of the three helpers he had just picked up off the street. Earlier I had thought that all workers for moving companies were highly trained and specialized in caring for and handling furniture—what a revelation. Anyway, I was happy to see them.

It was pretty hard on our parents for us to move to Michigan. Both families would have much preferred that their southern children not move "up there" and raise a family with all those "wops" and northerners. And even though we had lived in Champaign, Illinois, for three winters, we were totally unprepared to move to Michigan in the middle of winter. The ground was covered with snow, and we didn't see the lawn for three months. The first day of school we got three notes back from teachers saying, "Don't ever send these kids to school again without overshoes." So we went shopping that night.

One weather story I've told over the years is about attending an MSU–Ohio State football game one year on September 30, when it snowed so hard at the MSU stadium that we couldn't see the playing field; another is the one about mowing my yard in May when it snowed so much I couldn't see where I had already mowed. One lesson I never learned there was when to plant the garden. When there were some sunny days in March or April I would rush to plant seeds. Most years I would replant two or three times. The "natives" who never planted their gardens until Memorial Day (May 30) always made me look silly. But, as a southerner, I expected spring to arrive in March at the latest, and I just couldn't adjust to waiting another two months for it to finally arrive.

My primary job at Michigan State was a fairly simple one of working with the 4-H dairy program. Yet the post-Sputnik era of the Russian space program lay heavy on the United States, and my challenge was to incorporate science into the program. This was somewhat of a reversal for me, because it meant I was going back into extension and would be traveling again. That was why I'd left Kentucky—to go back to school so I could be a faculty member and not travel all the time. But MSU was well located, which meant I could visit the primary dairy areas of the state without overnight trips, except for the occasional travel to the Upper Peninsula.

Anyway, I launched into the job full speed, writing bulletins, holding workshops, visiting dairy farms, and getting acquainted across the state. We had a great reception and made wonderful friends, and our southern accents were a real asset among rural Michiganders. Actually, the migration of southerners to Michigan had been going on for three decades, and many of them were working on dairy farms. One meaningful event during my early days there occurred at a scientific-based seminar I was attending at Camp Kett, the 4-H camp in northern Michigan. One of the speakers stated that, on average, most workers would retrain themselves seven times over their careers. This infuriated me, because that was why I went back to school: so I would be set for a career and not have to train again. When I finally calmed down I suddenly realized I had already retrained myself twice and was in the process of doing it again. Yet I was unaware of what was happening in those terms. Over the years I have related this experience several times as I have continually retrained myself to meet specific challenges.

Our rental house was in Okemos, a small residential area adjacent to East Lansing and the university. Okemos had a good school system, ranked as the second "best" school district in Michigan. As usual, the ranking was based on dollars spent per student, so that Okemos ranked just behind the Birmingham district in Detroit.

The first few weeks, we explored some nearby areas and found Lake Lansing, which was frozen over with lots of cars and fishing huts on it. I started to drive out on the lake but Becky opened the door and jumped out. This ended our motorized skating, and I haven't gotten her on the ice since then.

Our house in Knoxville, which I was certain would be snatched up as soon as it went on the market, did not sell for three months. It was beginning to be a drain to pay heating bills and monthly payments on two houses. Clarence Beaman, our former neighbor across the street who'd sold the house to us, now sold it to someone else for $16,500. We had paid $14,250 and lived there for five years. We continued to rent our house in Okemos but ended up buying it for $21,500. The house with four bedrooms was quite suitable for our growing family. One April Fool's morning, when Beve and Beda were in the bathtub, I slipped in and poured cake coloring in the water. One of them contended that the color never washed off.

We visited several churches in Okemos and East Lansing. Most of the churches were nondenominational. The minister at the large Peoples Church in East Lansing had been in seminary with our former pastor, Joe Copeland, president of Maryville College. So we had wanted to go there, but it just never seemed to fit our needs for the family. We joined Eastminister Presbyterian Church in East Lansing in May 1963. At that time, we asked the minister if there were any plans for a Presbyterian Church in Okemos. He told us that the Presbytery owned some land in Okemos, but that it would be ten years before there was any action on a new church. Well, in August came a knock on our door: a chemical engineer from Dow Chemical Company in Midland. He had just completed seminary in California and moved into our subdivision, and was organizing a church. This presented a fast and vast change in our lives. We met in his home the next Sunday and for several thereafter, and then began to meet in the high school cafeteria. Every Sunday, we had to transport the organ and songbooks in a trailer behind the minister's little VW bug, and then set up and rearrange the cafeteria. The church was chartered with 100 members in less than a year, and we were soon at work raising funds for a building. On one memorable Sunday afternoon, the callers for the building-fund drive set up shop in our basement. Our goal was to raise $30,000 in pledges for the new building—actually we raised $37,000. Two years after the minister had first come knocking, we dedicated our new church building.

Each summer, in my work, I conducted the 4-H state dairy show at the stadium on campus and worked with 4-H dairy-cattle judging teams. I had a minor, part-time appointment in research but didn't allocate much time to it for the first three years. However, I did interact with the staff and graduate students in the reproduction laboratory which was located off campus adjacent to the Michigan Artificial Breeder's Cooperative (MABC) bull stud. I worked with Dr. Harold Hafs, especially, on some extension programs and some artificial breeding work at MABC. I began teaching the physiology course, including reproduction and lactation, to the two-year short-course students who were going back to the farm.

We developed fast friendships in our neighborhood, at the university, and in the church, and many of them continued through the years. The most notable is perhaps what we refer to forty years later as the "Michigan Group," which gets together annually to celebrate anniversaries. Four couples in the church—the Moshers, the Englanders, the Hinzes, and the Boyds—had anniversaries in the same month, and we formed a bridge club that met somewhat regularly. Only one of those couples still live in Michigan, but we continue getting together for two or three days each year. The Moshers, Englanders, and Boyds were in a YMCA program called "Indian Guides" with our young sons. We had some great times at the winter camps in northern Michigan.

Our first "big" purchase in Michigan was a chest-type Sears freezer, and it is still in use, having survived forty years and two moves. A frequent family joke about Becky's overflowing freezer is that some of the first foods put in the freezer are still there. We remained probably the only one-car family in our Michigan neighborhood for three years. But in December 1965 we made the move to a two-car family with the purchase of a 1966 Ford station wagon. We bought it from a church friend, Jack Gatrost, who worked for Ford Motor Company. The new vehicle did not arrive before Christmas, so Jack loaned us a car to drive to Kentucky for the holiday. There was a short in the lights and occasionally they would go out. I had to turn the switch off and on rapidly to get the lights to work. This process was repeated numerous times, which made night travel very interesting.

That was the year Nelson and Sue's house burned on Christmas night, and Becky, Daddy, and I made a fast trip from Murray to Sedalia in the snow. It was a new place they had just bought, and they'd been in the process of moving in. Finally, at the end of the holiday, we headed back to Michigan, and ended up driving on a solid sheet of ice from Fort Wayne, Indiana, to Okemos—all after dark with the crazy lights. Thankful to get home, yes!

The '66 Ford station wagon fit the times with its big body, but the motor didn't match the body—too little power. But we christened the big car anyway with our first family camping trip out West. We had never camped, but we were game to try it and got so excited planning the trip. We borrowed a homemade folding trailer from Ed and Marge Miller, our neighbors. It was big and quite heavy. We took it on a weekend short trip as a practice run.

We left Okemos early on a beautiful summer morning on the three-week tour to the West Coast. I must have been a little nervous, because on the bypass around Lansing I went twenty miles beyond our intended route and had to turn around and come back. We took the northern route around Chicago and into Wisconsin. The first night we didn't even unhook the trailer from the station wagon. We motored through Minnesota, then the Badlands; stopped to visit our dairy herdsman, Denny Armstrong, at his brother's farm in South Dakota; and then pushed on through Idaho, Washington, and down to Oregon to attend the ADSA meetings at Corvallis.

After the meetings we traveled the Pacific coastline through Oregon to Southern California. In the Yuba City–Maryville area, we visited three of Mother's step-siblings: Uncle Leon Bazzell, Aunt Myrtie Shockley, and Aunt Hattie, who had divorced Uncle Vernon Young and later married a farmer in California. On the return trip we came through Nevada, Utah, Colorado, and Iowa on the southern route. We stopped in Carroll, Nebraska, to visit Robert Bodenstadt, the pen pal I'd started writing in the second grade. It was the first time we had ever met.

We had a great time, but undoubtedly we were a comical sight to the genuine campers. We would pull into camp well after dark and would rustle around setting up and having supper long after everyone else had gone to bed. The next morning when we got up, everyone else would already be gone, so we'd be alone in the camp to have breakfast and leave at leisure. The station wagon got us back but it really was a struggle. There were some tough climbs in the Rockies and the motor almost choked down several times going up the Bighorn Mountains. Soon after that trip the motor developed a terrific thirst for oil, so I traded the car for a 1967 Ford station wagon with a larger motor.

With our survival of that trip, our appetite was whetted a bit, so we planned another camping trip the next summer. This time we used a lighter, commercial pop-up trailer owned by Jack Gatrost, the Ford man. We went to the World's Fair in Montreal and through the northeast, with two stops in Maine and at Cornell University for the ADSA meetings. In Maine we visited Bob and Marlene Courterier, who'd been at Illinois with us in graduate school, and Bruce and Betty Poulton at Bar Harbor. Bruce had spent a year at MSU as an administrative intern with President Hannah, and we'd become well acquainted, as he was a dairy professor and lived near us in Okemos. The most indelible memory of our visit, however, was the Maine lobsters. We went to the dock about 3:00 P.M., where the lobsters were cooked, and wrapped each in a newspaper. Four hours later they were steaming hot and absolutely delicious.

We had some fun experiences, like getting kicked off the New Jersey Turnpike because trailers were not allowed. A couple of those experiences have survived the years as frequent family jokes. All of us had an intestinal upset, occurring mostly in Maine. The morning after Becky's "siege" we were traveling over some sharp hills and valleys, and all of us, except Becky, were enjoying the roller-coaster ride. She tried to convince everybody that she was much sicker than anybody else—so for the ensuing years Becky has always been the sickest one in the family upon every occasion.

The other adventure occurred at our first crossing of an international border, into Canada. I had carefully rehearsed with the kids that we would probably be asked if we were all U.S. citizens, and I had prepared my response that yes, we are. At the crucial moment the officer asked me if I was a U.S. citizen, and in my flustered state I said, "Yes, I are!" That statement has been repeated to me hundreds of times—even Mama Conner at age 91 wrote it in a letter to be read at my retirement.

In the mid-1960s, the reproduction lab was moved from the dairy farm into Anthony Hall to be with the Dairy Department on campus, so I began working more with the group. Hafs, a highly respected good friend, was largely responsible for this move. We worked well together and collaborated in writing articles and in applied research. Eventually I was replaced in 4-H dairy, and I devoted my full time to reproduction extension and research while continuing to teach. Notoriously, extension workers always said that they couldn't teach because it was too confining—not for the extension workers, but for the farmers, county agents, and clients in the field, who would get mad if they called for help and found the specialist unavailable because he had to teach on campus. But I succeeded juggling all three activities (teaching, research, and extension) because I never told anyone that I couldn't help with a problem.

Hafs and I co-authored a highly successful reproduction booklet published by *Hoard's Dairyman Magazine.* This led to my recruitment to write a regular monthly column on reproduction in *Hoard's Dairyman.* The best efforts I encountered were in conjunction with the extension veterinarian in conducting three-day short courses on reproduction across the state. I was quite active in the artificial insemination (A.I.) field, and was invited to give lectures in other states. One winter day I was conducting a short course for farmers at the high school in West Branch, Michigan. I had taken several reproductive tracts from slaughtered cows and was using them to teach. The school's biology teacher learned that I was there, so he asked me to lecture to his class of eighth-graders. So I skipped lunch and brought the students in with the tracts and lectured on animal and human reproduction—parts, functions, hormones, cycles, birth control, fertilization, and pregnancy. Those beginning teenagers were crowded around and most interested.

Then the back door opened, and someone said, "Oh, here comes the preacher." So the county agent and biology teacher took off and abandoned me with the students. Turned out, he was the

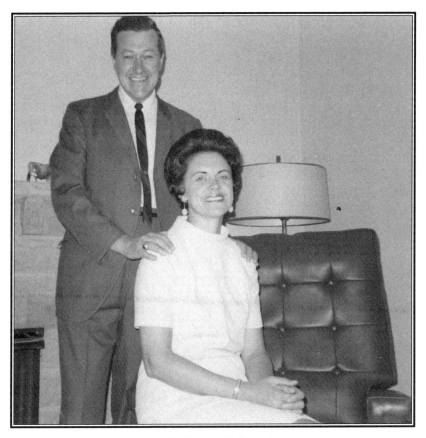

Louie and Becky, twentieth anniversary.

Church of Christ minister who was raised on a dairy farm in my home county, and I had double-dated with his younger brother, Will Ed Warren. The minister had read in the paper that I was going to be there, so he just stopped by to see me. He was indeed interested in the class lesson.

For our twentieth anniversary I had a clock made for Becky with our names spelled out on the face instead of numbers: "Louie" at the top and "Becky" at the bottom, with a dash at 9 and 3 to separate the names. This has remained a favorite conversation item in our home since that time.

The small Cape Cod house in Okemos was filled with our family, but we had a lot of fun while living there. Becky insisted on the family having all meals together—even breakfast—and most of them were with six seated around a small table in the little kitchen. There were lots of laughs and some continue down memory lane. Once Beda picked up a bottle of French dressing and began to shake it vigorously. The top was not screwed on securely so she sprayed salad dressing across my shoulder, over my forehead, and onto the window and wall. The laughing by five people continues to this day. Another remembered mealtime occurred after we had gotten our first puppy—a miniature Doberman Pinscher. After we had finished eating one night, I saw a "pickle" on the floor and reached down to get it. As I picked it up, I began to question what it was—as I held it up I said "O-wee, what's this?" It was a dried deposit from the dog.

In July 1968, the International Reproduction Congress was being held in Paris, France. Hafs was involved with the U.S. delegation, so he and I got grants to attend, and I presented a paper on the improvement of fertility by the addition of an enzyme to bull semen. Before the Paris conference we attended the British Society for the Study of Fertility meetings at Newcastle upon Tyne in England. This was our first overseas trip together, and Becky's first plane ride other than in that Piper Cub in Nashville in 1947. She looked down on the clouds over the Atlantic and was amazed at all the icebergs in the ocean—and she's been teased about *that* a few times since then!

Between the Newcastle and Paris meetings, Becky and I did some train and ferry touring in England, Belgium, and Holland, then went back to London for a few days with the Hafs. This was the first time we had left the kids so long, so we'd hired a graduate-student couple, Lloyd and Grace Swanson, to stay with them. This was not too popular with the kids, and to top it off, Beve had to be put to bed with mononucleosis two days after we left.

Becky started working part time for a certified public accountant in East Lansing in 1968. The CPA was the son of Professor

Weaver, who was the former head of the dairy department at MSU. Becky checked his math calculations and was particularly busy during tax season. She used her income to buy house furnishings, such as dining room chairs, a new couch, floor lamps, and silverware.

Beve graduated from high school in 1969 and started to Western Michigan University in Kalamazoo. Early in the fall term, Becky got a phone call from a doctor seeking permission to perform an appendectomy on Beve. I was out of town doing some research with the dairy herd at Michigan State Prison in Jackson. Becky started trying to find me and had a great deal of difficulty explaining to the operators that although I was at the prison in Jackson, I was not an inmate there. She finally made contact, and I went on to the hospital that night.

The overseas trip in 1968 whetted my appetite, and I wanted to take a sabbatical leave. I had achieved the goal of promotion to professor by age forty and wanted to make certain that I stayed ahead of the curve in the academic world. But first, I had to find the money. I went to the library and looked up all foundations and corporations that funded grants in my area of interest. I wrote to some with a preliminary proposal and sent inquiries to some international AI organizations. I ended up with two offers—one in Helsinki, Finland, and one with the British Milk Marketing Board in England. I chose England, maybe because I was too lazy to learn the Finnish language and maybe because I wanted to avoid the cold winter there. Anyway, I have never been sorry of the choice made.

Plans were finalized in March, and we began to get ready for a year in England. The hardest job was convincing Beve, the nineteen-year-old with one year of college, that she had to go with us. We applied strong pressure and were hoping she would go to the American University over there for the year.

Shortly before our departure, I attended the ADSA meeting in Florida, learned about an open position in Georgia, and was asked to apply. I was interested but could not apply because of our immediate plans. I was also being seriously considered for an associate dean position at MSU, but couldn't pursue that, either.

We had rented our house to a family from California who were coming to MSU for a year. I simply turned my house over to Bob Reynolds, our neighbor, and he handled everything—rent, repairs, payments, and all. We never saw the family with their three young boys, but it worked out beautifully. The house, furniture, and everything were in wonderful shape when we returned—just like coming back from a week's vacation.

We sold the station wagon to a dealer for $1,100, which was much too cheap, but I didn't want to try to sell it myself. I gave the old 1960 Chevrolet to Ed Convey, a young faculty member in the reproduction lab. It was using gobs of oil and smoking badly, but I knew how to accelerate and decelerate to minimize the exhaust smoke. Three days after we left, Ed was ticketed on campus for polluting the environment, which has provided some good-natured laughs since then.

Just two days before we left, a couple in our church volunteered to keep our dog, which took care of our last hurdle. We had to get to New York, as we were going over on the *S.S. France* and were flying back a year later. I had rented a station wagon and we had loaded it with enough clothes to last a year. It was a sad departure, as Beve and Beda were each leaving a boyfriend behind.

We had a smooth trip to New Jersey and spent the night near New York City. We drove to the dock the next day and got the family boarded. I then left to turn in the rental car and returned to the ship for our first transatlantic crossing. It was a gorgeous trip for all except Beve and Beda, who sat on the ledge of the porthole and wrote letters the entire trip. The kids were in one cabin, and Becky and I were in an adjoining cabin. The meals were fabulous, with unlimited wine on the table for both lunch and dinner. Of course, at that time we didn't drink any of it.

12

The Year in England

"You never meet opportunity strolling down Easy Street."

—J. W. FANNING

We arrived at Southampton in mid-July 1970. I was immediately detained by immigration because I had no work permit—only a letter about employment. That was soon okayed, but Becky and all the children were forbidden to work. We were met at the dock by gracious hosts with two cars and a van for the luggage. They took us to our furnished rental house in Reading. A new car for me was in the driveway, and the refrigerator was stocked with food. We were then taken to Streatley for lunch in a pub. After lunch we strolled along the Thames, and Beve asked the two guys in the group, "Are there any birds in England?" They laughed and said that there were two now. It took us a while in England to understand that joke. We returned "home" to unpack and build a nest.

Late that afternoon I just had to try that car but was somewhat apprehensive with the steering and gearshift on the wrong side. Our house was at the edge of town, on a little dead-end country lane with five houses on it. The first house was 150 years old with

White Gables, our home in Reading, England,
photographed twenty-three years later.

a thatched roof, and the last house was 350 years old with a thatched roof. Ours was the middle house and quite modern with central heat. We were just across the road from a dairy farm. Garth and I got in the car, and I drove carefully down the lane just to see if I could handle it. I made it so well that I just kept going and drove all the way to downtown Reading in rush-hour traffic.

Before we'd left Michigan I had bought a VW bus and was to pick it up at the factory in Hanover, Germany, and bring it to Michigan later. I had researched European cars and decided the bus was the only vehicle big enough for the family to travel in while we were there. So the next day Beve and I drove to Reading, trained to London, tubed to Heathrow Airport, and flew to Hanover to drive our new VW back. Upon our arrival I called the factory; the receptionist answered, "Wolksvagen Verks," and then "Oh, Mr. Boyd, your car won't be ready for a fortnight. We notified your dealer in Michigan ten days ago." So I called the dealer collect, and requested my money plus two airfares from London to Hanover. Then we flew back to London and went home. Thankfully, this happening kept us from becoming a "hippie family" noted for its travel in a VW bus.

The next day I went car shopping. Just a few days before we'd left for England, we'd gone to Murray to visit both sets of parents. Both fathers had had heart attacks and neither thought they would ever see us again, so they weren't very eager for us to move overseas. Well, anyway, as we were leaving Murray on our return to Okemos I pulled up behind a Volvo station wagon and really liked it—but we had already bought the VW bus. So it was easy when the bus fell through to buy a Volvo station wagon (with the steering on the left). It was shipped from Göteborg to London and then one year later shipped to New York at no cost. This meant Becky didn't have a car for a couple of weeks, and was stuck out in the country with no one to call or see and nothing cold to drink. It was some sad household for several weeks, and I was real happy to go to work every day or to go on a trip. Dr. Bob Zimbelman from Upjohn came over, and he and I drove to Cambridge University for a reproduction conference and celebrated his fortieth birthday while there.

We soon learned that sayings in England were quite different from what we had in the states. At the opening reception of the conference, Bob Zimbelman and I were talking to two female scientists who were working in the same area of research—with Melengesterol Acetate, MGA. We arranged to meet them for breakfast to continue our discussions of their research. Before departing the reception, one of the ladies gave us her room number and said, "come by in the morning and knock me up."

Before the Volvo arrived I took Becky grocery shopping several times in my little car. The first trip, we saw some bologna that looked good, and she asked for two pounds. Well, what we received was £2 (two pounds' worth), which was $4.80 in U.S. money. The British, of course, were on the metric system, and a "pound" was their money, not a weight measure. The bologna was good, but it had no preservatives and it spoiled in about three days. Later while grocery shopping Becky asked for a fryer—to cut up and have fried chicken. The grocer turned to get it then hesitated and looked back at her. Again she explained that she wanted a chicken to fry, and he smiled and said, "Oh, you want a *flyer*," and flapped his arms. He brought her a tough old dressed hen that was almost inedible even after baking. The locals, mostly with little or no refrigeration, went to the grocery every day. Also, the milk was delivered daily. At that time, pasteurization was not required in England, but the milk-delivery company was required to deliver pasteurized milk if the customer requested it. We had a quart of pasteurized milk delivered every day, not learning until later that we were the only ones requesting pasteurized milk and that the deliveryman had to drive to Maidenhead (about fifty miles round trip) each day just to get the one quart.

Immediately after our arrival we received our National Health Insurance cards through the postal service. And our introduction to the medical system came early. The third night we were in England, Anna and her son Roddy—they lived two doors from us in the 350-year-old cottage—had us down for dinner to meet her friends. One of her friends had read about two Americans who had been injured in a motorcycle accident and asked us to visit them in the hospital. The next day Becky and I did, and it was a sad experience. The facilities were so dilapidated and old that I told our family, "No one can get sick this year." When socialized medicine had started in England after World War II, the cost to workers had been based on the cost of operating expenses. Apparently, no provisions had been made for the cost of new facilities, so thirty years after the program started, the medical infrastructure was very much the same as it had been at the end of World War II. We soon learned that emergency surgery could not always be done on an emergency basis, and that many people might wait two to four years for elective surgery. Another vast change from the United States was that the medical doctors were paid quite low salaries, which were based on the number of patients "assigned" to the doctors. In 1970 the doctors were paid the equivalent of $4,000 per year. My British employers paid me only half of my U.S. salary, which was three times what the doctors and other professional people there were paid—so we fared quite well in England, even without my other half-salary that was still being paid by Michigan State.

The medical doctors there had very little prestige in the community. The prestigious and respected people in the community were the professors—the academic people—who had the status that the medical doctors have in the United States. Our trips to the surgery (doctor's office) were always amazing. There were neither appointments nor receptionists. The waiting room had wooden benches around the walls and a single light bulb in the ceiling. When the doctor was ready for a patient he would push a buzzer on the wall. The only way you could know it was your turn was to keep track of who was already there when you came in and who came after you. When you entered the doctor's room, you sat in a straight chair across the desk from him and told him your problem. He would then write you a prescription without examining you or checking any vital signs. However, we had no problem with our assigned doctor (Dr. Morrison)—we respected him and appreciated him. On two occasions he came by the house on his own just to check on one of the children who'd been to his office.

The first sick child was Tina, who'd had an allergic reaction to some ice cream. We'd craved anything cold soon after our arrival there, so on the way home from church we'd stopped at a little deli and bought some packaged ice cream to celebrate. The refrigeration was poor, and apparently the ice cream was old and had thawed and re-frozen a few times and had mold on it. It tasted good to us, but it did a number on her real fast. She was having a bad reaction—splotchy skin, swollen eyes—when we took her in. Dr. Morrison treated her and then checked on her the next day.

The second sick child was Garth, who came down with diarrhea for three or four days and became severely dehydrated. Again, the doctor stopped by the house to check on him. Although Garth turned out okay, Beve has had several laughs about the physical exam she had in England that was required for her to transfer to Michigan State. Apparently the doctor completed the form without any significant examination. Becky thrills at telling a different medical story: one afternoon I came home from work earlier than usual and was droopy, white, and sheepish. She asked what was wrong, and I said, "I've got to go to the doctor because I have an eraser in my ear." I had a lead pencil with an eraser on the end and had the habit of putting that end in my ear. The eraser came off and I couldn't shake it out, so I headed home in big trouble. Much against my wishes and better judgment, Becky wanted to look in my ear; she calmly got a pair of tweezers and lifted out the eraser. Oh, what a relief—but I have been teased unmercifully about it ever since.

But back to the purpose of my being in England. My research and extension activities in Michigan were focused on improving fertility in cattle, especially dairy cattle. Frozen semen was in full use, and much work was being done to control estrus in cattle as a means of expanding the use of A.I. in dairy and beef heifers. The British Milk Marketing Board handled the AI program in England and employed me for a year to do research in this area. Also, the Meat and Livestock Commission, which was responsible for the beef programs, cooperated by providing a technician and a place for me to work at the Institute for Research on Animal Diseases at Compton, near Newbury and Oxford.

I conducted research on estrus synchronization in cattle, with the primary concern of determining the cause of the low fertility at the first synchronized estrus. In addition to the work at Compton, I conducted a field study with six dairy herds and ten beef herds, which were located from the Yorkshire Downs across to Chester and down as far south as Stonehenge. Including these herds, I visited a total of thirty dairy or livestock farms and attended the Royal Agricultural Show in Stoneleigh.

During the year, I attended scientific conferences at universities, visited fifteen research centers, and presented papers or talks to eight groups. I also visited major research laboratories and AI centers in Sweden, Denmark, Holland, and France as well as the islands of Jersey and Guernsey. My chief employers, two veterinarians, were both wonderful people—Geoff Smith at the Milk Marketing Board and Dick Melrose at the Meat and Livestock Commission.

Adjusting to England was indeed an experience for us. Just before we left Michigan we had purchased our first ice maker in a refrigerator and had been using lots of ice. The little refrigerator in our new English home had a very small freezing compartment that held only six or eight ice cubes. Ice was out of the question, and we really suffered during the hot summer, craving something cold to drink. Even at my work there was only one drinking-water fountain in the entire research station, and it was located several buildings away from my office. It took us about two months to adapt to hot tea and to learn to quench our nagging thirst without iced tea or cold drinks.

My favorite British-told story takes place in a pub. The American is giving the Englishman a hard time about the British lifestyle, and he says, "You limeys just don't get it—you don't even have a Thanksgiving." The Brit says, "Oh, yes we do—we celebrate it on July fourth."

Labor Day was not observed there, but it was an excuse for us to venture out on a trip in our new Volvo just before school began. We started out at noon on Saturday and planned to go west to Bristol and drive along the coastline all the way down to Land's End, coming back along the southern coast to Southampton and then back up to Reading by Monday night. The whole trip was less than 300 miles and would have been a day's run in Michigan, so two days was ample time for the trip. I headed west on highway A4 on the wrong side of the road, and the steering wheel on the wrong side, too, for all the English cars we were meeting and trying to pass.

I drove hard for three hours and still hadn't gone 50 miles on the main road. So when we got to Bath we started revising the trip plan. We scrapped the Bristol visit and turned south toward Exeter. It was dark by the time we got to Exeter, so we stopped there for the first night. The next day we knew we would never make it to Land's End, but we did drive to Plymouth. That was fortunate, because we stumbled into a big celebration of the 350th anniversary of the sailing of the Mayflower from Plymouth, England. The American ambassador was there, and many people were dressed in Pilgrim costumes. That afternoon we headed back toward our new home and spent the night at Torquay on the coast. Then on Monday we headed back through Exeter to Bournemouth, to Salisbury, and on to Reading. We never actually drove the coastline as planned, but we had a pleasant learning experience.

School started, and the three kids were ready in their new uniforms. Beda and Garth were in a school at Thiele (a small suburb of Reading) and Tina was in a new Comprehensive School in Burghfield, a suburb of Reading. The schools were quite different from the Michigan schools, but in general they were quite good. The grade levels were not comparable, but all three of the children were able to resume their scheduled grades the following year back in Michigan.

In October we were ready for another trip, and took off for the Continent. We ferried across the English Channel and spent our first night in Luxembourg. I was having some pain in my right arm and chest while driving that first day and did not sleep well that night. The next morning I went to the hospital with a "heart" problem. Despite the language barrier, I learned that I had pulled a muscle and it would be all right, but I couldn't use my arm to drive. Becky was not a happy camper for some reason. I finally figured out it was because, much against her better judgment, I'd gone back to the research lab to play basketball the night before we'd left for our trip. And I fell, and that was where I got the muscle injury.

We finally got on our way with Becky driving and entered into Germany, arriving in Colonge at lunch time. I didn't have any German money, and the banks were closed for two hours, but the kids were hungry. As I was trying to explain (in English) my plight to the hostess in the restaurant, a person eating lunch saw my difficulty and came to my rescue. He gave me 100 marks and told me to feed the family, saying that by the time they were fed the banks would be open so I could cash a traveler's check. I didn't take the money, but he arranged for us to eat anyway and told the hostess he would pay if there was a problem. We had a real nice lunch, I got money at the bank, and we went to the person's chemist store to thank him for his kindness. He said that the American soldiers had been so helpful and kind to his family during the war that he was committed to helping Americans whenever he could. We left there very proud and happy. We headed south and stayed at Baden Baden, the entrance to the Black Forest. Ordering food was a challenge, so I asked for some translation in English. But Beve, the nineteen-year-old, insisted on ordering herself. When the food came it consisted of a big bowl of raw hamburger on a side table with a dozen or more condiments to be mixed with it. She had ordered steak tartare but couldn't eat any of it. So I gave her my steak and ate the highly seasoned raw meat.

The next day we ventured on side roads through the Black Forest, stopping for lunch at a little country hotel. As soon as the waitress took our orders we saw her leave and run down the street. We waited more than two hours as she went to the different grocers to get the food and then prepared it. This was quite different from the fast-food lunches we were accustomed to in the United States.

We stayed in Basel, Switzerland, that night, and the next night in Zurich. We had a day to spare so I asked where the family wanted to go in the Alps. Becky said she'd always wanted to go to Austria, so we headed out along the mountains in that direction. We crossed the border with ease, and visited and had lunch in a real nice city. Then we headed back to Switzerland, going to Lake Lucerne. On the return we visited Bern, Dijon, and Paris and crossed the English Channel on the Hovercraft, which was the roughest crossing we ever had on any kind of water vessel. A few weeks later, as I was retracing our route so I could identify our travel pictures, I discovered that we'd never made it to Austria. Actually, we'd stopped in Liechtenstein and had lunch in Vaduz, the capital. Of course, I blamed the navigator, and that experience has been revisited numerous times in subsequent travels. The memorable highlights for me were the mountain vineyards in the Alps, Lake Lucerne, and the White Cliffs of Dover.

During the year, we took several trips to sites around England, including the beautiful Cotswolds, Wales, Scotland, and the Isle of Wight. En route to Scotland we stayed overnight on Holy Island, which is accessible by road only at low tide. Near Glasgow, at Carluke, we visited Karen and Ron McPhail—Karen was the daughter of our friends Bill and Eleanor Cheney in Michigan. (On another occasion, Ron and Karen visited us in Reading.) A highlight of the Scotland trip was visiting Kilmarnock, the ancestral home of the Boyds. Also, we looked for the Loch Ness Monster, and waited till midnight for darkness to come. At the northernmost stop, Tina came back to the room from the bathroom down the hall and wanted her mother to go see the beautiful china on the shelf in the bathroom. The pretty pieces were actually chamber pots, to go under the bed in each room.

We were invited to several homes of new friends in England and were overnight guests at some of the dairy farms. While visiting a family in Tewkesbury we went out to see the Severn Bore, which is a "wall of water" pushed far inland up the Severn River by the rising tide. We watched the favorite sport of riding the tide in a canoe.

Although we were ever ready to visit with other Americans we knew there, especially for Thanksgiving dinner, we did enjoy learning the English customs. We were guests at a New Year's Eve party and also attended a Bobby Burns Birthday party. Seated on my right was a charming female agricultural extension agent. At that time, female ag agents were most unusual in the states, so I was interested in talking shop. When the haggis was piped in and being served from the sheep's rumen, Becky told the server that she didn't want any but that I really liked it. When I finally turned around, I found a plate heaping full and a tickled wife.

Our neighbors and friends were very helpful to us. It was a long autumn for Beverly, who had dropped out of college to accompany us. After the other three kids started school she was at loose ends. I had hoped she would enroll at the American University in London, but that didn't hold much attraction for her. Knight's Farm Restaurant was a real fancy place just across the field from our home. A neighbor arranged for Beve to work there, keeping a young child and working some in the restaurant. The restaurant was owned by a former airline stewardess with BOAC Airlines, and her husband was in business in London. They needed help and were delighted to hire her and, later, Beda, with no record of either girl's employment.

Beve's boyfriend, Tim, and Beda's boyfriend, Steve, both came over for Christmas. That was when we learned that our little dog, Cocoa, had died. He had slipped on the ice and re-injured his back, which had been broken previously. We were so sad to lose him, but we were so grateful to our church friends, the Beattys, who had kindly agreed to keep him for us.

Beve went back to Michigan with Tim after Christmas and stayed with the Lassiters until the winter term started at Michigan State. She had transferred from Western Michigan at Kalamazoo and was anxious to move into the dorm and start a new venture at MSU.

Winter and spring passed rather quickly for us. We had adapted and were enjoying our stay there much more. I took a nine-day trip in March to visit universities and key research laboratories in Sweden, Denmark, Holland, and France. This was a fabulous experience for me. I had arranged the trip with scientists I knew either personally or by reputation, and I was received graciously everywhere I went. Of course, I had to rely on others to translate for me in their homes, at dinners hosted for me, in their laboratories, and everywhere else. When guests came to visit us in the United States we fully expected them to speak our language, and it was embarrassing to me that now I could not speak my hosts' languages.

Two experiences from those trips have stayed with me over the years. The first happened when I was visiting in Utrecht, Holland, with Dr. C.H.W. deBois, who had just moved into a new veterinary building. My briefcase must have had a broken hinge, because as I picked it up off his new beautiful hardwood conference table, I made a deep gash and scar on it. I was so embarrassed. He was a good friend who later arranged for us to stay in his aunt's home on the North Sea coast while we visited the fabulous Tulip Festival in Holland and around Amsterdam. The other experience was driving on top of the major river dike along the Rhine. Returning from Wageningen, Holland, in the rental car, I got off the main road and drove on a gravel road on the dike for several miles, watching the ships sail right beside me.

Many of the farm workers at the research laboratory in England lived in public housing. They were paid about $55 per week, which was enough to pay their rent, buy a joint of meat to eat on Sunday, and pay for a pack of cigarettes and a "pinta" of beer each day. There was no incentive to make more money because of the excessive tax rate on anything above the usual weekly wages. Thus, they had adapted, and felt no real need for anything beyond this existence.

We encountered so many things there that I was certain we would never tolerate in the United States, such as having to pump our own gas, and dealing with lackadaisical postal workers and bank tellers. While we were there the postal workers went on strike for about six weeks. There was no way we could hear from our parents back home. Every week I would drive in to Heathrow Airport in London and ask a passenger loading on a flight to New York to mail letters for us on his or her arrival. (Once I asked a gentleman who turned out to be James Roosevelt, son of former President Franklin Delano Roosevelt.) This was the only way that our parents could hear from us during the strike.

Becky and the three children flew home to Michigan about a month before I left. The day they left I took the Volvo to the dealer in London to ship it to New York. It would take about three weeks for the car to get there, so I wanted to ship it so it would be in New York when I arrived. Meanwhile, Becky would be driving one of the Lassiters' cars, since we'd gotten rid of our other cars before going to England.

I was real busy winding up my work, but it was a lonely time after they left. I was getting anxious to return home, too. Dr. Vearl Smith (a friend from Utah and formerly at Wisconsin and dean of agriculture at Arizona) was working at the Institute of Dairying at Shinfield near Reading, so he shared our big house after the family left. Actually, he and I returned to the United States on the same day but on different flights.

Just a few days before I left England I attended a conference at Nottingham University, and on the way home someone ran into me at a construction site and banged up the back of my company car. So the morning of my departure I had to report an accident when I dropped off the car at the British Milk Marketing Board office in Thames Ditton. Before Becky had left the officials at MMB had entertained us royally at a going away party.

It was indeed a good feeling to be boarding that plane, heading home after a really good year in England. The plane was only half full, so I made a good bed and slept most of the way. Morty Cohen met me at the airport. It was the first time I had seen him in twenty-five years—since we were in the Army together in Manila. He was the only Army buddy I had stayed in contact with, but we had never visited. He entertained me at the theater, but I wasn't too alert after the flight. The next morning he took me to get my Volvo station wagon at the dock in New Jersey. I was ready to get it and

Home in Okemos, Michigan, 1963–1972.

head toward Michigan. I got to Okemos the next afternoon and was happy to be together with my family again.

We found the house in excellent shape. The people we'd rented it to—the California family on leave at MSU—had moved in after we'd left in July 1970, and had already moved out before Becky returned. The house was just like we had been gone on a short vacation, and there was nothing we had to do to feel at home. The biggest adjustment was to remember to drive on the right side of the road after driving on the left side for a year in England. And those big American station wagons looked gigantic to us.

13

Readjusting to Stateside

"You're never a loser until you quit trying."

—MIKE DITKA

We thrilled at getting home and really enjoyed the remainder of the summer. Of course, we made a trip to Kentucky to see our parents, as both sets had been convinced they would never see us again when we'd left for a year in England. I had to buy a car, so I took the yardstick and shopped for one with the most space in the back seat—for four kids. It turned out to be a 1971 Dodge.

When school started in September we were essentially back to normal for the family. The kids picked up with no loss of momentum even though the "grades" in England had been vastly different. However, it was certainly not that easy for me. Someone on the faculty had moved into my office while I was gone, and others had been doing my work in my absence. So I had a lost feeling and a reentry problem for a while. But it didn't last long, as I was teaching in the fall and was kept busy with 125 students in class. I soon got back into the swing as I was involved in research and extension, as well.

After a couple of months, I was contacted again about the Georgia job, which was still open after a year. This was rather amusing to us because one of the rare American shows we'd watched on British "telly" was the Great Wallenda, as he walked the tight wire across Tallulah Gorge in North Georgia. During the show both Becky and I had had private visions that one day we would be in Georgia. I arranged to go for an interview during the Christmas holidays at the university. It was about mid-December, and the University was closed down tight in Athens. I was staying at the Georgia Center, which was a conference center like the Kellogg Center at Michigan State, but I was the only one in the hotel part. I left a wake-up call that didn't happen, so when I awoke the group I was to meet for breakfast was already arriving. I jumped in the shower but there was no hot water, so I got quite a welcome to UGA.

Despite the inconveniences, however, the interview went quite well, and Becky and I were invited back for a second interview. I gave three dates when I could come, and they chose the latest one—March 1. I was giving an invited presentation at North Carolina State in late February, so we went from Raleigh on to Athens. Professor Herb Henderson picked us up in Atlanta, and we drove through some strange country on our way through Conyers and Monroe to Athens. We were lodged at the Holiday Inn. The next morning while we were having breakfast, a familiar-looking couple walked in. Becky said, "Who is that?" And I said, "It looks like Don Edwards to me." Don had lived in the adjoining neighborhood in Okemos. He heard me call his name and came back to our table. While we were in England, Don had been serving as dean at Minnesota, but now was being interviewed at Georgia as a distinguished professor.

We were hosted exceptionally well, with lots of interviews and parties. The dean took me to Tifton on March 1; corn was already up and growing in the Georgia fields, and azaleas and many other flowers were ablossom. Three days later Becky and I flew into Detroit in a blinding snow storm, so it was easy to accept the position in Georgia. I was committed to teach at Michigan State during the spring quarter, so we could not move until late June.

While we were visiting Athens in March, we had looked at locations, and Becky had looked at several houses. She'd found one she liked under construction in Cedar Creek, which was "the" place to live in 1972. It was especially attractive to us because a new high school—Cedar Shoals—was opening in the fall. But we couldn't get serious about a house until ours sold in Michigan. It finally sold in May, so I went to Athens on Mother's Day. We had been in contact with the realtor, and I told her that I would likely buy the house that Becky had seen in Cedar Creek. The realtor picked me up at the hotel late Sunday afternoon and took me out to the house. Construction had stopped for us to choose paint colors and so on before it was completed. I noted a few changes I wanted, as I had an appointment with the builder the next day at noon. The next morning the realtor picked me up, and we looked at three or four houses so I could compare to see how good a deal I was getting when I bought the house at noon. Two brothers were the builders of the house I was going to buy, so when we arrived at the site and I was introduced to one of the brothers, he said, "Oh my, my brother sold this house last night and he thought he was selling it to you."

Well, when that finally sank in I was one sick puppy, because I was going back to Michigan the next day without my mission accomplished. And then I thought, *what have I done? Committed to a new job, sold our home, no place to move—what will I do to provide for a wife and four children?* But, first things first—I had to go to the hospital to have a thorn cut from an infected finger, and then stop for some lunch. The realtor had a sick child at home, but I hadn't given her time to call home to check on the youngster. So we regrouped and rushed to a 2:00 P.M. appointment to see a house on the west side of town, in Timothy Estates. I actually liked the house, and the kids would still go to the new Cedar Shoals school in the fall because of cross-town busing. We looked at a couple of other houses, but I kept on liking the house in Timothy Estates. I called Becky and got her approval, and at 7:00 P.M. made an offer on the house. At midnight we signed the papers, and I returned to Michigan the next morning as planned. Someone asked me if the house had air conditioning and a furnace, and I didn't even know. I'd forgotten to check on that—but fortunately, it did.

From the initial contact by Georgia in December until I accepted the position in March, Becky and I had given thoughtful consideration to making a move. The final decision was that it was time to do so. In the late 1960s the Okemos school system had changed drastically. The "hippies" from college had returned as teachers, and the system had become ultra-liberal. Even students in junior high were aided and abetted by their parents in publishing underground newspapers in the school. In the high school there was a meditation room where a student could go any time he or she did not feel like going to class. We were not unhappy to leave the school system, even though we didn't know what was in store in Georgia.

As it turned out, we were in Michigan during the best of times for Michigan State and arrived in Georgia during the best of times for UGA. When we arrived in Georgia, gasoline was only 29¢ a gallon. The energy crisis that hit in 1974 really hurt Michigan State because so much of the tax revenue in Michigan was based on the automobile industry. This focused great attention on the Sunbelt—Georgia prospered, and the University of Georgia was getting tremendous support.

Yet we hated to leave our Michigan friends, and Georgia was not a popular destination with them. Georgia politics had given the state a bad image in the North, especially during the Talmadge years (when three people had claimed to be governor at the same time) and in the late 1960s, when the legislature elected Lester Maddox, the axe-handle racist, as governor. When we moved, Jimmy Carter was still governor, but Maddox was lieutenant gov-

ernor. My friend Clint Meadows, a native of Arkansas, told everyone that when Louie Boyd moved from Michigan to Georgia it improved the IQ in both states.

Beve's romance had survived the six months she'd reluctantly
spent in England, and her transfer to Michigan State had gone
well. She and Tim were planning to get married and were waiting
until September so both could work and save money during the
summer. It developed that friends in our church, the John Nellors,
were going to be gone all summer and wanted someone to live
in their house to take care of the dog and keep the grass mowed.
Becky was beginning to have some concerns about directing a
Michigan wedding from Georgia, so we "gently" encouraged them
to go ahead and get married before we left. They did get married
three weeks before we moved, and both worked during the summer while living in the Nellor home at no cost.

Since Beve was staying in Michigan, Beda wanted to do so, too.
Because of her good record in England, she had ample credits to
graduate, so she entered Michigan State and took courses there
during the spring term of her senior year in high school. Of course,
many of our friends and neighbors offered to let Beda stay with
them if she didn't want to move with us—which didn't help our
case much. We really wanted her to move with us but hadn't presented a strong ultimatum. We had told her that if she would move
with us and go to Georgia for her first year of college, we would
send her any place she wanted to attend after that—back to Michigan State or wherever. The uncertainty of what she was going to
do was not popular at all with Becky, but we refused to argue or
force a showdown when she kept telling us that she was not going
to move with us. Then, about two weeks before we were to move,
she and her boyfriend came in for our usual summer Sunday-
evening tradition of making homemade ice cream. She came over
and sat in my lap and said, "Guess what—I am going to move with
you to Georgia." That was one happy time for us!

The spring quarter at Michigan State was a busy time for me as

I tried to wind up my work and get ready to move. Tom Cowden, the dean of agriculture when I was hired at Michigan State, had always said that "if a person decides to leave, I want that person to get going right then." And I kind of agree with that philosophy, but I had agreed to teach a large class that term, and I was going to fulfill my commitment. It was indeed difficult to keep my mind on my job, but I think I did quite well. I had a large class, and I felt like I did the best job of teaching that I had ever done.

I had an interesting experience that term with a student enrolled in a new governmental experimental program at Michigan State. The idea was that if school dropouts on the streets of Detroit were placed in a college setting, they could adjust to the new environment and succeed. In my private work with this student I tried to explain what a *sire* was in animal breeding and used the term *father,* but he didn't know that word either. I spent more time with that one student than with the other 124 students combined. The main result of the program was that the friends of the participants flocked to the campus to sleep and eat in the dorms of the participants.

After school was out and the June 19 wedding was over, we spent our time packing and getting ready for the move. We got Bekins to move us because of the good experience we'd had with the move from Tennessee. Soon after the fourth of July we loaded up and headed south. It was late afternoon by the time the van left, and we kissed Beve and Tim goodbye and headed to Murray, Kentucky. It was well after midnight when we arrived at Becky's parents' home in Murray with two loaded cars, three kids, and a dog. Becky drove one car with two children, and I drove the other car with one child, the dog, and lots of flowers. Becky was just following me in kind of a trance, as she remembers nothing of the trip or of the stops we made during the last 200 miles.

We visited with both sets of parents and then drove to Dalton, Georgia, to stay in a pretty cheap motel. But we were headed to a new adventure, and we were excited. We arrived in Athens the next day in time for me to close on the house, get the keys, and show it to Becky and the kids for the first time. While we were waiting for the moving van, I was lying on the floor in the living room, and I heard a noise on the porch. When I looked up there were eight or ten kids from the neighborhood peering in to see the new neighbors.

The van arrived, and we began building our new nest and getting settled in. I had a week before I officially started to work, so I made the mistake of offering to do some interior painting. This turned into a big job, especially when you included the insides of all the closets. One day while painting I was getting quite warm, so I asked Becky to adjust the thermostat to make it cooler. After a couple of adjustments I kept getting hotter; I finally checked the thermostat, to find it set on eighty-five degrees. We had never had an air conditioner, and Becky thought that to get results with it you would turn it *up,* the same as we did with the furnace in Michigan.

14

Way Down South in Georgia

"Never let the fear of striking out get in your way."

—BABE RUTH

M y first day at work at UGA was July 12, 1972, and I reported to an empty room in the coliseum, a facility used both as the basketball arena and for livestock shows, as the agricultural people in the state were the ones who'd had the money appropriated for it. My first job was to set up an office and hire a secretary. My appointment was part time in cooperative extension, and my office was located near the Animal Science and Dairy Science Extension Department's offices. Extension was separate from the other departments involved in teaching and/or research, and it had its own personnel department for all its programs. But I didn't know that, so I proceeded to get applications from the university personnel office and to hire a secretary—much to the chagrin of the extension personnel when they learned what had happened. The new employee would have to go through a battery of additional testing to "comply with regulations" and determine that she was indeed qualified for the job.

My position was division chairman of the animal science division, which was composed of six departments at three locations: in Athens, two extension departments and two teaching and research departments; in Tifton, one research department; and in Griffin, another research department. The total faculty in the six departments was no more than in the one animal department at other institutions such as Michigan State or Kentucky—and here, only about one-third or less of the total faculty was responsible for handling an entire teaching load that would have been shared by all faculty at most other universities. Also, the division chairman had *no* money, as all money was handled by the department head and was allocated by the three college directors of teaching, research, and extension. My position was strictly "coordinating," with no financial carrot to influence programs. This handicap was not as limiting in the eight other divisions in the college (e.g., agronomy, agricultural economics, and plant pathology). Their chairmen also served as department heads, so they had funds to administer. Anyway, I hit the road and traveled extensively across the state to get acquainted.

We had not revisited the question of where Beda was going to college. When she'd agreed to move with us we had not pressed the issue of going to Georgia one year and then going anywhere she wanted to go. But one day, about a month after we arrived, she asked her mother for the car, and when she returned she said that she had registered for college at UGA.

Garth and Tina started school in September as sophomore and freshman at the new Cedar Shoals school. The Athens schools had been integrated only about five years, and the new school had a fifty-fifty mix of black and white students. This was indeed a new experience, because there had been only one black student in the entire school district in Okemos. The big difference was in the social arena, because parties and school activities other than sports were not an integral part of the recently integrated school program.

Also, on September 12, my parents celebrated their sixtieth

wedding anniversary. Nelson and Sue brought them and my sister, Kathleen, to visit our new home and celebrate the occasion. Just four months after that Mother had a stroke and was never aware of anything after that time. From the hospital she was moved to the nursing home, where she spent three years before she died on August 29, 1976. Daddy used to visit her daily. He knew everyone there and would talk about visiting those "old folks" in the nursing home. He was eighty at the time of her stroke.

Daddy had a rough time adjusting after Mother died. He came and stayed about a month with us. At first he was so weak he couldn't even walk to the end of our driveway. Becky kept pushing him, so that after a couple of weeks he was walking up and down the hills all over our neighborhood.

As new residents in Athens we visited four Presbyterian churches in the area, but settled on Central Presbyterian Church in the Beechwood area because of the youth program. We joined there in December 1972.

My first big task in Georgia was to plan and host the national meeting of the Society for the Study of Reproduction (SSR) already scheduled for the UGA campus in the summer of 1973. In late January Becky and I were in New Orleans to finalize plans with the SSR board, including Harold Hafs and several other friends I had worked with in SSR.

On the evening of January 22, 1973, our group was in a local restaurant and placed in a dining room with another national group. Our leader went over to talk to the "intruders" and came back with the news that they were the Planned Parenthood group and that the Supreme Court had legalized abortion that day (*Roe v. Wade*). Some in our group were elated, so a medical doctor from Ohio jumped up and gave a toast to the other group. He said, "Here's to the old woman who lived in a shoe—she had so many children she didn't know what to do." An attractive young lady in that group retorted immediately, "Here's to the old woman who lived in a shoe—Planned Parenthood could have told her what to do." The rest of the evening was jovial.

That winter Becky got Garth, at age fifteen, a job busing tables and washing dishes at Howard Johnson. One night while he was working we experienced our first tornado. Jim Edwards, Don and Clara's son, was spending the night with us, so we all huddled in the central hallway of the house and waited for the all-clear on the radio. We had very little damage, but a neighborhood just five miles away had extensive problems. It was the first tornado that had hit Athens in fifty years or more, but, oddly, another one struck Athens again just a month later. As usual, I was out of town, in an enclosed room in Macon attending a dinner meeting with a group of swine producers. We were totally unaware of anything happening except heavy rain when I headed home that evening. The 11:00 news on the car radio reported that a tornado had literally destroyed the university city of Athens, Georgia. I was so scared, but there was nothing I could do—cell phones hadn't been invented! I knew I wouldn't be able to get through if all the phone lines were down, so I just started on the two-hour trip home. Much of the drive was on a deserted road through the Oconee National Forest, and there was continuous thunder and lightning. Every time the lightning lit up the sky I would look all around to see if I could see a tornado. When I got to Athens I was scared to turn in to the subdivision, but I found all in good shape and everybody asleep, unaware of anything happening. Then I was really aggravated and even mad for worrying so much during the trip. It turned out that the tornado had struck precisely the same area as the previous one, and this time had done even greater damage.

As our first springtime in the Deep South arrived, we were excited and thrilled at the beauty of Athens all ablossom with flowers. Professor Henderson gave us tickets to the Masters Golf Tournament in Augusta, so Becky and I spent a glorious day there. It was astounding to walk on the "carpeted" fairways and enjoy

Party at "Boyd's Pub."

the great weather, the congenial crowd, the well-known golfers, and the beauty of the course. It was a day we shall never forget. Later in April, our special friends, the Hafs, came from Michigan, and we went to the beach at Jekyll Island for three days. You guessed it—we got really blistered, and Carol (Hafs) and I ended up with sun poisoning on our ankles and feet and could not walk for a couple of days.

Later in the season, Becky was planning our first summer vacation in Georgia. I said that I didn't care where we went as long as it was within three hours of Athens. I had traveled so much I was not eager to spend a vacation driving. She was fortunate to luck up on a cancellation at Callaway Gardens, and we spent a week there. It was most enjoyable, as there were abundant activities for Garth and Tina as well as for the adults. We enjoyed the Florida State University Circus that performed and worked there every summer.

As Kentuckians we began a ritual of having Kentucky Derby parties. Friends were invited to watch the race on television. Becky would serve Kentucky barbecue, baked beans, coleslaw, Kentucky Derby pie, and, of course, homemade mint juleps. This was indeed a favorite time of year in Georgia.

Later, we had a few Poor Man's parties, which were usually around April 15 when income taxes were filed. Invitations were written on irregular pieces of paper torn from a grocery sack, and people wore their scrubby "hard times" clothes. Becky served dried beans with ham hock, coleslaw, cornbread, and "tea cakes." We used oil lamps instead of electric lights and drank out of fruit jars.

The University of Georgia had doubled in size in the mid- to late 1960s. Many staff members had been hired rather quickly—while the money was available—and some who were hired were underqualified. Then Fred Davison, a veterinarian, became president in about 1967, and he soon began a concerted effort to transform UGA into a first-class research institution. He brought in top administrators to clamp down on promotions, which was a traumatic experience for some faculty accustomed to teaching in a small, provincial "party school" and never doing any research. In agriculture there were some (too many) staff who had not performed sufficiently to get promoted. Yet many felt that the state owed them their jobs because of family ties or political connections.

Professor H.B. Henderson retired as head of the dairy department in 1974. He was a person I had known and admired for many years; I had spent the night in his home in 1956 when I was interviewed and offered a job in his department. I tried desperately to hire a replacement and had top people, such as John Campbell at Missouri and Roger Hemken at Kentucky, come in for interviews. But we could not attract that quality to stay, because of our small department. So the college administration elected to combine the two departments—animal science and dairy science—into one animal and dairy science department, with me as head. Now I was department head in addition to division chairman, which gave me a budget. Indeed, this was the proper move for the university to make, but it threw together faculty who didn't want to be together and it displaced the head of one of the departments.

I continued to work with industry, and had a great relationship with livestock and agricultural leaders in the state. I spent a lot of time organizing and getting the Georgia Pork Producers Association (GPPA) started. Just a few years previously, the effective Livestock Producers Association, which had strong groups in every county, had been abolished and transformed into the Georgia Cattlemen's Association with a local group in most counties. This move was popular with the cowboy-boots-and-hats people but didn't provide anything for the hog producers. The GPPA got going quickly as a separate entity. They hired an executive secretary, and the organization is still thriving thirty years later.

There was also a strong dairy-producers association that was quite active. In fact, Becky and I joined a large group who went to Washington, D.C., on the "Milk Train" in January 1977 to attend Jimmy Carter's inauguration as president. In later trips to Washington with the Dairy Group, I had the opportunity to visit the Oval Office.

As I hired new, top-notch people, I tried to be fair and equitable with all faculty but encountered much difficulty. Some prima donna professors didn't want equitable treatment—they had dominated their previous departments and received preferential treatment, and still wanted it that way. They didn't want any competition for either funds or facilities. It is easy to build up a big opposition, especially when some of the opponents have cronies in high places.

Two examples will illustrate. One young, energetic teacher came in to teach animal genetics—a really hard course. He expected a lot out of the students and made that very clear, which was a vast departure from previous instructors in terms of course content and expectations of the students. The students rebelled strongly, and even the dean went along with the students and the good-ol'-boy professors who supported them, and he tried to fire the new teacher. The "hard" teacher persisted, and once the students got the idea of having to study they enjoyed the course. About three years later the students elected this new teacher as the outstanding teacher in the department.

Another young teacher caught a student cheating on a test. He reported the student to the Student Judiciary as required, but the same dean tried to get the young professor fired. The dean testified against the teacher at the student hearing, but the student was charged and kicked out of school at the beginning of the next quarter. The dean registered the student for 39 hours during the ongoing quarter and gave him grades enabling him to graduate before the expulsion from school became effective.

This same dean, a distinguished professor, the dean of the college, the dean of another school, and a couple of others finally got me. Not all of these individuals were together, but it is most interesting how some decidedly opposite types become strange bedfellows when there is an opportunity to join forces and get rid of someone they don't like. This happened to me after seven years as division chairman and five years as department head. One small group wanted me out, and the other group wanted my job, so it happened. This was traumatic for me, but you just have to go on and outlive your enemies, which I did. Within six months of my removal as division chairman and department head, two of the deans had been fired by the president and the other one had died. One of the opponents was effectively neutered when he lost his supportive deans, and within two years the other had retired.

Although it was hard to do, I tried to hold my head high and keep mingling in public. It would be easy to hide, but most inappropriate. The greatest weapon one has is to treat the oppressors kindly, especially when they expect and want you to rave with anger and try to get revenge. I immersed myself into making a contribution at the college level, working out of the dean's office. One redeeming event was that the next year I got the largest annual salary increase of my entire career. And later I watched with pride as several of the young faculty members I hired became department heads and laboratory directors at various institutions.

My first new challenge after that was with Sponsored Programs, which involved chasing grant dollars for research and other sponsored activities. Traditionally, all research in agricultural experiment stations was funded by appropriations from federal and state funds. But as research money became more scarce, it was necessary to find other sources of funding. During the last twenty years of the 1900s the percentage of grants in the college's research-funding mix increased from about 10% up to 25% of the total funding. I also worked closely with the Ag Alumni Association and fundraising for the entire college.

When I first came to Georgia, the revitalized Ag Alumni Association had been going about twenty years. It had been organized by alumni of the college, mainly through the Georgia Department of Agriculture, and was almost exclusively organized so state appropriations could be funneled through the college to do projects that the alumni wanted to do out in the state. In other words, its focus was "what can the college do for its alums"—directly opposite what it should have been, namely, "what can alums do to support and benefit the college."

Shortly after my arrival in 1972 I got two good programs started. One was a lifetime membership in the association, similar to one at the University of Illinois whereby an alumnus could pay $100 and be a life member instead of paying annual dues. I took this proposal to the part-time secretary of the Alumni Association, and soon it was implemented as the Eterna Club. That fund has grown over the years to support numerous scholarships and other programs for the college. I also set up the Georgia Dairy Memorial and Scholarship Fund, copied from a successful program in Michigan, to endow scholarships for dairy students. It, too, has been quite effective.

But back to the Ag Alumni Association, which was run by a part-time secretary. I worked with the association officers and ag leaders in the state to move toward having a full-time alumni secretary, to be funded by the college, and to hire a person to raise funds for the college from alums, corporations, and other donors. Of course, the biggest hurdle was to change attitudes toward giving to help the college. The prevalent feeling was that if the college needs something it doesn't have, it could go to the legislature to get the money appropriated. There was never a hint that alums should support the college directly.

A big factor that was most helpful in changing attitudes was to get the local alumni officers active in an organization called NAADA, which was the National Agricultural Alumni and Development Association. At yearly meetings, alumni directors, agricultural fundraisers, and alums from ag colleges across the country got together to share ideas and programs that really work. The national meeting was held on the UGA Campus in 1987.

We set up accounts in the University Foundation for the departments and for specific purposes for the college, and rather successfully moved the alums and friends of the college toward believing that it was appropriate to contribute money to enhance the college's programs. In 1985 the college hired Donya Lester, the first full-time person to work with alumni and to do fundraising for the college. She was subsequently hired by Purdue University and was replaced in the college by Tammy Tate, who later moved on to university-level fundraising. Within fifteen years we'd had three full-time and several part-time employees involved in alumni and fundraising activities for the college.

Let me pause to focus on some general activities I enjoyed working on during the late 1970s and the 1980s. First was a joint program with Fort Valley State College at Fort Valley, Georgia. If the kind reader is not aware of what a land-grant university is, please hasten to learn. (For a quick introduction see Appendix II, The Miracle Club.) I am an enthusiastic disciple of the land-grant university system and am completely convinced that this unique system of early higher education, with its teaching, agricultural experiment stations, and cooperative extension programs, is solely responsible for the phenomenal progress in food and fiber production in this country. This great system of education with its clever funding was started by the U.S. Congress in 1862. However, the colleges were not open to the black population in the southern states. Thus, in 1890 land-grant colleges for the black population in the South were established by Congress. Yet they were not funded very well, and following the integration of schools in the 1960s the southern states were mandated by the federal courts to provide comparable education programs for all races.

This is a long introduction to the University System of Georgia Committee I served on for ten years to ensure that the University of Georgia and Fort Valley State College (FVSC) cooperated and had comparable programs in agriculture. This was a fabulous experience. There was considerable federal money available to FVSC, and we were charged with its prudent use. I pushed the goat-production program there, but at first the faculty did not want to be identified with goats. However, there was no scientific information on goat milk and meat production and products, so the project prospered and has fared well for twenty-five years—even expanding to other 1890 institutions.

Another favorite activity was serving on the board of directors for Coble Dairies, Inc., in Lexington, North Carolina, from 1974 until 1992. Quarterly meetings were held, and the summer meeting each year was always a family gathering at Myrtle Beach, South Carolina.

In 1974 I was elected to the board of the American Dairy Science Association (ADSA), a scientific organization for academics and industry workers. I'd joined in 1949 as a student, and became a life member after forty years. At the end of my board term I was a nominee for president but was defeated by seven votes (out of 2,000 members) by a member employed by the U.S. Department of Agriculture. In 1981 I was elected to the board of the American Society of Animal Science (ASAS), a similar scientific organization including all large animals (although in the early days ADSA was distinctly separate). I was told by my former major professor at Illinois, Dr. G.W. Salisbury, that he and I were the only two people who had ever served on both boards—ADSA and ASAS. However, I never checked on it and don't know if that is accurate. As the two societies enter the new century, they are much closer and hold joint meetings as Federated Animal Science Societies (FASS).

In the early 1980s I was appointed by ADSA to represent that society on the Council for Agricultural Science and Technology (CAST) board. CAST was an exciting organization, composed of thirty or more agricultural scientific societies, whose express purpose was to provide scientific facts to decision-makers such as the U.S. Congress. I was on this board for five years, serving as president in 1984–85.

Among some personal events, I mention the loss of the Volvo station wagon (Ole Yellow Mustard) we brought back from England. Garth and a neighbor girl were on their way to the high school one Saturday morning in April 1974 to take their SAT exams when a lady rammed into the back of the station wagon. Garth was stopped at a traffic light, and the lady behind him went to sleep and buried a little VW bug in the back of our car. Fortunately, no one was hurt, but it buckled the frame and totaled the station wagon.

In May the same year I was asked to give the commencement address at Sedalia High School, where Becky and I had graduated eighteen years before. I was tickled for Becky to sit on the stage as a member of the official party.

The next year, on March 22, 1975, Beda married Steve Smith, a "Georgia cracker" from Jesup, Georgia, which is in the rural southern part of the state. This was a big event, with many of

Steve's Army buddies gathering from across the country for the wedding. Beda graduated from college that summer and started teaching, while Steve was on the Athens police force.

Just two years and three months later we received the phone call that every parent dreads. The call came from a neighbor and friend, Dr. Butch Mulherin, who said, "Louie, we have your daughter here in the hospital; she has been in a serious automobile accident." It was July 4, 1977, and we had just driven that day from Murray, Kentucky where we had visited Becky's parents and my daddy. We'd been returning from Colorado, where we had visited Garth (who was working at a dude ranch in the Rockies). We had arrived home at about 5:00 P.M., and Beda and Steve had been returning from a visit with his family in Jesup. His family started calling us about 7:00 to see if we had heard from them, because they couldn't reach them by phone (there was no such thing as a cell phone then). I refused to worry, but was plenty anxious about three hours later when Butch called from the hospital. That frantic trip to the hospital started such a whirlwind—Beda was six months pregnant, but conscious, with unknown injuries. Steve, the big burly policeman, lay there asleep so peaceful. The doctor told us he might not wake up for a while but I just knew he would be up and taking charge of the situation in a couple of hours. How wrong I was, and it was all so tragic and unnecessary. We were to learn that two carloads of blacks were out celebrating the July 4 holiday and were racing side by side on a two-lane road—Highway 15—below Greensboro, Georgia, and had rounded a curve and hit Beda and Steve head on. The driver of the car causing the accident was the only occupant injured, and he had a broken leg. He was brought to Athens Hospital also, and after a week I went in to see him (I had the chief of hospital security go with me so I wouldn't be tempted to choke him). I finally forgave him, but it indeed took a long time. The only penalty he got for the severely disrupted and altered lives he caused was probation and suspended drivers license for one year.

Louie presenting Outstanding Student Award to Garth, 1979.

Beda came home to our house after about ten days with several broken bones in her ankles and a broken nose. Steve had a severe brainstem injury, and indeed did not come out of the coma for six weeks or more. When he did, he had no memory. He went to Emory for surgery after two months. Jeremiah was born on November 3, 1977, and all was well. All, including their big dog, Wally (who'd also been in the wreck), were at our house, but Beda was anxious to get her brood back to her home and take care of them. They did move to their home in Winterville in early December for the first time since July. Three days later—when I was out of town, of course—Beda had an attack of kidney stones in the middle of the night. Tina was out in the other car but soon came in, and they hurried to Beda. Becky took care of the month-old baby and Steve, while Tina took Beda to the hospital for surgery. All of this was on the same day (December 13, 1978) that Beve had her first child, Meghan, in Elkhart, Indiana.

Of course, Becky wanted to be there but she couldn't go. Becky took Jeremiah to the hospital every few hours to nurse and then went back to Winterville to take care of Steve. All came back to our house when Beda was released from the hospital. Garth had left on December 9 for Colorado to work the ski season at Winter Park. I insisted that Becky go to Indiana to be with Beve, Tim, and their new baby at Christmas. We have laughed many times about the hotdogs Beda, Steve, and I had for Christmas dinner. I don't remember where Tina was for Christmas dinner.

The New Year of 1978 began with Beda soon ready to move back to her home to meet the many, many challenges she faced.

In July 1979 we headed to Colorado for the wedding of Garth and Lynette—a Colorado girl he'd met at Beavers, the dude ranch at Winter Park. The wedding was on July 21, 1979, at an outdoor chapel at the YMCA of the Rockies in Frazier. It was a beautiful setting. From there, Becky and I drove on to Tucson, Arizona, for the American Society of Animal Science meetings. When we returned to Athens those so discontented with me had been quite active and had laid plans for me to be removed as department head and division chairman. It took several weeks to accomplish their feat because I didn't resign my position as they had planned. A couple of months later we were at a meeting at Jekyll Island when Nelson called to tell me Daddy had died—November 11, 1979. That fall and winter were not the best of times.

15

University of Georgia– Florida Football Game

This annual football game, played on a neutral field at the Gator Bowl in Jacksonville, Florida, is widely known as "The World's Largest Outdoor Cocktail Party." It is indeed a tradition for football fans, and our family joined the crowd after moving to Georgia in 1972.

For many years we would go to New Smyrna Beach for the week preceding the game with Charles and Linda Butterworth in their condominium. We would play golf all week, then go to the game on Saturday. It was always a sight to behold, with intense rivalry between the fans of the two teams.

The weather usually seemed to go to extremes—either scorching hot or cold and extremely uncomfortable. We have tailgated in mud over our shoe tops with no coats to keep warm. On more than one occasion, we have gone to the game in shirtsleeves on a sunny, warm afternoon and left the game very wet and cold by halftime.

Port-O-Let toilets are set up in the parking lots, and they are quite busy—so everyone knows to get in line well before it is absolutely necessary. One year Becky and Linda got in a line, and after several minutes Charles and I got in another line. Just as Becky was ready to go in the toilet I bolted out of line and ran up to her and said, "Hey, lady, can I go in with you?" And we both went in and closed the door.

In the 1990s Charles and Linda stopped going to the games, so now we stay at St. Augustine Beach either the week before or the week after the game, and visit with friends from Athens.

The first week of November is a perfect time to be in Florida—the summer crowds have gone, the winter residents haven't arrived, and the weather is gorgeous—except for game day!

16

Did the Guide Tell about that Eccentric Ol' Woman?

"Strangers are friends you have yet to meet."

—ROBERTA LIEBERMAN

For our thirty-fifth anniversary I planned a special surprise trip for Becky. It bugged her mightily not knowing where we were going, especially because she didn't know what clothes to take (she has always been so proper and careful about her appearance). All I would tell her was to be prepared for some dressy occasions and to take some casual clothes, too.

Well, we headed out early on Thursday morning for the Atlanta airport. Actually, I had arranged for a long weekend at the theaters and other special places in New York through two close friends. Mortimer Cohen, a special friend from Long Island, was the only Army buddy with whom I'd maintained constant contact since we'd been discharged thirty-six years earlier. During that time, I had seen him only once—that was in July 1971, when I returned from the year in England. (Becky and the children—only three of them, as Beve was already in Michigan at college—had flown home a month ahead of me, and I had shipped the car at the same time they flew home. Morty picked me up at the airport, and I spent

Becky and Louie, thirty-fifth wedding anniversary.

the night with him, then picked up the Volvo at the port the next morning and drove to Michigan—back home after a full year.)

Becky and I arrived at La Guardia in New York by noon and checked into the Marriott there. Unfortunately, Morty was summoned for jury duty while we were there, but he did arrange to pick us up and take us to his home for dinner that evening with his mom and him.

During the afternoon following our arrival, we took a Gray Line boat tour around Manhattan. It was most enjoyable; a memorable sight along the Hudson River shoreline was Columbia University. There was a bright, shiny concrete wall about five feet high extending for several blocks along the shoreline. But in the middle of the extensive concrete wall there was a little red-brick building that, from a distance, appeared as a little red doll house with a window in it. The tour guide told us that when Columbia University was expanding there was an eccentric ol' lady who would not sell her property, so the university just bought everything around her and extended the concrete wall for several blocks beyond her property.

That evening Morty picked us up in his new Lincoln Continental to go to his home in Woodmere, on "Long-Gyland." On the drive out, Morty asked what we did that afternoon and Becky told him about the boat tour around the island. He asked if the guide had told about that eccentric ol' lady, and when we laughed, he said that eccentric ol' lady was his mother! That evening we learned that the little red doll house was actually a thirty-foot-wide, two-story building that extended 300 feet in from the river. It had well over 100 apartments that rented, at a sizeable sum, to long-term renters employed at Columbia University and Hospital. This had been Morty's sole occupation after his father had died—managing his mother's rental properties (the job consisted mainly of collecting rent).

We had a lovely evening. Becky could tell enriched stories about the elaborate twelve-place setting of fine china, crystal, and silver that had been set for months or perhaps years on the oilcloth table cover. Yet, only three of us ate dinner there, as Morty's mom and the (perhaps) illegal-alien housekeeper were busy serving us. Despite the choices of crystal glasses, we were more comfortable drinking our Pepsi out of the can with our meal.

Even though I saw Morty's mom only twice, I loved her. She was a great person. Naturally, I'd always favored her because of the constant flow of care packages—cakes, cookies, and goodies—that she'd always sent to her baby Morty in boot camp and when we were overseas.

That evening, when Morty took us back to the hotel, he treated us to a splendid midnight tour of downtown New York, including Times Square, Wall Street, and the brilliant lights of the famous skyscrapers.

The next day we were on our own and did many of the touristy things, ending up at 42nd and Broadway in mid-afternoon. I was fascinated with the kinds of people on the street—we were accosted frequently to buy jewelry, watches, cameras, and other items. At this famous intersection, I just stood and watched as a big Lincoln Town Car parked illegally at the curb on 42nd Street. Soon a young boy, twelve to thirteen years old, ran across the street and got in the back seat of the car. A young girl about the same age approached from another direction and also got in the back seat. As we watched, both kids emptied their pockets and handed two or three wallets each to the burly driver. He removed the money from the wallets and returned them to the kids. The kids got out of the car and the driver drove away.

Morty had warned Becky not to wear any loose jewelry, but this incident, which we observed in broad daylight with policemen around, got to me. As we strolled around the theater district that afternoon, it was so obvious that we were out-of-place targets that I became over-cautious and a little frightened. We ended up going into a hotel and relaxing for a couple of hours before dinner. We were having dinner that night nearby at Mama Leone's and then going to the theater to see *My One and Only* with Tommy Tune and Twiggy.

After the theater, the entire area became transformed from its seedy daylight appearance to a glittery display of tuxedos, evening gowns, and limousines; it felt perfectly safe and enjoyable. We hailed a cab for our trip back to the hotel at La Guardia. The cabbie got on the expressway and almost literally flew, at ninety-five miles an hour, making the trip from 42nd and Broadway to La Guardia in twelve minutes. I tipped him right well for a fast, safe trip, but I wouldn't want to ride with him anymore.

The next morning I told Becky we were checking out and must be ready to go by 9:00 A.M. She wasn't satisfied with my feeble, evasive answers as to where we were going and what she should wear. When we went down to the lobby, we were greeted by our very special friends from Michigan—Harold and Carol Hafs. A few years after we left Michigan State in 1972, Harold became vice president of Merck and Company. So there they were, waiting for us with a company limousine to spend the day in New York, go to the theater that evening, and then accompany them to their home in Mountainside, New Jersey.

It was a splendid day. We had lunch at one of the theater-district diners frequented by noted actors and actresses, and that evening we dined at the Russian Tea Room. Then went to see *42nd Street*— a great play. After the theater, we joined the elite who were being escorted into the waiting limousines clogging the area streets.

The next morning Carol had a champagne breakfast for us. She had invited Ed and Linda Convey—other friends from Michigan State who had joined Harold at Merck. That afternoon Harold took us to Newark for our return to reality and to start our thirty-sixth year. On the same plane were late-arriving, bleary-eyed gamblers from Atlantic City. Some of them had hands and pockets full of money and counted it all the way home. But, many, many more of them—without money to count—were most content to sleep all the way to Atlanta.

17

Back to Work with Expanded Horizons

Returning to my work experiences—I want to relate an important aspect dealing with international agriculture. For more than ten years I handled International Programs for the College of Agriculture.

Following World War II, the United States made great efforts to develop the war-torn countries of the world and to give assistance to underdeveloped countries, especially in Africa and Asia. Most of the assistance was in food production to relieve rampant hunger, so agriculture was heavily involved. Many colleges across the country were targeted to provide expertise to these countries. However, in the late forties, the fifties, and even into the sixties, international work was not held in high esteem by universities. This was a place to send the misfits and faculty that administrators wanted to get rid of. In fact, my first job at Tennessee was to replace a person who had been "shipped off" on an overseas assignment. When he later returned, I kept my position, so he retired.

Another factor in those years was that American farmers did not want to teach other countries how to grow crops that would compete with U.S. markets. "They" preferred for all countries to get their food from the United States. The isolationist attitude of most U.S. farmers at the time overshadowed the hunger issue and the fact that the severely underdeveloped countries had no money to buy food.

The assistance program was mainly taking big tractors and our modern (at the time) system of farming and trying to apply it to all countries. A lot of time, effort, and much money were expended, but it didn't work then and still won't work today. One does not suddenly disrupt social customs and traditions and accomplish very much in a short period of time.

In the early 1960s, a new program called the U.S. Agency for International Development (USAID) was started by the State Department. President John Hannah at Michigan State University was the chief architect and first director of the program. I mentioned earlier that when I was being interviewed in September 1962 by President Hannah at Michigan State that he took a call from the secretary of state about this budding program, and that I was impressed. The program was designed to take the abundant expertise in U.S. universities and share it with the world. It had credence, but it, too, was ahead of its time. The assistance and food were used frequently by the State Department to "buy" friends and influence in other countries. And American farmers still hadn't fully accepted the aid to foreign countries. Strengthening grants ($500,000) were given to universities to select countries and acquaint faculty with their needs and the ways in which the faculty could assist them.

By the mid-seventies (thirty years after WWII), the world was becoming internationalized rapidly. The United States was blanketed with products made overseas, and faculty were well aware that they needed to be involved with their international peers and that students needed international experience to be competitive in the U.S. workforce.

One of the best international programs developed was called CRSP (the Collaborative Research Support Program), by AID. The U.S. government appropriated the funds, but the program required each grant recipient to select a university or agency in a less-

Louie and Becky, fortieth wedding anniversary.

developed country and submit a collaborative proposal. Half of the money was to be spent in the less-developed countries, and the results of the work had to be of benefit to both those countries and the United States. This program helped build up the infrastructures in other countries and also helped train resource people there to become independent and operate a thriving program once the project was completed.

This was the setting I was in for almost fifty years—from the mid-1940s to the early 1990s. And I was all across the spectrum, from the bad to the good. My Army experience had taught me that Americans were superior and that Philippinos and all other "foreigners" should be grateful and respectful. This carried over forcefully through college and my first faculty experience at Tennessee. I felt strongly that because these foreigners were going to school in the United States, they should adopt our ways and eat our food and change completely because we undoubtedly knew and did the best of everything. Oh, how I learned over the years. There is nothing that will make one a better American than to spend time in the homes of friends in other countries—to really visit, not just take a quick tourist ride through the country.

The following is a presentation to an agricultural faculty group at the University of Georgia in 1991.

Building Faculty Resources:
An Administrative Perspective
by Louis J. Boyd

Thirty-five years ago I assumed my first faculty position at the University of Tennessee, shortly after World War II, when many "foreign students" were coming to the United States for graduate study. One day I was in the cafeteria line just behind a new arrival from Pakistan. He could not speak English and was holding up the line unduly, trying to communicate why he would not accept a slice of bread that the cafeteria worker was handing him with a pair of tongs. I was very impatient. The problem that eventually surfaced was that she had previously used the tongs to pick up a hot dog, and the "foreigner" would not take the bread from the tongs that had touched the meat.

It made me furious. In my opinion, the foreign students should immediately learn and practice our way of life. After all, we were the best and had all the answers. Ten years earlier I had spent a year in the Philippines as an eighteen-year-old in the U.S. Army. The United

States had won the war, and we did things our way, even in "their" country.

In those days the common practice in higher education was that, if a professor was not doing his job and could not get along with the administrative structure in the system, then that person was shipped off on a four-year foreign assignment. That is precisely why my first position became available, as I filled a vacancy created in this manner.

So, my concept was that we brought foreign students here to learn our ways and that we sent our worst professors on foreign assignments to upgrade our domestic system. Unfortunately, this idea extended far beyond me, and *most* unfortunately, these concepts still prevail in some universities today.

Thus, *attitudes* are the greatest deterrent to a thriving international program in any university. If we as faculty don't like our fellow man or have a problem with integration in higher education, then we will definitely have a serious problem with our international program.

My greatest personal revelation was an overseas experience. It was for a year in a well-developed country, but how I craved a hamburger and ice cream. I struggled to associate with other Americans—to eat turkey and celebrate Thanksgiving. I wanted desperately to cling to my customs and to eat our own familiar foods. I was doing precisely what I'd been so critical of that day in the cafeteria line.

Successful corporations and successful universities are value-driven. Internationalization depends upon values. As a university we must produce graduates who are humane and productive citizens of the world. The assessment of our internationalization in higher education is in the ability to get inside the lives of our students.

Attitudes and values of administrators, like those of all faculty, change with international experiences and involvement. Many people feel that designated funding is essential to internationalize a college or university. However, attitudes and values of administrators and faculty will do as much as financial resources to enhance internationalization. There must be a commitment.

I, and the administrators of this university, must never again be-come so arrogant that we believe our principles and values are the best for the world.

My work in international agriculture was indeed fabulous. In the Partners of the Americas Program, Georgia was a partner with the state of Pernambuco in northeast Brazil. My first over-seas trip from Georgia was to Recife, Brazil, where we had a coop-erative program with the Federal Rural University. We had faculty exchanges, and several faculty members there were trained here at UGA. Becky went with me once to visit there in 1991. We have good friends there who have also visited us in Georgia.

Georgia was linked with Burkina Faso in West Africa through its Strengthening Grant in AID. Our program was with the Uni-

Baptiste, president, and Romero, research director,
at Federal Rural University in Recife, Brazil, 1986.

versity of Ouagadougou (wahga-*do*-goo) in the capitol city of Oua-gadougou. We were involved with the agricultural part known as the Institute of Rural Development. Several of their faculty were trained at UGA. I was there in 1986 and again four years later.

My second trip overseas was to Israel in 1986 to evaluate possible cooperative programs in agriculture. I was exceptionally well hosted by the National Jewish Federation, which provided a limousine and driver for a week. I spent a weekend in a kibbutz hosted by the daughter of Chris Noll, a friend here in Athens. She had married an Israeli and lived at the kibbutz where her husband was in charge of the agriculture program.

Another memorable trip was to the Republic of Georgia. We had a cooperative project in operating an environmental institute in Tblisi. En route Dean Bill Flatt and I spent some time in Moscow, which was memorable.

Georgia managed two CRSP projects in USAID. They were the Peanut CRSP and Bean-Cowpea CRSP, and each had cooperative projects at several locations throughout the world. I served on the board of directors of both projects and made several trips in connection with board meetings and site visits. The destinations included Senegal, Puerto Rico, India, Thailand, and the Philippines. Becky went with me in 1991 to Thailand, India, and to Manila. I wanted to show her where I'd been stationed at the University of the Philippines at Dilmon, near Manila. After forty-five years I found the building and even the office I worked in at the headquarters commandant's office.

We had a student exchange program with Hohenheim University in Stuttgart, Germany, and visited our students once while they were there for the summer. We also had a faculty exchange program with Kagoshima University in Kagoshima, Japan; I never visited there myself, but I did have the privilege of hosting many Japanese visitors from there. In general, the most distinguished visitor I had the opportunity to host was the president of Hungary, Arpid Goncz. I had him for a full day and had a southern luncheon at the UGA Botanical Gardens. He had been a political prisoner for several years but became president after the former government was overthrown. He was an agriculturist but became a playwright while in prison.

Amid the work and travel, we decided to investigate a new country club that was being talked about in Oconee County—way out in the country in 1986. Three days before I left for Israel one of my colleagues and I went to Atlanta to see Governor Joe Frank Harris about probable projects between Georgia and Israel. On our way back to Athens my friend told me that the country-club development was already underway and how to get to it. So on Sunday after church Becky and I drove out to a trailer in a muddy field and found a person we knew who was involved in the project. He loaded us in a four-wheel-drive Jeep for a ride over muddy roads that had just been laid out. Well, we ended up buying a lot and joining the club in less than an hour. We got home and wondered what we had done. The next morning I left for Israel.

We never dreamed that we would ever live in the new development but thought it was a good investment and planned to hold the lot. Well, as time went on and the golf course began to take shape, we began to think we might build and move after retirement. A bit more time passed. Our friends, the Donohos, were building a house at Lake Oconee. One Saturday night in early March 1988 they were over for dinner, and he said, "Louie, why don't you go ahead and build your house and enjoy it before you retire?" That sounded appealing, so after they left we called the builder and he said, "I'll meet you at the lot tomorrow afternoon."

He gave us several books of house plans that Becky and I studied separately. Her first choice was my second choice, and my first choice was her second choice, so we combined features from both and had our house plan. On March 30 we broke ground and started building the sixth house to be built in the new development. We moved in on September 2, 1988. Since we had downsized we planned to rent a motel when all of the out-of-town fam-

The Boyd clan, Christmas 1988.

ily visited. But the first Christmas in the new house no one would stay in the motel. All in Beve's and Garth's families—four adults and seven kids—were here for the holidays and we had a great time. An expected activity when the grandchildren visited was a daily trip to Hodgson's Pharmacy for ice cream.

18

International Travel

"Laughter translates into any language."

—LJB

The best part of my international travel was the wonderful people I associated with in the different countries. This was so true for our year in England, as we have enjoyed so many good friends through the years since we lived there. Likewise, the international agriculture work provided the opportunity to develop great friendships in several countries—especially in Brazil, Burkina Faso, and the Republic of Georgia.

One of my most memorable trips was the time I went to Burkina Faso and had a problem with my luggage. I had to come home before the other travelers in order to leave immediately for a meeting in Kansas. A most capable young lady in the university international office, LaQuita Booth, was the chief arranger of the trip. She wanted to become a travel agent, so I poked a lot of fun at her and blamed her for my travel problems described in the following "Luggage Ode."

The Luggage Ode*
by Louis J. Boyd

International travel offers unique learning experiences, as the Georgia delegation to Burkina Faso discovered during their July trip. Sometimes, just getting from Point A to Point B presents the greatest challenge of all! One member of the delegation has set down his international woes in the tale that follows. A true story, it serves as a warning to all who would undertake world travel lightly.

Once upon a time, a budding travel agent serving as a tour guide arranged a trip to Burkina Faso for three lonely travelers. The byword became "Never fear, you're in good hands."

While awaiting initial departure at the Atlanta airport, a traveler commented that it surely was an uneventful trip. But, alas, the trip had not really begun!

Arrival in New York was delayed due to congested air traffic. The tour guide vowed that the delay was not her fault. The travelers said it wasn't *their* fault. The travelers followed the tour guide hurriedly in circles and through tunnels to reach the connecting flight just in time to board the plane. After the travelers were safely aboard, the engines started and they were on their way. But, wait. Engine number one misbehaved and another delay was imminent. The tour guide said engine trouble was not her fault.

One-and-a-half hours into the delay the tour guide sprinted into action—TWA cringed. There were only two hours between connecting flights in Paris. If their departure was delayed by two hours there would be no need to go to Paris. After all, there were only two flights per week from Paris to Burkina Faso. The tour guide drove a hard bargain with TWA for her travelers. TWA agreed to house the travelers in Paris for four days or provide free return to New York if the travelers missed their connection. It was a good deal for the travelers.

---

*Originally published in *International Travel*, a publication of University of Georgia International Programs (1986, p. 172). Ever so slightly edited here.

Paulo Tavarres Correia and wife Suzanne of Recife, Brazil, at Boyds' in 1992.

Alexio Da Silva family, Recife, Brazil.

The engine was repaired and it behaved. They were off to Paris, just two hours late in departing.

The travelers deplaned in Paris just twenty minutes before departure time for Ouagadougou. Of course, the departure gate was not nearby. The deplaning passengers were moving much too slowly, so the travelers leapt the rail and ran to the loading gate. The plane was already loaded and the agent was not about to admit the travelers because they had not been there in time to be issued boarding passes. The tour guide cast a spell upon the agent. After their French-English conversation, the travelers were reluctantly issued boarding passes. This traveler was literally the last person aboard as the plane was departing.

This traveler bet the other travelers and the tour guide twenty-five cents each that the luggage did not make the flight. The optimists eagerly took the bet, and this traveler was hoping he would lose. A change of clothes in a hot climate is worth much more than seventy-five cents.

They arrived in Ouagadougou on time. A most pleasant delegation met the travelers. It was HOT—even at 4:30 P.M. The travelers cleared customs and waited, waited, and still waited as the luggage carousel halted. This traveler won the bet.

Much help and many interpreters were needed in filing the lost luggage claims. The tour guide said the lost luggage was not her fault. The travelers were certain it was not *their* fault. Their luggage would be in from Paris on the next flight—just three days later. Meanwhile, enjoy your stay in the hot climate.

The travelers began to recognize each other at great distances after the second day. The fact that they wore the same travel-weary clothes all the time was not the only tell-tale signal.

The tour guide stormed the embassy and much assistance came forth. Return schedules were confirmed, and all were excited about the luggage arrival. This traveler was to depart on the very plane that was to bring the long-awaited luggage.

There was a man named Josef who came out of the land of the

Becky and Louie, Rio de Janeiro, 1991.

Colleagues from Tblisi, Republic of Georgia, 1991.

Cumminses and Boyds, Manila Hotel, 1991.

embassy. He was in charge of international travel and was suddenly promoted by the tour guide to be in charge d'affaires of lost luggage.

This Josef had taken tickets and baggage-claim checks long ago. This traveler and the tour guide were to meet Josef at the airport at 6:00 P.M. to retrieve luggage on the arriving plane at 6:30 P.M. This traveler was to depart at 7:15 P.M. on the same plane.

The man Josef was well known in his land. He took this traveler's passport and got him checked in, obtained a boarding pass, and checked his luggage, which hadn't even arrived yet, all the way through to Atlanta. The plane arrived at 6:40 P.M. Josef disappeared. This traveler, who had no ticket, passport, or baggage claim in hand, was clearly nervous. The tour guide said it was not her fault. The terminal around the baggage area began to fill with incoming passengers. The resting luggage carousel was watched eagerly. It was 7:10 P.M.; the departing flight was called in French (the traveler thought). Forget the luggage, this traveler wanted to board the plane, but he had no ticket and no passport. It was 7:15 P.M. and time for the plane to leave; the luggage carousel jerked into motion. The luggage had not appeared—neither had Josef. It was 7:20 P.M.; the traveler was more nervous. Suddenly Josef and the Air Afrique luggage claims agent appeared with the traveler's luggage. The traveler bade farewell to the tour guide as Josef whisked him through the security area while the guards, with big guns strapped on, wondered what was happening. It was 7:22 P.M., and the traveler started his walk to the plane, which was parked a long way from the terminal. Josef and the agent personally put the traveler's luggage on the plane. The traveler met them as they were returning from the baggage compartment. He bowed down and thanked them profusely. The traveler was less nervous now and gaining some courage. It was 7:26 P.M. as he boarded the plane. He thought he heard the tour guide shouting that it was not her fault. The plane departed at 7:30 P.M.

How great it was to commence a thirty-six-hour trip in clothes that had been worn for five days. But it was so comforting to know that there was a suitcase full of fresh clothes on the plane.

The quiet and uneventful trip included a three-hour layover in Abidjan, Ivory Coast. The traveler arrived in Geneva, Switzerland, at 7:30 A.M. on a crisp, pleasant Saturday morning. After a two-hour layover, the Pan Am flight to New York was called. Before boarding, each connecting passenger was requested to identify his or her luggage, which was just outside the terminal. Yes, it's true—the traveler's luggage was *not* there. Pan Am agents contacted Air Afrique to have the luggage brought over immediately. It was learned that the luggage had remained on Air Afrique and had already gone to Paris. Arrangements were made, hopefully, to have the luggage transferred to Pan Am in Paris.

The traveler arrived in Paris just ten minutes before the Pan Am flight left for New York. Despite a futile attempt by the traveler, there was no way to check on the luggage because the baggage compartment on the plane had already been closed. The traveler boarded, hoping his luggage was aboard.

It surely was an uneventful flight to New York. The traveler arrived in New York and hurried to the baggage area. He waited and watched very carefully until the carousel emptied and quietly stopped. No luggage. It was easy to clear customs. The Pan Am agent said to trace the luggage in Atlanta, since that was the final destination. However, it still had to clear customs in New York whenever it arrived.

Upon arrival in Atlanta the traveler proceeded immediately to the claims agent. He was not very optimistic about ever seeing the luggage again, but made arrangements to have the long-lost clean clothes sent to him in Kansas. After filing the claim, the traveler stopped by the luggage carousel on his way out of the airport. Eureka! There was his luggage, merrily going around on the carousel. He retrieved it, canceled the claim, and quietly and happily left the airport. The traveler arrived home at 9:00 P.M. and prepared to leave at 8:00 the next morning on a two-and-a-half-week trip. It didn't take long to pack, since his suitcase was filled with clean clothes. How, when, and where the luggage cleared customs and got to Atlanta remains a mystery. But one does not have to worry when arrangements are handled by a competent tour guide!

19

When Did I Have Time to Work?

I retired on March 31, 1992. I was really enjoying my work and felt like I was more effective then than any other time during my career. I told Becky that with so many friends and multiple contacts, I could get more work done in an hour on the phone than I could get done in a day in earlier years. But I wanted to retire before I felt like I needed to so I felt good about retiring. Becky was working part time when I retired, and I was so free. It took me only about five minutes that first morning to get accustomed to retirement—I could go where I wanted to, when I wanted to, and didn't have to tell anyone where I would be, when I would be back, or how to contact me. Free at last! (Remember this was before widespread use of cellular phones.)

The first day of retirement I called my three major professors for my graduate programs—Dr. Dwight M. Seath at the University of Kentucky, and Dr. G.W. Salisbury and Dr. Noland L. VanDemark at the University of Illinois. I thanked each one for his marked influence on my life and major contribution to my career. I was so pleased that I made the contacts, because Dr. Seath died just a few months after I talked with him and Dr. Salisbury died a couple of years later.

The only thing hanging over my head after retirement was a

presentation I had reluctantly agreed to give in three weeks at the National Association of Animal Breeders (NAAB) Technical Conference in Wisconsin. It had caused me some mental anguish, as a friend from Michigan, Bruce Bean, who was manager of the Eastern Artificial Insemination Cooperative, had insisted that I face up to the predictions I'd made about artificial insemination (AI) twenty years earlier at the fourth NAAB Technical Conference. He even had the courage to enclose a copy of the article I'd written for the presentation in Chicago in 1972. What caused my main heartburn was that I had never once thought about that article for twenty years, and that I had not worked directly in the animal field in the last ten years. But I still claimed some real good friends who excelled in the AI field, so I drew heavily upon their vast knowledge and sound judgment.

The summer of 1992 was busy, as we met our Michigan group in Kentucky in June and continued visiting there en route to Columbus, Ohio, for the American Dairy Science Association(ADSA) meeting at Ohio State. For July 4, we had a family gathering for a week at a dude ranch on Bull Lake in the Ozarks (in Theodosia, Missouri). Twenty-two of us lived in two large cabins for a week— and survived.

In late July, while I was enjoying myself immensely, I was called back to the university to do part-time work as executive secretary of the College Research Advisory Board. I agreed to do this, which would involve about 20% work time but could be done as per my scheduling. This turned out to be a fortunate happening, because I was already beginning to miss my contacts with colleagues and friends in the state. But before I got deeply involved in conducting the first meeting of a newly appointed board of about thirty people across the state, we were off to another conference and a trip to Alaska. We spent a week on the Pacific Coast at Newport, Oregon, attending the National Agricultural Alumni and Development Association meeting. As related previously, this organization had been extremely helpful in getting the alumni association here

The family at Bull Shoals Lake in the Ozarks, 1992—
four children, twelve grandchildren.

tooled up and going in the right direction to support and raise funds for the College of Agriculture.

From the conference, we flew from Portland to Fairbanks, Alaska, where we joined the Butterworths (Charles and Linda) for a land tour that included Denali Park, Kotsibu, Nome, and Anchorage. Then we had a one-week cruise back down to Vancouver and Seattle, and then the trip home.

This retirement bit was beginning to be real fun because in November that year we flew out to Arizona for a week with Bob and Norma Seerley, visiting such sights as the Grand Canyon. Following that trip, the Seerleys bought a home near Phoenix and have lived there for several months each year.

In 1993, we started in January with a cruise along the California-Mexico coastline with a group from our church. This was one of our best cruises, and we discovered fabulous places like Cabo San Lucas, Mexico. Two months later we flew to Hawaii

Seerleys and Boyds at Grand Canyon.

and cruised around the islands for a week. This was the whale cruise, which we greatly enjoyed after seeing the whales along the Alaskan coast the previous year.

The big event of March 1993 was the blizzard of the century for Georgia—even south Georgia. We were in Kentucky for a Boyd family reunion honoring the 100th birth dates of Mother and Daddy—both deceased. Garth and his family drove through bitter cold from Colorado, and they came on to Georgia with us, but we were stranded for a day and a night in Chattanooga by closed Georgia roads.

In May we spent a few days in San Francisco with the Butterworths on a trip that included a train ride through the wine country of Napa Valley. The next month we were in College Park, Maryland, for the ADSA Meeting. I found it to be much less demanding and more fun to attend scientific meetings as a retiree.

The long-awaited trip to England came in September. It had been twenty-two years since we had lived there, yet when we'd left there in 1971 we'd been totally convinced that we would go back often to visit friends.

We arrived at Gatwick Airport early in the morning, got in our rental car, and headed to Reading. It was rush-hour traffic, and we met thousands of cars creeping into London. Almost immediately I noticed something strange (besides the fact that we had to drive on the wrong side of the road), and began to count. We saw only seven women drivers during the two hours of heavy traffic. The men drove the cars to work, and the women took the trains. We got to Reading and checked into Kirton's Resort, which had been built on the dairy farm directly across the little lane where we'd lived while in England. The resort hotel was on one of the gravel-pit lakes, and our room was out over the water.

It was such a thrill to see our house, which was then owned by the resort for its employees, and to visit our former neighbors and friends. We visited Mrs. Betty Melrose, whose husband I had worked for, and our former next-door neighbor, Bettina Webster,

Betty Melrose in Reading, England, with Louie, 1993.

who had moved across town. Both of these ladies had lost their husbands since we'd lived there. We spent much time with our favorite "Aunt" Lucy and her sister-in-law, Kath Hannington. Kath and her late husband, Phil, had operated Kirton's farm while we were there. (Phil and Lucy's husband, Roy, both had died since then.) The fun part of our trip was showing the resort to Lucy and Kath; although they lived real near the hotel, neither one had been inside it.

Upon leaving Pingewood (Reading), we headed north and stopped in Streatley for lunch in the same pub where we'd eaten upon our arrival with our family twenty-three years earlier. We drove just a few miles up on the downs to Compton and visited the research center where I'd worked for a year. The director told us that Dr. McGregor Henderson, the director while I'd been there, still lived in Streatley. I regretted not seeing him while we were there for lunch but did talk with him by phone. That afternoon we drove on to Tewkesbury and stayed at a hotel on a golf course; it

"Aunt" Lucy Goswell and Becky, 1993.

was owned by the same resort chain as Kirton's Resort in Reading. That evening we drove out in the country to find a dairy-farm family with whom we had visited overnight while living in England. This was the family that took us to see the Severn Bore early one morning. We found the farm, but it was vacant—no dairy herd, no family in the house.

We stopped at another dairy farm nearby to inquire about the family. The lady of the house who was renting it had no connection with the dairy herd, but she was a well-known interior designer in London. She invited us in for a drink, and we had a wonderful time visiting with her. She knew the family we were seeking. He (Eric Wynters) and his wife (with five children) had divorced, and he was pursuing a new life as a photographer. Our hostess rang Eric up and he promised to stop by the hotel to have breakfast with us the next morning, but he never showed.

Our next stop was up near Chester to visit friends, Tony and Ann Fair, who formerly ran the dairy farm for the Duke of Marlborough. Recently, the Fairs had purchased an estate at Market Drayton and had a large dairy farm on it. Tony and Ann had visited us in Georgia, and one of their sons had visited us while he was in college in North Carolina. They had just built a new home to fit the Heritage Society requirements, and we had a great time visiting with them.

From there we drove to London for the remainder of our stay. En route we drove by the golf course where the Ryder Cup Golf Match was being played. Of course, we could not get in to watch, but there was high interest in England. The Europeans were leading big on the final day, and when we stopped at a pub for lunch the limeys were really razzing us—the Americans. Becky shot back to just wait till it's over, and sure enough, by the end of the day the Americans had won.

We stopped in a small town north of London to deliver a gift (a jacket) to the retired director of the International Agricultural Research Center in Niami, Niger. He had worked with us on the

Visiting Tony and Ann Fair at their new estate home in Market Drayton, England.

Peanut Collaborative Research Support Program (CRSP) project managed by the University of Georgia. Dr. David Cummins, the project director, had sent the jacket to him. From there we drove into London, turned our car in, and checked into our hotel. David Melrose, the son of my boss (Dick Melrose) when I'd worked in England, arranged for us to stay at the Selfridge Hotel adjacent to Selfridge's Department Store. David was managing a hotel in New Jersey, and the manager of the Selfridge was a good friend. We stayed there almost a week, going to the theater daily and visiting familiar sights after twenty years. Upon checking out we learned that our stay was gratis.

We were walking in the theater district one afternoon when a lady yelled—"Louie and Becky!" It was Suzanne Ginn, from Atlanta, whom we had known since our arrival in Georgia. Just the day before we left for England we had attended her son's wedding, but neither she nor us knew that the other was going to London.

In March 1994 we took a cruise of the ABC Islands in the

Becky, at a chance meeting with Suzanne Ginn and her friend in London, 1993.

Caribbean, and in June we were in the western Caribbean on the *S.S. Norway.* Harold Ford and I played golf on St. Maarten Island. We especially enjoyed the *Norway,* as we had made our first ocean voyage as a family on it in 1970 from New York to Southhampton when we went to England for a year. In those days it was the largest passenger ship afloat and had sailed as the *S.S. France* (later refurbished and renamed the *Norway*). In December we went to Jekyll Island for the Georgia Farm Bureau meeting, and then on down to the Butterworths' in Florida for a few days of golf in the Orlando area.

The morning we started home, Becky noticed something odd about her stool, and she had some abdominal discomfort while traveling. The next morning the problem was worse, so her doctor sent her to the hospital. No source of bleeding could be found, but her hemoglobin was very low. The doctor wanted to give her a blood transfusion, but Becky felt so strong and feisty that she would not agree to have one. After four days her hemoglobin went

Fords, Donohos, and Boyds on *SS. Norway,* 1994.

up slightly, sufficiently so that the doctor did not force the transfusion issue. He and the gastroenterologist who was called in did insist on a colonoscopy, but they were not overly concerned about the scheduling of it. Likewise, we were not anxious to rush into it, because we had too many things we wanted to do and didn't want to take time out for such a nuisance as a colonoscopy.

We had a big Christmas and scheduled the colonoscopy for February 6 following a busy January. We were in Kentucky in the middle of January and went to Carmel, Indiana, during the last of the month to visit Beve. We stopped in Lexington for a University of Kentucky ag alumni event and Kentucky basketball game. The Butterworths were there, and they stopped overnight with us on their way back to Florida.

February 6 arrived, and we hustled off to the hospital all prepared for the colonoscopy. I took my briefcase along and was busy working and making phone calls from the waiting room. We were both a little perturbed that we were having to take time for this test when there were so many things we wanted to do.

I had just realized it was taking a little longer than expected for this procedure when a nurse came after me. With Becky, I was told that cancer was found in the colon and that surgery had already been scheduled for the next morning.

Wow, did life ever take on a new meaning—no more schedules or deadlines, just long days and nights. Following surgery the next day, I stayed with her that night and lay on a cot next to her bed. She was still anesthetized right much, but she was breathing so clearly and was so peaceful. I could have spent the rest of my life just listening to that "Sound of Music." The following days we learned loads about the cancer's invading the lining of her colon, about the positive lymph nodes (seven of thirteen), about oncologists and chemotherapy. Chemotherapy started on March 6, with daily injections for five days and then weekly injections for fifty-two weeks. By the third treatment that first week she was very much nauseated, and I had to literally force her to take the next two treatments. The subsequent treatments on Monday mornings continued with the same nauseating results, but after three or four months she began to feel better during the latter part of each week—just in time for the "poison" injection to knock her down again the next Monday morning.

By the end of June we were wearing down right much, so we decided to go to Garth's in North Carolina to get away for a few days between treatments. Shortly after we arrived, the two younger boys wanted "Meenaw" to go on a bike ride with them, but she didn't feel like it. She promised to go the next morning, which we did. The bike she was on had a raised seat and her feet wouldn't touch the ground, so when she dismounted she fell on the concrete driveway and broke her hip. More new experiences—a house call by Garth's local doctor, a trip to the local hospital for x-rays, and then on to Wilmington for surgery that night after midnight. To make matters worse, the orthopedic surgeon was a Clemson graduate. This was on Wednesday night, and on Friday Caitlin, our fourteen-year-old granddaughter from Indiana, surprised us at the hospital as she was at Wrightsville Beach vacationing with her friend's family.

On Saturday morning—just two days after the surgery—I loaded Becky in the car and headed to Georgia. Oh, what a frightful sight we were, traveling from Wilmington with Becky in her gown, and carrying a walker and high potty seat. At one rest stop in South Carolina we bucked a long line of women waiting to use the restroom. I finally got a female attendant to take her inside and help her with the walker and potty. Were we ever glad to get home and especially to find Beve and Beda there waiting for their mother. The next Monday morning we were back for her regular chemotherapy, and she never missed a scheduled treatment during the year. We just added another doctor to the list to handle the hip recovery. Our cruises and travel were definitely on hold during 1995.

The last chemotherapy treatment was February 25, 1996. A month later I had a surprise champagne breakfast for her at Jennings Mill Country Club. About 150 people helped me celebrate her successful treatment regimen. Becky kept fairly active and gradually recouped her strength—along with a full growth of gray hair. The last of April we attended our fiftieth high school reunion at Sedalia. Three weeks later, we went on a Mediterranean cruise starting in Athens, Greece, and visiting the Greek isles (with one day in Israel). I was thrilled that Becky could visit Jerusalem and Bethlehem. In July we flew out to Oregon for the dairy-science meetings, and in August we drove to Branson, Missouri, for our first reunion of Army buddies. In November Becky had elective gallbladder surgery, and was playing golf a few days later.

In 1997 I began my year as president of Jennings Mill Country Club. It was indeed a rough and tough year financially for the club, not to mention the fact that dissident groups were trying to either take over or scuttle the club. Yet we resumed our travels with a cruise through the Panama Canal, starting with three days in Costa Rica. I wanted Becky to see the canal, since I had gone

Relay for Life victory lap, 1996.

In Athens, Greece, 1996.

The Nardis (England), Giards (Canada), and
Boyds (US) on Mediterranean cruise, 1996.

through it on a troop transport ship forty-one years earlier. We boarded the *Radisson Diamond,* which had twin hulls (or hulks) and was touted to be smoother on the ocean, though we couldn't tell much difference from a regular cruise ship.

March arrived and we had the second big scare: two spots showed up on Becky's liver with a routine x-ray. Our dear friend Bob Rhodes, the radiologist, took us in to see the results. Again, we got a fast and furious education, as we didn't even know that surgery was an option for liver cancer. The surgeon at Emory was at a conference in Chicago, but we got an appointment just three days later, on a Monday. He was upbeat and encouraging but would do surgery only if there were no other spots on the liver and if no other organs in the body were affected by cancer. Many rounds of multiple tests were conducted. Fortunately, all tests were clear and surgery was done on April 24. It was indeed a long week, as they kept Becky completely knocked out for three days after surgery, and I sat outside the recovery room waiting for her to wake up. The surgery was most successful with no subsequent treatment recommended. We got home in early May, and Mother's Day was a special time in our family.

In a month we were moving again, as we met our Michigan group at Callaway Gardens and then flew to Guelph, Canada, a week later for dairy-science meetings. The end of July we were in Nashville for animal-science meetings, and then returned home to a flooded house. This created considerable disruption, including the installation of new carpeting. In November we missed the annual Georgia-Florida football game to attend a CAST meeting in Chicago. It was the twenty-fifth anniversary of the Council for Agricultural Science and Technology, and all past presidents were invited to participate in the meeting.

In 1998, a big year, we had planned a trip to Australia and New Zealand, along with the big "five-o" celebration on June 12. I guess I had been hankering for a little medical attention, so I decided to

Invitation to fiftieth anniversary celebration.

have surgery for diverticulosis. I had been having increased abdominal pain which had perhaps started some years before. The
first bout for which I'd been diagnosed thusly was during and after
our trip to India and the Philippines in 1991. So I elected to do
something about it before our trip "down under." I had surgery a
month before our trip and was fully assured that I would be fully
recovered and ready to go. But, alas, it didn't happen that way—
there were some complications with an occluded vein from the
scrotum which caused much discomfort and prolonged abdominal pain. So the trip had to be cancelled.

I was functioning for our golden wedding anniversary in June.
The four children put on a big event at Jennings Mill Clubhouse,
and our family and many friends turned out again (as they had
for the champagne breakfast) for a gigantic celebration. All of the
grandchildren (eleven of them) except Meghan Gallagher were

there. She was on a study program in Melbourne, Australia—we'd wanted to go while she was there, but my diverticulosis intervened. In August we went back to Branson, Missouri, for another meeting of our Army buddies. One of my special buddies, Ed Hammett, lives in Branson, so it is a great place to meet, and with his connections it is very inexpensive.

Seed-packet favor for golden anniversary.

Fiftieth anniversary—Louie, Beve, Beda, Tina, Garth, and Becky.

The Louie–Becky clock.

Army buddies at Branson, 1998: Earl Griffin (Alabama), Louie Boyd (Georgia),
Morty Cohen (New York), Ed Hammett (Missouri), Neal Kennington (Florida),
Harry Reinke (Kansas), John Burns (Missouri), and Warren Fusselman (Florida).

20

A Most Memorable and Special Place
Revisited after 18,520 Days

In early June 1998 we were planning our annual trip to meet the Michigan group—the Moshers, the Hinzes, and the Englanders. The Hinzes were in charge, and we were meeting at Lake Barkley in western Kentucky.

We left home early on Saturday morning to take a leisurely drive toward Kentucky, spend the night on the road, and then go on to meet our friends at the resort early Sunday afternoon. As we were going through Nashville I got off the expressway to drive through downtown, with the excuse that we hadn't seen it in a long time. I stopped at the Double Tree Hotel, and Becky was becoming a little suspicious. Actually, I had reservations there, so we checked in.

We went out for a drive and I started out Shelby Avenue. After several blocks I mentioned that I wanted to try to find the house where her Uncle Jonah Cobb and Aunt Alta used to live—where we had visited more than fifty years ago. We found some familiar landmarks, but not the house we remembered visiting on Labor Day weekend in 1947. I really didn't care about that part, because we drove into Shelby Park and found the spot I'd been seeking.

Shelby Park was only a block or so from the Cobbs' house. In the early evening of Labor Day 1947, Charles Butterworth, Linda

(Becky's sister), Becky, and I had walked up to the park. Becky and I had sat down on a grassy knoll overlooking the park, and that was where it had happened—that was the very first time that Becky told me that she "loved me." It was 18,520 days later when we visited that special spot for the second time.

A significant family heritage event occurred on this same trip. I wanted to make sure that the farm Daddy had inherited from his father and that I had then inherited from Daddy remained in the Boyd family. Nelson's son, John Wilson Boyd, was living on the adjoining farm, so we sold our farm to him. We went to Mayfield to close the deal when we were at Kentucky Lake. Thus, the farm has been in the Boyd family since 1881.

21

Health Concerns Again

"There are no hopeless situations; there are only
people who have grown hopeless about them."

—Clare Booth Luce

In late summer (1998), changes were surfacing in Becky's
health, but nothing that could be identified. Routine tests conducted by Dr. Firth, our treasured family physician and neighbor,
found an increase in blood protein. Extensive further testing re-
vealed no problem, and she felt great. But by Christmas she was
not feeling as perky. We spent the holidays at Beve's in Carmel,
Indiana, and Becky was definitely under par—she didn't even
want to go shopping (which was *definitely* abnormal). Early in
the new year the Butterworths stopped by for a couple of days,
and Becky was dragging. Again, nothing showed up—until January 21, when she was showing signs of jaundice. So the next day
we were at Emory Hospital, where a stent was inserted into her
bile duct. This immediately corrected the problem, and Becky was
feeling great right away.

Continued extensive testing, however, could find no cause for
the occluded bile duct. The radiologist "thought" there was a

growth nearby, yet biopsies (through the liver) in that area showed nothing. We came home with the news that the stent in the bile duct would have to be changed every three to four months for the rest of her life.

The considered opinion of all involved doctors at Emory and in Athens was that there was probably some cancerous tissue in that area, perhaps in nearby lymph nodes, and that radiation therapy was recommended. The next morning we sat in the oncologist's office while he explained the situation. We selected a radiation therapist and were in his office an hour later. He spent two hours with us, and again we got a gigantic education learning a new word— *palliative treatment,* that which would not cure but would make life more comfortable for the patient.

We spent that afternoon in the hospital, where they took measurements and built a "saddle" to use each time so the x-rays could be directed to a precise location. The very next day Becky started her twenty-eight-day radiation treatment. Since there was no affected tissue that could be targeted, the doctor (Dr. Shiv Khandelwald, a wonderful person) zeroed in on the end of the stent at the juncture of the bile duct and the liver, giving a shotgun scattering of x-rays in that general area. The radiation therapy was not as debilitating as the chemotherapy. It lasted only a month instead of a year, and she wasn't nauseated—just tired.

A couple of months after completing the therapy, we went back to Emory for the first "change of the stent," which was to be done three or four times a year for the rest of Becky's life. The doctor, Dr. John Affronti, removed the stent, but instead of replacing it immediately, he hesitated, watching the bile flowing freely through the bile duct, and decided not to insert another stent. Each anniversary of that date (May 25, 1999) I have written Dr. Affronti with a progress and travel report and thanked him for taking the time to watch the bile flow!

During this time I was still fretting and complaining. I had not recovered from my abdominal surgery to my satisfaction. I was still

Becky and Louie in Sydney, 1999.

having chronic pain and could get very little relief. The gastro-enterologist and surgeon kept saying it was a urological problem. After several months of repeated and varied tests, the urologist was emphatic that it was not "his problem." So, I finally convinced the surgeon to go back in for exploratory surgery, which was done fifteen months after the first surgery (in which a short section of the colon was removed to help the diverticulosis). I learned there was a short loop of intestine that might have been a problem, but that the probable cause was adhesions and scar tissue, which would not be helped by further surgery. Even though there were no post-surgical complications, it did in fact take longer to recover than I wanted. However, we were able to go to Indianapolis for animal-science meetings in late July. And we did go on the post-poned Australia–New Zealand trip on November 15 for three weeks. It was delightful.

22

A Trip Back to the Old High School

You are young at any age if you are planning for tomorrow.

—READERS' DIGEST

The president of our twenty-four-member senior class of 1946, Billy Kreisler, died on November 17, 1998. The remaining living class officers were Carolyn Boyd Herndon in Alabama and Rebecca Conner Boyd in Georgia. It was an easy decision for Carolyn and Becky (they let me help) to solicit contributions from our classmates and plan a memorial for Billy.

The remaining classmates collected more than $500. Carolyn and Becky decided on a watercolor painting of the Sedalia High School building (built in 1940) and a nice globe to be presented to the school in Billy's memory. The big event was planned for April 30, 1999, with all classmates invited.

Sedalia High School was terminated about 1984, when it and several other high schools in the county were consolidated into Graves County High School, located in Mayfield, Kentucky. I was invited to give the commencement address at my school on May 28, 1974, which was within ten years of the last graduating class from the high school that graduated its first class in 1914. I

251

requested that Becky sit on the stage, too, so it was a proud moment for me. The building is now used as an elementary school for grades one through six.

The big day arrived, with fifteen classmates along with some spouses attending. Including the Kreisler family (Dorothy, the widow; three children; and Betty Lou, Billy's sister), there were attendees from nine states.

During the morning, the classmates gathered and had lunch in the Sedalia Restaurant, which was in the same building where Billy Kreisler's father had operated a store during the years we were in school. It was a beautiful time for reminiscing. There were three of us—Billy Warmath, Junior Terrell, and I—who'd gone into the Army together immediately after graduating from high school. Our own Army chaplain, Billy Warmath, led a meaningful devotion honoring four deceased classmates—Anna Lamm, Jim Leech, Linda Ray, and Billy Kreisler—and our beloved class sponsor, Mrs. Geneva Denham.

After lunch we gathered in the high school gymnasium along with some local residents and about a hundred sixth-grade grade students. Following the presentation of the memorial painting and globe, the principal, Mr. Billy Kinsey, urged the sixth-graders to ask questions of the graduating class members of fifty-three years ago. The kids were interested in the World War II years—it was a fun dialogue. I created a minor stir among the students when I asked Becky to stand and told the students that she and I had been in two plays on the stage in this gym, and that she had been my mother in one of them. I also told them they'd better be careful who they were sitting by, because Becky and I were the only ones in our class to marry another classmate. The kids erupted with shrieks and began to scram. The principal had to calm them down after a while.

I was asked by Carolyn to write and present the memorial citation for Billy. This is what I said in introducing the citation:

Not many of us who occupied this building fifty-three years ago knew very much about Fritz Kreisler—as to who he was and what he did. But even before television we did know there was such a person, because one of Billy Kreisler's nicknames here in school was *Fritz*.

One story is that a woman rushed up to violinist Fritz Kreisler after one of his resounding concerts and gushed, "Oh, I would give my life to play as you do." He answered soberly, "That's exactly what I did." [Fritz] Kreisler had made a great sacrifice of time, effort, and personal desires to attain the heights of such human accomplishments.

It is abundantly clear that there was a much greater similarity between Fritz Kreisler and Billy Kreisler than any of us could ever have imagined— one as an accomplished musician and one as an exceptional education leader.

23

In Remembrance of
Dr. Carl William Kreisler

D r. Carl William Kreisler is fondly remembered as the senior-class president of the Sedalia High School Class of 1946. He was affectionately known throughout elementary and high school years as Billy, Bill, Kreisler, Ruffles, or Fritz.

"Billy" was actively involved in dramatics, sports, glee club, FFA, and Boy Scouts, and served as editor-in-chief of the senior annual. He was voted by his peers as "Wittiest Boy," "Most School Spirit," and "Most Likely to Succeed."

And succeed he did.... Despite his love for hunting and the desire to be a backwoodsman, he was one of the early graduates of Sedalia High School to obtain a doctoral degree. He had an outstanding career as professor at Western Kentucky University, and served as president of Parsons College in Fairfield, Iowa.

Immensely popular in school, Billy entertained us with his wit and charm; he opened up new vistas and expanded our horizons with his "wild ideas." Billy's personality and accomplishments made his life a glowing testimonial to our senior-class motto: "Before us lies the timber, Let us build."

In all those he touched, Billy built a memory. Therefore, we, his classmates of 1946, dedicate in his memory a painting of the Sedalia High School building, constructed in 1940. May all of those who walk these hallowed halls be reminded by this memorial painting that a former graduate—a country boy from Sedalia—made a difference through his service to his fellow man.

Billy Kreisler was a truly great man.

FROM HIS CLASSMATES
CLASS OF 1946, WITH LOVE
APRIL 30, 1999

Prepared and presented by Louie Boyd

Billy Kriesler and I were among the first graduates in Sedalia High School's 33-year history (first class was in 1914) to get doctoral degrees. One other person, Joe Vance McClain, had obtained a doctorate of education as Billy had received, but I was the first graduate to be awarded the PhD degree.

❧ 24 ❧

Cars We Have Owned

Before "our" cars, I digress to the "beginning" of cars—at least in my family. I don't remember when the buggy was the sole mode of travel for my family. But there were pictures of Daddy in his convertible buggy with his spirited horse. He was quite a sport. Then there were pictures of the horse and buggy that Kathleen and Nelson drove to school each day at Lynn Grove.

Our first car was a 1926 T Model built by Henry Ford. It was an open-sided car that, apparently, had side curtains, although I don't remember them ever being used. Nelson tells a story about the T Model that I never knew. One day Mother was driving back from picking strawberries at Mr. Noah Roger's at Browns Grove. As a baby, I was lying on the back seat of the car. She hit a rough spot in the road near the Mayfield Creek and it pitched me out of the car into the ditch. Could that lick have been the problem I've had all these years?

The T Model was traded for a 1931 A Model Ford in the mid-1930s. This car, a mainstay, got Nelson through his dating years. In 1944 it was traded for a 1941 Plymouth, which was built just before the building of cars in the U.S. stopped in late 1941 due to the massive war effort. I learned to drive in this car, and Daddy kept it until after I went into the Army. In 1946, Daddy bought his first new vehicle, which was a 1946 GMC pickup truck.

New-car production started in 1946, after the war. But Becky and I didn't have a car during the first two years of our marriage. Despite the money I'd saved while in the Army, we still resisted the urge to buy a car for a while.

Cars—old and new—were scarce for five or six years after the war. In the spring of 1950, I rode the bus from Lexington to home (in Murray, Kentucky) to buy a car. Sylvester, my brother-in-law, took me around to several dealers trying to find one. I finally bought a two-door, pea-green Chevrolet in Paris, Tennessee, for $1,600. Though we had the money to pay cash for the car, I still had to borrow money from my brother, Nelson, to buy gas to drive the car back to Lexington.

This first little car served us exceptionally well. I drove the car across the state of Kentucky for two years while working in dairy extension at the University of Kentucky. But its most notable service was that it brought four children home from the hospital. For fourteen years we lived 300 miles from our home in western Kentucky—in Lexington for five years; in Champaign, Illinois, for three years; and in Knoxville, Tennessee, for six years. When we drove to the family home from Lexington between 1951 and 1953 with one child, the car was fully packed. In 1958 and 1959, when we drove home from Knoxville with *four* children, the car was still fully loaded—but there was always enough room for everything, including Christmas presents.

After ten years, we bought another car—a 1960 four-door Chevrolet—for $2,200 cash at Maryville, Tennessee. We still couldn't afford two cars, so I sold the old 1950 to Doug Stamper, a University of Tennessee student worker, for $165. I had just purchased a new battery for the car before I sold it, but later Doug had some trouble with the car, so I gave him $50 back. So much for my sales ability. The 1960 Chevrolet was destined to stay with us for ten years, just as our first car had done.

Three years after our move to Michigan, our perceived "prosperity" meant we could have a second car. So in December 1965 we joined the big station-wagon trend and ordered a 1966 Ford station wagon through our friend Jack Gatrost, who worked for the Ford Motor Company. Our first big trip was a three-week camping trip to the West Coast. It was a big station wagon, but it had a small motor—only 192 horsepower. On our trip we borrowed a heavy, home-built camper trailer. The station wagon didn't handle the load too well, especially in the Rockies and the Big Horn Mountains. It soon started using lots of oil and expelling volumes of exhaust smoke, so I traded it for a 1967 Ford station wagon with a bigger motor. This one took us on another camping trip with another borrowed camper trailer (destination: the northeast coast and the Montreal World's Fair in 1967). Just before we moved to England in 1970, I sold this station wagon to a dealer in Michigan for $1,100.

The old 1960 Chevrolet was well worn. It was using lots of oil, which I purchased in large quantities, and smoked badly. But I was able to baby it along, and drove it to work every day. When we were leaving for England, I gave the car to Ed Convey, a colleague at Michigan State. Shortly afterward, he was ticketed for polluting the environment and had to get rid of the car. Over the years we've had lots of laughs about my gift to a good friend. In Michigan I could not "give" a car so the transfer title listed the price as $1.00.

While planning our one-year stay in England, I studied the British autos carefully in order to get a vehicle that would accommodate our family of six and enable us to do a lot of traveling, both in England and on the Continent. The decision was that a VW bus (very popular with the 1960s hippies) was the only way to go. So I bought a 1970 VW bus and paid the dealer in Michigan for a pickup delivery at the VW factory in Hanover, Germany, in late July 1970. Our second day in England, Beverly and I flew to Hanover, Germany, to pick up our bus and drive it back to England.

Upon arrival at the airport, I called the "Wolksvagen Verks" and was greeted with, "Oh, Mr. Boyd, we notified your dealer that your vehicle would not be ready for a fortnight."

I placed a collect call to the Michigan dealer, telling him to refund my money plus two round-trip airline tickets from London to Hanover. I got the certified check in a week, but I had a lot more trouble cashing the check in England than I had in getting the check in the first place. Finally, the City Bank of New York there in London cashed the check, and I was indeed grateful for the service.

Anyway, we were back in the market for a new car. A few days before we left for England, we visited our parents in Murray, Kentucky. As we were leaving Murray, I drove up behind a vehicle I really liked but was not familiar with it. It was a Volvo station wagon. I wished that I had known about it before I had ordered and paid for the VW bus. Now was my chance, so I ordered a left-hand-drive 1970 Volvo station wagon from a dealer in London, and it was delivered from Sweden in three weeks. When we came back to the United States in 1971, the Volvo company shipped the vehicle to New York for us at no cost. The Volvo—called "Ole Yellow Mustard" by us—was a great vehicle for traveling, both in England and back in the United States.

Upon our return to Michigan in July 1971, I took a yardstick to shop for a new car. With a college student and three teenagers in the family, I wanted lots of room in the back seat. The roomiest one was a 1971 Dodge.

We moved to Georgia in 1972 and were in good shape with the Volvo and the Dodge for a while. In the spring of 1974, Garth was on his way to take his SAT exam early one Saturday morning when a lady asleep at the wheel rear-ended the Volvo while he was stopped at a traffic light. The little VW bug was going so fast it literally buckled the frame of the Volvo and totaled it, but neither Garth nor his passenger, Cindy Noles, was injured in any way. This sent me car shopping again in a hurry. I couldn't afford another

Volvo at U.S. prices, so I bought a 1974 two-tone brown Dodge. It was a demonstrator that had been driven by Mr. C. Swanton Ivy, the retired Dodge dealer in Athens.

After five years, this car was traded for a 1979 Dodge—another one that had been driven as a demonstrator by Mr. Ivy. For a few years in the late 1970s we became a three-car family, again with a connection to the Ivy Dodge dealership. Miss Cossie Rice, an elderly old-maid friend in our church, took care of her sister and brother-in-law, John Allgood. When her brother-in-law died, Miss Cossie wanted us to have his little car. He was the longtime manager of the service department for Mr. Ivy, and Mr. Ivy had in 1964 given him a new Dodge Valiant. It was a neat little "antique," with power steering and pushbutton automatic gear-shift on the dash.

These three Dodges were the only used cars we ever owned. All our other cars were purchased new. After a few years we sold the little Dodge Valiant because we didn't have a place to keep it and it was rusting out.

In 1982 I bought a little Plymouth Reliant—the reliable "K Car" built by Lee Iacocca, who saved the Chrysler Motor Company from the brink of extinction. In 1986 I switched from the big Dodge cars to the Oldsmobile and bought an Oldsmobile 98. In 1987 I traded the little K Car for a different one. It was another dependable small car.

When I retired in 1992, I bought another Oldsmobile 98. The large trunk space was the primary factor in the decision, because we wanted to travel with luggage, golf clubs, and so on. In replacing the little K Car, I went shopping with my golf bag. I wanted a small car to drive locally but with a trunk large enough to handle a golf bag conveniently. I ended up with a 1995 Dodge Stratus.

In 1997, with a five-year-old big car, the bug bit again, and I went shopping for another Olds 98. The big problem was that Olds had stopped making the big 98 sedan in 1996. I looked at several other cars, but nothing suited me. Actually, the radio and temperature controls on the steering wheel became a big factor. So I called around until I found a dealer who still had a 1996 Olds 98 on the lot. Then I went to Columbus, Georgia, and bought a one-year-old new car, which was exactly like our black 1992 Olds.

The car bug kept nibbling at me, because I was never well satisfied with the 1995 Dodge Stratus. It wore out a set of tires in 8,000 miles. So I traded it for a 1997 Chevrolet Malibu. Thus, the latter two cars—the 1996 Olds 98 and the 1997 Chevrolet Malibu—took us to the end of the twentieth century.

In the fifty years from 1950 to 2000, we had had sixteen cars. We kept each one anywhere from one to ten years. All except three were purchased new, and all except one (which was financed) were paid for at the time of purchase. We never put more than 90,000 miles on any car. The first car cost $1,600, and the last one cost $33,000. A conservative net cost for purchase of all these cars would not exceed $100,000, which is not much according to 1999 standards.

There is no way this country can support the American dream with the automobile in the future like it has during the last five decades of the 1900s. Previously, everything was based on desires and economics—everybody got what he/she wanted. But in the first two decades of the new century, traffic gridlocks, air pollution, and economics (high gasoline prices) should bring forth some alternative transportation.

❧ 25 ☙

The New Millennium

The big event for the coming year was the beginning of a new century—January 1, 2000. There was considerable disagreement as to when the new millennium actually would begin—January 1, 2000, or January 1, 2001. However, the beginning of 2000 was an important time in this country, and had an impact on the economy. The big problem was that when computers were invented in this country, only two digits were allotted to designate the year—thus, "03" designated 1903, and "48" meant 1948. In the new century, there would be no way to differentiate between 1901 and 2001. So millions and millions of dollars were spent by businesses and institutions across the country to adopt a new system of record keeping. The costly projects preparing for 2000 were known as "Y2K," and many people were convinced that the whole country would crash at the stroke of midnight on December 31, 1999. There were widespread rumors that time-keeping mechanisms, electrical systems, banking, and all businesses would shut down. Many people stored up water, food, and other supplies in preparation for the emergency. Actually, nothing happened other than the calendar changed to a new year.

Meghan graduated from Purdue University in May, and in July Becky and I resumed our cruises with a tour of the eastern

The new millenium for Becky and Louie.

The clan at Thanksgiving 2000 at Sky Valley.

Caribbean in the company of the Ellises from Bowling Green, Kentucky. Floyd was a college classmate that we have kept in touch with since 1947. In August we were back in Branson again with several of the Army buddies. On November 4, we were back in Indiana for Meghan's wedding to Tom Lentz, another Purdue graduate. At Thanksgiving all of the family came to Leisurely, a place in the mountains at Sky Valley, Georgia. We'd bought into a partnership of a furnished house in 1995, and we have use of it four weeks each year—one week each in winter, spring, summer, and fall. It is a marvelous place and all our family had a delightful Thanksgiving, 2000.

Well, after a few months of partial relief from abdominal discomfort following my second surgery, the pain did indeed return. I must have done a lot of complaining and checking with different doctors. Everyone explained the chronic pain as adhesions and scar tissue, and no one would operate again for fear of making the situation worse. So by the end of the year I finally mus-

Army buddy Ed Hammett, Becky, Chris Hammett, and Louie in Branson, 2001.

tered enough courage to go to a pain-management specialist. This resulted in having a nerve block on December 21, 2000. I floated through Christmas and felt great—no pain, and it never returned.

For Becky and me, the new millennium was to begin January 1, 2001. We preferred to start the new century with the year one (01) instead of year zero (00), so we took a cruise of the western Caribbean from December 28, 2000, to January 6, 2001. It included a gala celebration on New Year's Eve, but the weather was lousy all week. We were out on the veranda only once all week because it was so cold and rainy.

In April we attended our fifty-fifth high school reunion in Kentucky, and the next month we were back in Branson, Missouri, but this time with our Michigan group. A golfer's memory of that trip is that I got a hole-in-one at the resort where we stayed (Thousand Hills). It was my second such feat, as the first one had been at our course at Jennings Mill in 1995 when Becky was taking chemotherapy. (Actually, it was my third hole-in-one, but the other one had occurred at a little par-three course at a hotel on Fiji Island en route to Australia–New Zealand. It was kind of a fluke that happened while Becky and I were playing, so she wouldn't consent for me to take credit for it. Oh, well, lots of people never get even one.)

Summer of 2001 included another trip to Indiana for Travis Gallagher's graduation from high school, and Jeremiah Smith's wedding on June 16 to Kim Bennett; and a trip to Kentucky for Mama Conner's one hundredth birthday. From there we went on to Indiana again for scientific meetings. It was a great summer, as I remained pain-free and Becky was feeling great.

On September 11, 2001, our country was devastated by the terrorist attacks with airplanes on the World Trade Center towers in New York and on the Pentagon in Washington, along with another plane to crash in Pennsylvania. These dastardly events have forever changed the trusting, genteel, and free way of life we have always enjoyed in this country. All air traffic was grounded for about a week—but just five days later, Becky and I went on our scheduled trip to Ireland. Then in December I went to Raleigh, North Carolina, to attend the memorial service for Dr. Noland L. VanDemark, who was my major professor for my Ph.D. program at Illinois. "Vandy" was a wonderful person whom I greatly respected. Just the year before, I'd been asked to write about someone who had influenced my life. The following is what I wrote about Vandy.

❧ **26** ❧

A Sensitive, Creative Giant
(December 15, 2000)

"A master can tell you what he expects of you.
A teacher, though, awakens your own expectations."

—PATRICIA NEAL

One person outside my family who impacted my life is Dr. Noland L. VanDemark. In college and in my first job I had learned about this person's reputation—as a highly respected, productive researcher who had published numerous scientific papers on animal reproduction.

I met him for the first time in the summer of 1953 as I began an assistantship in a graduate program at Champaign-Urbana, Illinois. I went there to study under another professor, but in my peon labor I became better acquainted with Vandy and changed to him as my major professor. [My wife and I] had one child and he had three young children. Our families became friends, and we would visit in their home to watch a new invention called TV. Thanksgiving in their home along with other graduate students was always special. One year after we had all eaten too much he put a big turkey leg on my empty plate. Of course, I ate it but later paid the price for overeating. Our second daughter was born in 1954, and we named her after his wife, Beda.

But, what was his influence? He was not only a great research scientist but an excellent teacher. He was always opening up new vistas to put everything in proper perspective. He had a wonderful outlook on life and easily encouraged you to do your very best. We had many stimulating conversations. He not only led me to discover what to do and how to do a project, but he emphasized why do it. His constant goal was to benefit mankind. When I wore down or encountered rough going, he was ever ready to give a boost but never one to take over and do things for you, just there to encourage, urge you to come up with your own solution and determination to overcome the difficulties. He was most influential in my career and served as a role model.

After I received my degree, he later served in administrative roles at two major land grant institutions. During those years he specialized in helping others expand their creative horizons and published a book entitled *Breaking the Barriers to Everyday Creativity.* He wanted each person to recognize, develop, and utilize creative potential through better understanding of yourself and the people you live and work with. His book illustrates how mutual respect, trust, and love contribute to the creative process at home, at school, and in the workplace. One point of pride is that he was named a distinguished bicentennial professor at

UGA and spent three months here in 1985 teaching a graduate course on nurturing creativity.

In June, while in Raleigh, NC, I called to arrange to visit Vandy and his wife in a retirement center in Durham, NC. As she answered the phone she said, "Oh, Louie, Vandy has been placed in a security unit with severe dementia." I did not get to see him, but I send cards and hear from him through his family. Vandy was only five feet tall and never weighed more than 120 pounds, but he was and remains a GIANT to me.

27

New Branches
on the Family Tree

"The most important thing a father can do for his children
is to love their Mother."

—THEODORE HESBURG

The new year of 2002 began with a big snow—enough in this
area of Georgia to last two days and to postpone the annual
Polar Bear Golf Tournament at Jennings Mill. On January 15 we
left for a cruise on the fabulous *Queen Elizabeth 2*. We met Bill and
Marilyn Hinze in Aculpulco for two days, then boarded the QE-2
for California and Hawaii, where we spent a few days in Honolulu.
Just before we left, Becky had two teeth extracted, which left a
black-and-blue bruise on her face for most of the trip. Of course, I
was blamed for the obvious abuse she showed.

Our big trip was to China and Tibet. We started in Beijing, then
moved on to Xian and Wuhan for five days on the Yangtze River,
including a tour of the renowned Three River Gorges Dam just
five months before it was opened for service. The cruise ended in
Chengdu, where we stayed overnight before going to Lhasa, Tibet.
We returned to Chengdu for a couple of days, then traveled on to
Hong Kong for another two days before returning home.

Becky and Louie on the Great Wall of China, 2002.

Monks-in-training debating scripture in Lhasa, Tibet, 2002.

The Michigan Group—Erv Moshers, Don Englanders,
Bill Hinzes, and Boyds—in Florida, 2004.

Well before recovering from our jet lag we left for Kentucky, Illinois, and Door County, Wisconsin, for our annual get-together with the Michigan group. After three weeks in China, this was the most enjoyable drive I ever made. The beautiful farm homes, open countryside, and towering church steeples were thrilling sights.

June 29, 2002, was a milestone with the birth of our first great-grandchild: Loganne Marie Wilson was born to Cameren and Scott Wilson. Another first came on July 8, when I got my first traffic ticket (speeding) after sixty years of driving. Surely it was overdue after several years of my bragging to our many-ticketed children and grandchildren about never getting a ticket for a traffic violation. Of course, the most recent bragging was with Garth's family over the July 4 weekend—when the speeding ticket was issued on our return trip to Bogart. Another milestone was the gathering in Kentucky on July 19 for Mama Conner's 101st birthday.

As a former president of CAST, I was invited back to meet with the CAST board in Phoenix in September. This was a fun experience, as Dick Stuckey, the former executive director of CAST, arranged for us to stay in a condo at Sun City West in Surprise, Arizona. We got to visit grandson Travis Gallagher and friends Bob and Norma Seerley, and enjoyed five days of golf—even golfing at 6:00 A.M.

Another great year came to a close with the annual Georgia-Florida football game in Jacksonville and a week in a condo at St. Augustine Beach. This was followed by a winter week at Leisurely in the mountains at Sky Valley, Georgia.

The following year (2003) was likewise memorable, with the gathering of great-granddaughter Loganne, her mother, Cameren, her grandmother Tina, and great-grandmother Becky in Kentucky for a five-generation photograph with Mama Conner. Our best friend, Harold Ford, was honored as outstanding alumnus of Murray State University, so we made another trip to Kentucky for the festivities.

We went on a cruise to Bermuda with Charles and Linda Butterworth to celebrate our fifty-fifth wedding anniversaries. In the summer, Becky and I and our friends, the Englanders, had a wonderful river-boat trip from Budapest to Amsterdam on the Danube and Rhine rivers. This was our first time to visit Budapest, Vienna, and Nueremburg. It was a beautiful and most enjoyable trip. We were saddened on Christmas Day when Mama Conner passed away at 102 years, five months of age.

The red-letter event of 2004 was the birth of our second great-granddaughter, Makenna Marie Lentz, in Huntley, Illinois. On the return from our first visit with Makenna, we went to Kentucky for a reunion of our 1946 graduating class from high school. This special gathering was prompted by the sale and possible demolition of our high school building, which had been new in 1941 when our class was in eighth grade. The event called for an "undedication" of the beloved building. Also, our class promoted an open house for all graduates of the high school and the awarding of diplomas to those students who'd been called into service and

Five generations in 101 years–Gladys Conner, Tina Mize,
Becky Boyd, Cameren Wilson, and Loganne Wilson.

were unable to graduate with their classmates. It was a grand day
for Becky and me. It has been a long-lasting joy to maintain contact with our high school classmates. At our private luncheon, fea-
turing long-remembered barbecue and six-ounce bottles of Coca
Colas, I told them that as many places as we had lived and as much
as we had traveled, the dearest place and deepest love for Becky
and me was right there—with our classmates.

Later in the year we went on a cruise to the Scandinavian cap-
itals and to St. Petersburg, Russia. We wanted to see Helsinki,

Becky and Louie in Budapest, 2003.

where I had an opportunity to go in 1970 on sabbatical leave, and to see St. Petersburg. We also went to the famous Greenbriar Resort in West Virginia with the Butterworths and played golf there.

The highlight of 2005 was a return cruise to the Mexican Riveria. I had been enamored with Cabo San Lucas, Mexico, twenty years ago—before it was discovered by the hordes of tourists and residents. We visited some of the fabulous golf courses. The fulfillment of a long-time dream was a golfing trip to Ireland. Harold Ford and I went with a group, and we had a jolly good time there. The pinnacle was a beautiful golf course called "Old Head," perched high above and literally out in the Atlantic Ocean. The wind was blowing thirty-five to forty miles per hour, but the caddy assured us that it was a "good" day!

The treasured high school building at Sedalia was sold, resulting in another Boyd heritage event. A bronze plaque had been installed at the dedication of the building in 1940 that had Daddy's name on it as a member of the county school board. With the im-

Wanda and Harold Ford—friends, absolutely.

pending sale of the building, Nelson and I had tried at all levels from the school janitor up to the school superintendent to get that plaque for Nelson as a family keepsake—all to no avail. But, when the building was sold, Nelson went to the successful bidder and told him he wanted the plaque, if possible. In two minutes with a crowbar and hammer, he had the plaque in hand.

As we progress into the new millennium, I am ever mindful of the wonderful friendships developed during our married life and before. In our moves while living in five states of this great country and in one foreign country, we continually added to our long list of friends. For more than thirty years in Georgia there have been four couples of us in a bridge group that usually met monthly—Gene and Ruth Younts, Allan and LaVerne Barber, and Hugh and Georgia Logan. All three couples were special. Also there was what we called our "Kentucky group," which consisted of John and Ann Kohler, Jack and Pat Gritton, and Bob and Micki Parcells. Any possible excuse we could find to get together, we used.

We have thrilled at so many long-lasting friendships.

✎ **28** ✎

Greener Pastures
Just Over the Next Hill

"It's easy to make a buck. It's a lot tougher to make a difference."

—TOM BROKAW

As mentioned earlier, my first "life's ambition" was to have a dairy farm. In fact, the site had already been selected as a place near a creek that our school bus passed twice daily on the long ride to and from Sedalia School. The Army and perhaps many other reasons ended that early teenage dream.

My mother, bless her heart, wrote me when I was overseas in the army encouraging me to think about a career. I had to respond, so I told her that I would not be satisfied until I became postmaster at Mayfield. That was the only thing I knew about. Carolyn Boyd's father, cousin Byron, was the postmaster at Sedalia and it appealed to me as a "good job"—much better than suckering tobacco!

The next "vision" came as I progressed through college. First, it was as a fieldman for a dairy plant like Pet, Carnation, or Kraft, which were large milk-processing companies in those days. The fieldman would work with the dairymen (milk producers), perhaps live on a farm himself, raise a family, and have a great life. Certainly a motivating factor for this possible vocation was that Becky's uncle Bob Jenkins was the CEO of Pet Dairy Products Company in Johnson City, Tennessee. But, as I continued on for a master's degree, that kind of work began to fade away.

My next dream was to teach at a state college like Murray State, Western Kentucky at Bowling Green, or Southern Illinois University. Most states had several state colleges with agricultural programs, and at that time a Ph.D. was not required for their faculty members. The main reason that a master's degree was satisfactory for state colleges is that there was a shortage of Ph.D.'s so soon after World War II. Again, one could live on a farm, have a good life, and teach at the college in a small college town.

This was a predominant dream during my master's program, and as I completed it I considered a position at Southern Illinois University in Carbondale. However, it was temporary, for one year only, to replace a faculty member going on leave. So I ended up taking another temporary position at Kentucky immediately after finishing my degree. This was done at the urging of my major professor, but there were other strong motivators—Becky was eight months pregnant, and we could continue to live in the same veterans-housing units even though I was a faculty member. So, we didn't have to move at that time.

The first greener pasture outside the academic arena surfaced in the fall of 1952. I had been working a year and traveling a lot across the state, which was not real pleasant with a new baby at home. A Purina Company district salesperson in Louisville (Mr. Montgomery) tried to get me to go with Purina in feed sales. Purina was a very successful and popular feed company selling to dairy and other livestock producers. I was making $4,000 a year, and his feed salesmen were averaging $18,000 per year. This was truly a greener pasture—with the real "green"—but I resisted. I guess the main reason was that we in extension at the university were telling dairymen that they could prepare their own feeds that would be just as good and be less expensive than the commercial feeds.

After that encounter, I began to lean toward a career in academia at the university level, which meant that a Ph.D. was a necessity. So preparation for more graduate school began to evolve.

The next two offers of greener pastures came at Tennessee while I was working in my first real, full-fledged faculty position. George Brinks, a person I had known casually for about three years in Knoxville, had just started a new company (Brinks, Inc.) selling dairy-processing equipment. I agreed to spend a day with him, so he gave a full tour and accounting of the company and wanted me to join him in the business—undoubtedly a fine opportunity, but it just didn't interest me.

The other temptation to leave academia came a couple of years later. In my diligent efforts to organize a FarmHouse fraternity chapter at Tennessee I had become acquainted with Mr. James Skidmore. He was an FH alumnus from the Midwest and was president of Security Mills in Knoxville, a very successful small feed company. He had been quite helpful to me with the FH alumni activities in the fledgling student chapter, and I had great respect for him. He wanted me to come in to handle a sizeable expansion of the company, particularly in Florida with the large dairy herds that were getting started. Then, after two years, I would become his replacement. The money paid to management in a small company was astounding to me, especially since I was still making less than $10,000 per year, and this was after four children and ten years out from my first job in Lexington, making $4,000 per year.

This offer I indeed gave serious consideration, but I soon concluded that it really wasn't what I wanted to do. Though I turned it down, I did get Mr. Skidmore to hire one of our students who was just graduating. He was hired not for the job Mr. Skidmore wanted me to do, but to do public relations work for the company. Emmett Barker did real well for Mr. Skidmore and later for the American Feed Manufacturers Association—and still later as executive of the National Farm Equipment and Industrial Equipment Association.

Immediately after the move to Michigan, I was contacted about coming back to Knoxville as manager of the East Tennessee Artificial Breeders Association. I felt sure I would not be interested at all in this venture, but I had so many good friends on the board of directors that I had to meet with them. I met with the board in Hershey, Pennsylvania, to listen to the grandiose plans they wanted implemented. Even if implementation had been a possibility, however, I would not have been interested.

The last and final industry opportunity to which I gave any thought at all came about five years later. Dr. Harry Herman was retiring as the long-time executive secretary of the National Association of Animal Breeders (NAAB). By this time Becky was comfortable in the academic environment and didn't want to give up her security blanket of friends and contacts across the country. Likewise, I knew that I could never be content in that type of work. So at age forty, even before the mid-life crisis hit, I was firmly set with my career in the academic setting.

A discussion on job opportunities outside the academic area would not be complete without the story of a brief internal struggle in the late 1960s. Our work in organizing a new church in Okemos, Michigan, was a fine experience. The organizing pastor, Dr. Howard Kehde, was a Ph.D. chemical engineer at Dow Chemical Company who'd gone to seminary at forty-four years of age. He spoke frequently of his burning motivation, which was Christ's admonition to Peter—"If you love me, feed my sheep." As I worked with him closely as an elder and heard his story many times, it began to work on me. I tussled with this for a while, even to the point of choosing the Louisville Seminary as the place I would go, and tried to deal with the fatherly question of how in the world could I do this with four children and no job and no money.

Late one night I awakened Becky to talk about it. Her comment was that if it was something I felt I must do, then we would find a way to do it. She fell promptly back to sleep—problem solved! I indeed gave this possibility serious consideration over several months and eventually resolved it clearly in my mind. And I have never regretted the decision that I made.

Even though I never feasted in the greener pastures of industry, I have always been satisfied with my progress in the public sector of a land-grant university. I started at Tennessee at $6,800 per year in September 1956. Thirty-five years later, during some bad and good years economically in the states we lived in, I had averaged a $2,000-plus per year increase in salary. I only asked for a salary increase once in my life, which was on my first job in Kentucky, and I always wished that I had not done it there.

Though I never made more than $80,000 per year, we perhaps stayed a little ahead of the inflation rate over the years; we had a good standard of living and prepared well for a comfortable, self-sufficient retirement. The main reason for our economic success was Becky's frugal household management and her contentment with and appreciation for a simple lifestyle without unnecessary frills and expensive luxuries. With our childhoods during the stifling Depression in the 1930s, we could never depart from the philosophy of living within our means and, if that's not possible, readjusting our standard of living and lifestyle—downward.

❧ 29 ❧

Slavery, Religion, War

"The time is always right to do what is right."

—MARTIN LUTHER KING, JR.

I wish to comment briefly on three topics that impacted my life. The first was slavery, with which I had no contact at all, in any form. Early South Carolina history relates that some of the Boyds who came from Ireland and settled in the Newberry area were covenanters in the Reformed Presbyterian Church. One of the principles of the covenanters was opposition to slavery, and they were forbidden to accept slave holders as members of the church. A reference in the *Annals of Newberry* cites a David Boyd who set his slaves free but, when they were unable to care for themselves, was forced by the authorities to take them back and become their guardian.

It is unknown whether the covenants or practices of the covenanters as neighbors had an effect on our family members who moved westward. However, no record has been found that any of our branch were slave holders. Another reason might have been that none of our immediate ancestors had plantations. However, in the late 1930s and perhaps earlier, some black families did attend the Boyd reunions in Kentucky. I have only a faint recollection of this, but Nelson relates a story that at one of the reunions a black lady asked Mother where she fitted into the family. As Mother told her, the lady said, "Well, it doesn't matter cause we're all related anyway." My brother-in-law, Sylvester Paschall, told the story about his ancestors as they moved westward with their slaves. One night there was a violent thunderstorm, and they thought the world was coming to an end, and in their fear they released their slaves. The next morning the sun rose as usual, and they were ready to move on, but their slaves had all disappeared.

The second topic is religion, which had great influence on the immigrants who came to this country. There is little doubt that the Boyds were among the Reformed Presbyterians who moved from Scotland to Ireland and then on to the new land called America. In South Carolina they were absorbed into the Associate Reformed Presbyterian (ARP) Church of America. Of my direct ancestors, John Boyd was very active in the ARP Church as he moved into Kentucky and was one of the organizers of the Beech Grove Cumberland Presbyterian Church. Thomas Pressly Boyd was also an active participant, serving as an elder in that church. My grandfather, Lewis Gray Boyd, was a lifetime member, but he was less active as he apparently married a Southern Baptist who never joined his church. I have no knowledge of the situation when Daddy was growing up, but he later was a Baptist, and I presume it was because his mother was a Baptist.

In my immediate family all I can remember is the Baptist Church, as we were members of Salem Baptist Church at Lynn Grove, Kentucky. As far as I knew, my folks had been members there all their lives. But I had a revealing experience in Nashville when I went with Becky and Linda and Charles Butterworth to visit the girls' relatives over the Labor Day weekend in 1947. We were visiting Mr. Jonah Cobb, who was a brother to Miss Emma Cobb Mills (who lived at our house as a teacher), so they knew my family. Mr. Jonah married Aunt Alta, a sister to Becky's Grandmother Byrd (Little Mother). Aunt Essie, an old maid sister to Mrs. Cobb, and "Little Mother" lived with the Cobbs. The household there was much divided, as Mr. Cobb was a strong Baptist and his wife and her sister were Church of Christ members. Aunt Essie, the old maid, asked me if my mother used to be a member of the Church of Christ, and I said no. She replied that, yes, she had too been a member. I never asked Mother or anyone about it, but I surmise that she felt compelled to join the Baptist church because Daddy was a strong Baptist. Grandma Bazzell, Mother's mother, and Mother's sister, Aunt Nona Meadows, were members of the Church of Christ, and I suspect there was slight friction over the issue. In the area where we lived, and generally throughout the Bible belt, there was intense rivalry and even some displeasure between the Baptist Church and the Church of Christ.

The morning I was getting dressed for our wedding Mother told me how proud she was that I was marrying Becky and said that she just wished that we were both members of the same church. I assured her that was not a problem for us and then rushed off to the wedding. In reflecting back over the five decades since that day, I presume there was a deeper meaning in her comment than I got from her spoken word. Actually, it took us eleven years and four children to resolve our religious preferences. Settling on a church was never a problem for *us*, as we approached it with love and respect for each other. Our overriding concern was always how the parents would react. At one time I told Daddy that I was going to join Becky's church, and he didn't say anything. And I truly made an honest effort, but as time progressed I just couldn't force myself to do it. As the search and faith journey continued, we both were led to the right choice, and we have been entirely happy with the decision.

The third brief topic is war. Southerners have always been attentive to the Revolutionary War and the Civil War. Tracing lineage to become a member of the Sons of the American Revolution (SAR) or, especially, the Daughters of the American Revolution

(DAR) has been big in the South. However, I have found no record or hint that any of the Boyd ancestors served in the Revolutionary War. The main reason is that I have no traceable record prior to 1807. It is possible that John Boyd's grandfather or even his father could have been in the Revolutionary War—if either of them immigrated here before the 1770s. It is also possible that our branch of the Boyds came here after the United States was formed as a new nation in 1775.

I have found no record of any ancestors in the Civil War. John Boyd would have been in his late fifties when the Civil War started and was probably too old to serve in any official capacity. Thomas Pressly was about thirty years old, married, and had three children when the war started. It is likely that his family status kept him out of the war. However, any attempt to give a reason for his involvement or lack of involvement would be pure speculation by me. It was an accepted practice In the early years in this country that a person could hire someone else to serve for him in the service. Also, it is possible that some able-bodied farmers in that area were not engaged in the war, since Kentucky was firmly on the Mason-Dixon line and very close to the border (Ohio River) separating the Union from Kentucky.

Mother would tell a story about the Civil War that was passed down in her family. Her grandfather, John Turnbow, was a lover of fine horses, and they were kept in tip-top condition. One day a group of soldiers rode up to the barnyard gate, dismounted, and leaned their guns against the fence. They then put their worn-out horses in the lot, caught John Turnbow's fine horses, and rode them off. All the family could do was to watch the beautiful horses taken away. The sequel to that story is that, although John Turnbow was a slave owner before the war, his slaves refused to leave even after they were given their freedom, because they were treated so well by him.

Then came World War I from 1914 to 1918. This apparently was the first time that U.S. soldiers were sent from this continent to fight aggression in a foreign land. Daddy was not in service, and I presume that his marital status was the reason. He'd been married two years before the war started, and their first child was born in 1915, soon after the war began. Uncle Jap was in service but he was single. I am sure there was always a little resentment there by Aunt Tola and Uncle Jap. I can remember little remarks being made about serving your country in the military.

And then it had to be done all over again just twenty-three years later, when World War II, the war of all wars, began in December 1941. It affected Nelson and me, who are the only ones I am aware of in this direct line of ancestors to serve in the armed forces.

✤ **30** ✤

A Perfect, Fun Day Visiting Protemus, Kentucky

"Life is a journey in growing old—not in becoming old."

—J. W. FANNING

While Becky was in Florida playing golf and bridge with her sister Linda, I went to Kentucky a couple of days to visit my brother Nelson and Mama Conner. On April 17, 2000, Nelson and I tried to play golf, but it was much too cold. So we took off to visit the places where our Boyd ancestors had lived. We went to Grandpa Boyd's home place near Tri City—the farm that I had inherited and owned for twenty-five years and sold to Nelson's son, John Boyd, in June 1998. Then we went to Beech Grove, where the Beech Grove Cumberland Presbyterian Church once stood. A historical marker was installed recently to commemorate the site, and the cemetery there is well maintained. We visited the gravesites of our great-great-grandparents, John Boyd and Jane (Jenny) Montgomery Boyd; our great-grandparents, Thomas Pressly Boyd and Mary Elizabeth Turnbow Boyd; and our grandparents, Lewis Grey Boyd and Hattie Murphy Boyd.

From the cemetery we went a few miles to Protemus, where John Boyd and his wife settled in the early 1830s. We saw the log

Louie Boyd and Nelson Boyd.

cabin where John Boyd lived; it has been preserved by the resident owners of the farm. Dr. John Thomas (Tommy) Murdoch, a teenage friend of mine, bought the farm when he retired from the University of Wisconsin. He and his wife Sue live on the farm near his son, Ricky, and Ricky's family. They are doing a fabulous job of farming employing modern techniques. They raise forages and cattle, do a bit of fish-farming, and have a vast, computer-based consulting business located on the farm.

We drove back to Tri City and, while having lunch in a little country restaurant, I asked Nelson about the Jetton Graveyard. We had always heard that some of our ancestors were buried there but we never had seen it. As luck would have it, a person Nelson knew who lived in the Protemus area was eating at a nearby table. Nelson asked him if he knew where the Jetton Cemetery was, and he said, "Yes, it's on my farm and I'll take you to it."

This person was Ferral Miller, who was raised in Lynn Grove near Salem Baptist Church; as it turned out, we'd gone to church there with several of his older brothers and sisters and his ancestors. Mr. Miller played basketball under the renowned Coach Edd Diddle at Western Kentucky University in Bowling Green in the 1960s. After college he returned to the Murray, Kentucky, area and soon began training bird dogs. He now lives on a farm adjacent to Tommy Murdock and is a highly successful dog breeder and trainer. He has won all of the major field trials in the United States and Canada. His trophy room fills the whole house—there must be hundreds of trophies and pictures of his prize dogs. He has made a vast amount of money with the dogs, and he currently owns 2,200 acres of land in the Protemus area—so it's no wonder that the cemetery was on his farm. Let me further digress to say that the Protemus I remember of fifty or sixty years ago was nothing but red, sandy-clay, eroded hillsides that were very poor for farming. The land was infertile and the soil largely depleted. Today, the entire area is beautiful with lush green grass growing—ideal for quail and training bird dogs.

He put us in his four-wheel-drive truck and took off across the fields to the Jetton Cemetery. It was fenced and reasonably cleared of underbrush and trees. During a quick look through the cemetery we found three Boyd graves. They were those of William J. Boyd, born June 21, 1831, and died January 31, 1857; Eastee C. Boyd, born June 8, 1839, and died January 16, 1859; and John Boyd, born January 11, 1846, and died September 23, 1856. I did not have my records with me so without documentation, at this point, it was assumed that all three of these young people were children of John and Jenny Montgomery Boyd. Thus, they were probably brothers and a sister of Thomas Pressly Boyd, who was born June 27, 1832.

Also, we found the grave for Louis U. Jetton, born January 8, 1827, and died October 12, 1916. Again, I assume that he married one of John Boyd's daughters and that Louis U. was the father of Mr. Malcolm Jetton, our neighbor where I was raised. As a child I always "knew" we were related to the Jettons in some way, but I never knew how. Our family frequently attended the Jetton family reunions, and I always called Mr. Malcolm "Cousin Malcolm" and his wife "Cousin Nancy" as long as they lived.

Crossing one of the fields near the cemetery we passed a concrete cattle-water tank where the water was bubbling up in the middle. It was running from a continuous-flowing spring about 100 yards away. Mr. Miller told us a story that Mr. Gordon Crouch had told him. (Incidentally, Mr. Gordon Crouch, a former Sunday-school teacher of mine and a wonderful, wonderful person, had been buried at Salem Church the day before at ninety years of age.) Mr. Gordon, who used to hunt quail in this area, told Mr. Miller that in the early 1920s and 1930s the whole hillside around the spring was covered with black kettles where the women would come to the water source to wash their clothes. It was fascinating to me to learn that Protemus had an early version of the modern laundromat.

Mr. Miller spent a couple of hours taking Nelson and me all around the countryside between Lynn Grove and the Kentucky-Tennessee state line. We saw where our sister, Kathleen, had lived for several years after she and Sylvester were married and where several acquaintances had lived fifty to sixty years ago. You see, it was a wonderful day!

Upon checking the above names and dates with previously collected family records, it is most evident why genealogical searches are right much confusing. For example, the tombstone for William J. Boyd shows his birth date as June 21, 1831, but all family records show his birth date as August 24, 1834. If he was born in 1831 he would have been the second child and one year older than T. P. Boyd. I feel confident that T. P. Boyd was the second child and that William J. was born in 1834, which is confirmed by the 1850 census showing him to be the third child and two years younger than T. P. Also, the tombstones show that Eastee (Ester) C. died January 16, 1859, and that John W. Boyd, another son of John and Jane Boyd, died September 23, 1856. Again, family records

The three Boyds—Louie, Kathleen, and Nelson, with Becky and Sue.

show that all three children died the same year—William J. died January 31, 1857; Eastee C. died January 16, 1857; and John W. died September 23, 1857. I strongly suspect that the three children, ranging from eleven to twenty-three years of age, did die the same year, yet it is difficult to understand why the discrepancy in dates appears on the tombstones. The birth dates also differed for Eastee C. and John W. Boyd. The tombstone listed Eastee C. as born June 8, 1839, and John W. as born January 11, 1846; whereas family records show Eastee C. as born August 6, 1839, and John W. born November 1, 1846.

31

The Second Anniversary Celebration

"In case you are worried about the younger generation, it's going to grow up and start worrying about the younger generation."

—J. W. FANNING

Our engagement occurred at 12:01 A.M. on Sunday, February 29, 1948. The *exact* second anniversary of our engagement occurred at 12:01 A.M. on Sunday, February 29, 2004. That day of that month falls on that day of the week every 28 years.

In preparation for the second occurrence, I alerted the four children several months in advance to hold the date for a celebration in Bogart, but didn't tell them what it was until much later. All was to be a big surprise for Becky.

As Sunday, February 29, 2004, approached, Beverly told her mother that Tim had a meeting in Atlanta on the last weekend in February and that she was coming with him for a visit. With this development, I suggested that Becky contact the other three children and see if they could come the same weekend for a family gathering. This she did, and she was right much shocked that all so readily agreed to come on that date. Becky had planned the family dinner for late afternoon on Saturday.

Louie and Becky, "second anniversary," 2004.

Garth and his family were coming in from North Carolina, arriving late the night before the get-together. They were staying in a motel, and Beve and Tim were at our house. So I arranged for us to meet early the next morning to have breakfast together ahead of her planned gathering.

As Becky walked into Jennings Mill Country Club that morning all our children and another 100 people were there for a champagne breakfast to celebrate our second anniversary. She was completely surprised.

The third anniversary will be in 2032.

32

The Family Tree
The Tree of Life

*"I don't know who my Grandfather was.
I am much more concerned to know what his Grandson will be."*

—Abraham Lincoln

I first became interested in the Boyd history about the time I married—age twenty. By that time, however, all my good sources of information were no longer available. Grandpa Boyd died six months after we were married; while I was growing up, I never had a conversation with him on any subject, so I did not learn anything from him about his family or his life. Family history and family business were never discussed with the children nor talked about at the dinner table. Thus, I learned almost nothing about my grandparents and very little about the early years of my parents.

As a teenager I do remember Grandma Boyd telling about the Boyds coming from North Carolina—when they got to the Tennessee River in the fall, they had to wait until winter for the river to freeze over so they could cross with their wagons. Her maiden name was Murphy, and she told that her family came from Murphy, North Carolina, to Tennessee, and then on into Kentucky. She had a stroke before I returned from the army so I was unable to talk with her when I really wanted to learn about the family. The only personal sources I had to talk with were some of Grandpa's brothers and sisters, but I still did not get any reliable new information. Mother was the only one who encouraged me to delve into family history, and she was very helpful in keeping me interested.

College, marriage, a new job, and a growing family took precedence over family history in the early 1950s. One valuable bit of information during this time came from Kenny Young at the Kentucky Artificial Breeders Association near Louisville. He had just bought a Jersey bull for the KABA bull stud from Henry Parr in South Carolina, and he told me that Mr. Parr had married a Boyd and lived on the Boyd farm. This chance occurrence turned out to be good information.

During this time I did check the Beech Grove Cumberland Presbyterian Church cemetery in southeast Graves County, Kentucky, where my great-great-grandfather, John Boyd, my great-grandfather, Thomas Pressly Boyd, and my grandfather, Lewis Grey Boyd, were buried. I also checked the 1850 census records for Calloway County, Kentucky, and found that John Boyd was born in Newberry County, South Carolina, in 1807. So our line of the Boyds had come from South Carolina instead of North Carolina as I had originally understood from my grandmother. Perhaps she was relating that *her* ancestors had come from North Carolina.

In 1957, after a graduate degree, two children with another one on the way, and a few months into my first faculty position, I started writing this record. The first pen to paper occurred on a faded yellow legal tablet in a flea-bag motel en route back to Knoxville from the West Tennessee Experiment Station in Jackson. I also did a little searching of records and reading before I got sidetracked again, and again, and again (as will become abundantly evident).

I also visited the farm where the Boyds had settled near Protemus, in southwest Calloway County, Kentucky. I found a house that consisted of the log cabin built by John Boyd. It had been built onto and around so that only a small portion of the logs was visible. Tenants were in the house, and it was in serious need of repair, but I took a picture showing the logs.

Another fortunate find was a Mrs. Margaret Bright, near Lewisburg, Tennessee. Part of my research out of Knoxville was at the Dairy Experiment Station in Lewisburg, which was operated jointly by the University of Tennessee and the U.S. Department of Agriculture in Washington. Apparently there was something in the local paper about me, and she wrote me at the university. Her maiden name was Montgomery, and she and I were related through my ancestral grandmother, Jenny Montgomery, who had married John Boyd. She and I corresponded, and I talked with her and went out to visit her and her elderly mother. They lived on the old Montgomery farm in Marshall County, Tennessee. Apparently, John Boyd and wife Jenny, along with some of the Montgomerys, headed westward from Newberry, South Carolina, in about 1829. They arrived in Tennessee in what is now Marshall County, about sixty miles south of Nashville, and stopped there for a while. Later, the Boyds moved on into Kentucky while the Montgomerys remained in Tennessee. She told of frequent correspondence and of her mother's reminiscing about occasional visits with their beloved cousins in Kentucky.

Then my historical pursuit slowed again. The family had increased to four children and job demands, including a new job in Michigan, meant very little activity in the 1960s. But upon moving to Georgia in 1972, I found a Boyd Parr as a veterinary student at the University of Georgia. Indeed, he was a son of Henry Parr in Newberry, South Carolina. Within a year or so our family made a weekend trip to Newberry, finding the farm near Kinard late Saturday afternoon. They were having a big picnic that night with her family, so Mrs. Parr (a Boyd!) insisted that we join the party, and she prepared another basket of food.

Another year or so later Nelson was visiting us in Athens, and he and I drove over to the Parr farm. Mr. Parr had told me on the first visit that he would take me back on the farm to the old Boyd graveyard. So that is what we wanted to do, even though it was a cold day and we had to walk a couple of miles. Mr. Parr was quite old then, at least compared to Nelson and me, but we could not keep up with him walking. The cemetery was in poor condition, and I did not find anything helpful during the short visit. I was hoping to find the parents of John Boyd, but nothing like that surfaced. However, I have never checked the census data or courthouse records in Newberry, and I believe that would be a good place to get valuable information.

Then another busy time ensued, with hard work at Georgia extending on into retirement with hard play and travel, so that thirty years later I still have not pursued the genealogy nor assembled what information I have gathered over the years. I do want to record what data I have, and I am fairly certain of the accuracy of the dates, although I have made little attempt to document or cross-reference sources of information.

33

Children of John Boyd and Jane Montgomery

Admitting my prolonged failure to stumble across the linkage with the Boyd line prior to 1800, I will commence in chronological order.

John Boyd was born in Newberry County, South Carolina, on December 25, 1807. He married Jane (Jenny) Montgomery, who was born in Newberry County, South Carolina, on January 10, 1807. The date of marriage is listed as February 1827 in the probate file of Robert Montgomery in Newberry, South Carolina. Undocumented evidence from the Montgomery line indicates that John Boyd and Jenny Montgomery were "double first cousins."

John and Jenny had a son, H. Spence Boyd, born in South Carolina in 1829. It is believed that they moved westward through Tennessee to Kentucky between 1829 and 1832. My great-grandfather, Thomas Pressly Boyd, was born in Kentucky on June 27, 1832. The 1850 census for Calloway County, Kentucky, shows the following for the John Boyd household: John, age forty-two, born in Kentucky; Jane and H. Spence, listed as born in South Carolina; T. P. Boyd, age eighteen, born in Kentucky; along with seven other children born in Kentucky. This census record shows a discrepancy from all other information, which points to John Boyd's being born in South Carolina. I believe that the birthplace listed for John Boyd is truly a census recorder's error and that the record should have shown his birthplace as South Carolina (the same as for Jane Boyd and H. Spence, their son).

When I saw the original Boyd farm in South Carolina and the stopover place with the Montgomerys in Tennessee, I was much amused at the place where the Boyds had finally settled in Kentucky. I was reminded of the saying, "Location, location, location," as the determinant of demand and increased values for property. I have witnessed many examples of farms selling at greatly inflated prices because they were in the pathways of rapidly expanding cities, industries, roads, or housing developments. But this was not a Boyd trait. They left good farmland in South Carolina; and the stopping place in Tennessee where the Montgomerys stayed was splendid farmland, just like the Bluegrass area of Kentucky. Yet, the area where John Boyd eventually settled was some of the worst farmland in many states—or at least, that is the way I knew it in my teen years. The soil was hilly, infertile, red, and highly erodable.

Mrs. Margaret Bright told me that her ancestors had always told *her* that the Montgomerys ran out of money and had to stop their westward trek in Tennessee, while the rich ones (the Boyds) went on to Kentucky. I assured her that was absolutely untrue. Even today, 175 years later, the Kentucky destination is very rural and isolated and no match for the Tennessee or South Carolina farmland that they left. The farms of the three succeeding generations (my great-grandfather, grandfather, and father) were some improved over the original settling site but were not even remotely evocative of "location, location, location," and incomparable to the Tennessee and South Carolina farms.

John Boyd

Born: December 25, 1807
Place: Newberry County, South Carolina
Married: Jane (Jenny) Montgomery

John Boyd (1807–1891).

Date Married: February 1827

Died: March 24, 1891

Buried: Beech Grove Cemetery, Southeast Graves County, Kentucky, at site of former Beech Grove Cumberland Presbyterian Church.

Inscription on Monument:

John Boyd

Born December 25, 1807

Died March 24, 1891

Age 83 years, 2 months, 29 days

The pains of death are past

Labor and Sorrow cease

And Life's long warfare closed at last

His soul is found in Peace.

Jenny Montgomery Boyd (also called Jane)

Born: January 10, 1807

Place: Believed to be Newberry County, South Carolina

Married: John Boyd

Date Married: February 1827

Died: August 11, 1895

Buried: Beech Grove Cemetery

Inscription on Monument:

Jane

Wife of John Boyd

Born January 10, 1807

Died August 11, 1895

Age 88 years, 7 months, 1 day

Farewell dear mother, Sweet Thy Rest

Weary with years and worn with Toil

Farewell till in some Happy Place

We shall Behold Thy Face Again

I have scanned several documents that trace the Boyd name to Ayr, Scotland, at Kilmarnock. A book entitled *Belle Boyd—Confed-*

erate Spy, by Louis A. Sigaud (1944), gives the early history of the Boyds. In general, some Boyds moved from Scotland to Ireland about 1550. They stayed in Northern Ireland for 200 years and apparently emigrated to the United States in the 1700s. Their main reason for leaving Ireland was to pursue religious freedom. The book entitled *Newberry County, Historical and Genealogical,* by George Leland Summer Sr. (privately printed, 1950), gives an accounting of the Boyds in Newberry and their leaving Londonderry and Bellemena, Ireland. Three brothers—James, John, and Thomas Boyd—received land grants from the King of England during the early to mid-1700s and settled in the Newberry, South Carolina, area. Thomas arrived just prior to the Revolutionary War. They were staunch Presbyterians siding with Prince William of Orange and fled Ireland to escape the religious tyranny of Kings William II and William III.

I will reiterate that I have made muted efforts to trace my ancestry to find those born before 1807, but I simply don't know whether my great-great-grandfather, John Boyd, descended from one of the three brothers or from other Boyds who came at different times. I am fairly certain that our line did come from the Scots via Ireland. I had the opportunity to visit Kilmarnock and the Boyd Castle in 1971 when we lived in England. The Boyds are still prominent there, as the Lord Mayor was a Boyd when we visited the town. I hope that future generations will bridge this gap and extend the direct line far back beyond 1807.

I make no claim as a genuine genealogist and cannot attest to the absolute accuracy of dates and events cited, except for those involving my immediate family and occurring during my lifetime. Earlier I mentioned historical information from Newberry, South Carolina, and personal contacts with relatives. Undoubtedly, the closest and best source of information is "Material on the Ancestors of Maude Lee Boyd," compiled and printed by her daughter, Margaret Howard Adams, about 1995. Her mother, Maude, who was my daddy's first cousin, died in 1993 at 104 years of age. She retained a keen memory and had gathered many family records. In addition to retaining the personal stories from her mother, Margaret did an exceptional job of researching legal and church records. I have relied heavily on her information about John Boyd and Thomas Pressly Boyd.

It is believed that John Boyd and Jane Montgomery Boyd had nine children. Known children were as follows:

H. (Hugh) Spence Boyd, born in South Carolina on January 25, 1829; died July 20, 1924 in Graves County, Kentucky; buried at Beech Grove. Married Jincy Boyd (daughter of Wilson Boyd and Sarah Wilson), born March 12, 1829; died January 16, 1929.

Thomas Pressly Boyd, born in Kentucky June 27, 1832; died January 9, 1921 (see chapters 34 and 35).

William J. Boyd, born August 24, 1834; died January 31, 1857; buried in Jetton Cemetery near Beech Grove.

Mary Ann Boyd, born June 8, 1836; died November 26, 1880; buried in Jetton Cemetery. Married Louis U. Jetton, born January 8, 1827; died October 12, 1911. They had seven children, including Malcolm S. Jetton, who was our neighbor (I called him Cousin Malcolm). A bachelor brother lived with him (I called him Uncle Wes).

Ester C. Boyd, born August 6, 1839; died January 16, 1857; buried in Jetton Cemetery.

Sarah Jane Boyd, born February 6, 1841; died January 19, 1915; buried at Beech Grove. Married John Hay Andrus, born October 4, 1845; died October 1, 1902; buried at Beech Grove. They had six children, including Voris Andrus, who married Allie Murphy, a sister to my grandmother Boyd (Hattie Murphy). Voris and Allie had five children and lived in Murray, Kentucky. I remember our taking Grandma and Grandpa Boyd there for visits. Coy Andrus, was the oldest son, and Daddy was very fond of him. He was principal of Symsonia School near Mayfield and was of Sedalia High School when Becky and I were in junior high there. Later

Coy served in the superintendent's office of Graves County Schools for several years. Two younger sons of Voris and Allie were neighbors of Becky's parents in Murray during the 1980s.

Rachel Rebecca Boyd, born June 19, 1843; died September 26, 1875; buried in Jetton Cemetery. Married James W. Brown on November 5, 1865.

John W. Boyd, born November 1, 1846; died September 23, 1857; buried in Jetton Cemetery.

Rosie Elizabeth Boyd, born November 1, 1846; died March 12, 1929. Married Benjamin Franklin Enoch on March 8, 1866. They had eleven children.

Apparently the last two children of John and Jane Boyd were twins. They are both listed in the 1850 census as four years old, confirming their birth date as November 1, 1846.

Three of the nine children died quite young, at eleven, eighteen, and twenty-three years old. They were buried at the Jetton Cemetery near Protemus. Apparently yellow fever struck the community in 1857, and the younger children were victims with William J. and Ester C. dying in January that year and John W. in September.

As was customary, given the limited travel and communications in this newly developing country, the Boyd children married into nearby families. As mentioned previously, H. Spence married Jincy Boyd, the daughter of Wilson Boyd, and Thomas Pressly married Mary Elizabeth Turnbow, all living in the same community. These families, as well as the Jetton, Andrus, Brown, and Enoch families, came to Calloway and Graves counties with land grants.

Undoubtedly the Boyds were staunch Presbyterians, which lends credence to the story of their flight from Ireland to the new democracy in the United States. Margaret Howard Adams has church records (signed by John and Jane Boyd) showing the organization of the Beech Grove Cumberland Presbyterian Church in November 1833. Apparently the original site was north of Bell

City, Kentucky, near the Tennessee state line. The church was moved to the Sugar Hill schoolhouse in 1868 (near Tri City, Kentucky) before the church was built at the site near Protemus where the Beech Grove Cemetery is located. I attended church there many times as a child and my grandfather's funeral in 1949, but in 2003 the building is gone and only a marker remains on the site.

Church records show that John Boyd and H. S. Boyd were elected elders on November 27, 1860, and that on February 24, 1861, the session met at the schoolhouse (Sugar Hill) with elder John Boyd attending. The register of elders shows John Boyd as "ordained" on November 27, 1860, and in the next column as having "ceased to act" on March 24, 1891. In the register of deaths John Boyd is listed as passing on March 24, 1891, which indicates he served as elder until his death, a total of thirty years.

Also, Margaret Howard Adams shows a copy of John Boyd's will made on March 5, 1891, just nineteen days before he died. My great-grandfather, T. P. Boyd, was named executor of his estate. He willed his granddaughter, Sally J. Paschall, daughter of Rachel Boyd Brown (deceased), 100 acres of land, and he described explicitly where this land was located that was to be her entire part of the estate. The remainder of the estate was willed to Jane Boyd for the rest of her life to manage and control as she saw fit. At her death and after all expenses, the remainder of the entire estate was to be equally divided among his five heirs—his sons H. S. Boyd and T. P. Boyd, the heirs of Mary A. Jetton (his daughter, deceased), and his daughters Sarah J. Andrus and Elizabeth R. Enoch. He also appointed T. P. Boyd as agent and councilor for Jane Boyd for remainder of her natural life. The will was attested by J. W. Broach, B. F. Enoch (his son-in-law), and C. W. Crawford.

Records kept by T. P. Boyd show the amount he paid for the funeral, burial, and monument as $146.50, and the amount paid for taxes as $19.75 in 1891 and $16.70 in 1892. The record of what he paid for his mother, Jane Boyd, in 1891 and 1892, showed one bottle of syrup $1.00, dress pattern and trimmings $6.15, bottle of tonic $1.00, mending buggy tire $0.50, recording will and getting copy $4.15, surveyors and expenses for division of land $23.00, transfer of deeds $2.50, shoes $1.00, and buggy and harness $75.00. The income from stock in two banks and interest at a bank and from individuals who owed John Boyd money amounted to $1,560.75. All of these records had a notation across them as "Settled August 19, 1897" which was two years after his mother's death. Also, receipts showed that T. P. Boyd paid $34.00 on August 12, 1895, for his mother's burial case and robe, and that he paid $30.00 for her tombstone on November 6, 1894. On February 25, 1896, he gave $25.00 as payment in full for his mother's medical account. This receipt was signed by C. W. Crawford, who also witnessed John Boyd's will—he apparently was their doctor.

Rich history abounds from Maude Howard's memory of her grandparents as she recounted to her daughter, Margaret Howard Adams. Maude had just started to school at Sugar Hill just shy of six years old when her father, Thomas Jefferson Boyd, rode up to the schoolhouse on his horse to get her to take her to her great-grandmother's funeral at Beech Grove Church. My daddy was only two years old then (in 1895). Maude recalled the casket and how her grandmother (Jane Boyd) was dressed, and that she wore a black bonnet trimmed in black lace.

John Boyd was a tanner. The tan yard was located away from the house but on occasion the odor was prevalent. He used the leather to make shoes and harnesses. He sold hides and did tanning for the neighbors. He was also a blacksmith.

The house where John and Jane lived had a large kitchen with a big fireplace for cooking. The boys slept upstairs, above the fireplace. Maude visited the house in 1912 or 1913, when her cousin Jane Jetton Sims, daughter of Mary Ann Boyd Jetton, lived in the house. As the houses were in those days, the cooking and eating area was usually separate from the living and sleeping area but connected by a covered area called a "dog-trot," which could be closed on the sides when needed. The Simses (Frank and Jane Jetton) had built onto the original log house. This was the same house I saw in the mid-1950s—more additions had been built, yet the logs were still visible in the area that was covered as a porch. In the late 1990s the property had been purchased by the John Thomas Murdock family (believed to be descendants of H. Spence Boyd). The original logs from the Boyd house were salvaged to build a log-cabin office on the farm.

The extent of the John Boyd estate is unknown, though it is believed to have been substantial for the 1890s. Records show a land grant to John Boyd in 1834, and in 1836 he bought land from John H. Edwards. Other purchases were made for land east of Bell City in the Protemus area. Records in Graves County (Mayfield), Kentucky, reveal a court case in which Wilson Boyd filed suit against John Boyd for 100 acres of land and won the suit. The reason for the suit and the relationship of Wilson Boyd to John Boyd are unknown. Records show that Jincy Boyd, daughter of Wilson Boyd and Sarah Wilson, married Hugh Spence Boyd, the oldest son of John Boyd. Tradition amongst later generations was that Jincy Boyd and H. Spence Boyd were cousins.

As mentioned several times previously, I do not know the Boyd ancestry before 1807, when John Boyd was born. In 1994 I had contact with Terry Kanago in Veradale, Washington. A descendant of the Montgomerys, she had found most interesting information on her family. She had uncovered records in South Carolina showing that Jane Montgomery was a child of Thomas Montgomery and Ann Spence. The ancestor of Terry Kanago was Robert Montgomery, brother of Thomas Montgomery, and he married Esther Spence, a sister to Ann Spence. Thomas Montgomery (my great-great-grandmother Jane's father) died in December 1808, when Jane was almost two years old. His brother Robert was named co-administrator of the estate with the widow, Ann. Robert Montgomery died in 1825 and later his wife had to sell the farm to settle debts. In the process, John Boyd, on behalf of

Thomas Pressly Boyd (1832–1921).

his wife, Jane Montgomery, filed a suit against Robert's estate to get money owed to her from her father's (Thomas's) estate. An affidavit in the probate file of Robert Montgomery stated that Jane Montgomery and John Boyd were married in February 1827. Apparently, when the estate was settled (about 1829), Esther Spence Montgomery moved to Bedford County, Tennessee, with her young children and widowed sisters. It is believed that Ann Spence Montgomery (Thomas's widow) was in this group, along with her daughter, Jane Montgomery, Jane's husband, John Boyd, and their young son (H. Spence Boyd), as the group moved westward. The

1830 census shows the Montgomerys and Boyds in Bedford County, Tennessee, but it is unclear whether Jane Montgomery Boyd's mother, Ann, accompanied them when Jane and husband John Boyd moved on into Kentucky.

The family name and South Carolina connections were evident in the naming of John and Jane Boyd's children. Their first son, Hugh Spence, was apparently given her mother's maiden name, *Spence.* It is pure speculation on my part that my great-grandfather Thomas Pressly Boyd was named after a Reverend S. P. Pressly, who was pastor of the Prosperity Associate Reformed Presbyterian Church from 1825 to 1832. The little town of Prosperity was located seven miles south of Newberry.

Thomas Pressly Boyd

Born: June 27, 1832
Place: Calloway County, Kentucky
Married: Mary Elizabeth Turnbow
Date Married: Unknown
Died: January 9, 1921
Buried: Beech Grove Cemetery in Graves County, Kentucky
Inscription on Monument:

T. P. Boyd
Born: June 27, 1832
Died: January 9, 1921
Asleep in Jesus
He lived to be 88 years, 6 months, and 12 days of age.

Mary Elizabeth Turnbow

Born: September 12, 1837
Place: Calloway County, Kentucky
Married: Thomas Pressly Boyd
Date Married: Unknown
Died: February 4, 1888
Buried: Beech Grove Cemetery

Inscription on Monument:

Mary E.
Wife of T. P. Boyd
Born: September 12, 1837
Died: February 4, 1888
50 years, 4 months, 22 days
Behold this grave it doth embrace
A virtuous wife with Rachel's comely face
Sarah's obedience, Lydia's open heart
With Martha's care and Mary's better part

It is believed that Thomas Pressly was born in Kentucky, as shown on the 1850 census, but apparently his marriage record lists Carroll County, Tennessee, as his birth place. Family lore has it that he was born in a log cabin about two miles south of Protemus in Calloway County. When he was a young child, his family moved a few hundred feet away into another log cabin, which I visited in the late 1950s and early 1960s. At that time, additions had been built onto the log cabin, and it was known as "the Virgil Lassiter place." By the year 2000, the original log cabin had been preserved on the same farm, now owned by Dr. John Thomas Murdock, a descendent of Hugh Spence Boyd.

34

Children of Thomas Pressly Boyd and Mary Elizabeth Turnbow

Thomas Pressly married Mary Elizabeth Turnbow, daughter of Lewis and Mary Gray Turnbow, who lived nearby in Protemus. The newlyweds settled between Protemus and Bell City, near Mount Pleasant Cumberland Presbyterian Church. Mary Elizabeth was five years younger than Thomas Pressly. They had eleven children, six girls and five boys. They were:

Mary Jane Belvedere Boyd, born January 14, 1857; died June 2, 1936. Married John Leech Yarbrough, July 28, 1874, and had thirteen children. Lived near Boaz, Kentucky, between Mayfield and Paducah.

Rosa Azalee Boyd, born September 19, 1858; died March 5, 1941. Married William J. Gregory in 1874. Lived in Mayfield and had five children, including twins who died as infants. Their son William Voris Gregory was a U.S. congressman from western Kentucky from 1927 until his death in 1936. Another son, Noble Jones Gregory, was elected to replace his brother and served in Congress from 1936 to 1959.

William Ether Boyd, born April 7, 1860; died October 28, 1938. Married Virginia Emma Dulaney in December 1883, and had eight children.

Thomas Jefferson Boyd, born March 3, 1862; died December 7, 1961. Married Willie Amanda Alice Jones December 7, 1887, and had seven children. They lived in South Graves County, Kentucky, near my grandfather, so I knew Uncle Jeff and his family better than I did any of the other brothers and sisters of my grandfather.

Sissie Boyd, born March 8, 1864; died November 6, 1864. Buried in Jetton Cemetery. Apparently never named.

Lewis Grey Boyd (my grandfather), born January 19, 1866; died December 31, 1948. Married Hattie Murphy, March 20, 1892, and had four children. Lived in South Graves County near Tri City (see chapter 36).

John Broach Boyd, born June 8, 1868; died October 31, 1947. Married Nancy (Nannie) Furchess, December 24, 1893, and had four children. Lived near Sinking Springs Baptist Church in Calloway County between Lynn Grove and Murray, Kentucky.

Pernecia Boyd, born April 11, 1871; died July 6, 1957. Married I. W. (Newton) Rogers, November 1888, and had two children. Lived in Florida for several years.

Sally Boyd, born June 25, 1873; died March 25, 1957. Married Ernest Furchess, December 6, 1893, and had four children.

Rachel R. Boyd, born March 7, 1876; died November 3, 1963. Married William Wayne Howard, December 6, 1893, and had two children.

Walter Boyd, born April 20, 1878; died March 27, 1947. Married Sallie Harding, December 26, 1900, and had one daughter. Lived in Oklahoma.

Mary Elizabeth (Turnbow) Boyd died at fifty years of age. One child (Sissie) had died; six children ranging from ten to twenty-two years of age were still living at home when she died. Pernecia, at age seventeen, was married nine months after her mother died. Four years later my grandfather was married at age twenty-six, and the next year (1893) three of the other children, John (age twenty-five), Sally (age twenty), and Rachel (age seventeen), were married during the same month. Sally and Rachel, in fact, were both married on the same day: December 6, 1893. Eighteen days later John Boyd married Nannie Furchess, who was a sister to Ernest Furchess (whom Sally Boyd married).

35

Children of
Thomas Pressly Boyd and
Pamelia Lassiter Baugh

L ooking back at these events after 100 years, one might suspect that the rash of marriages occurred because their father,
Thomas Pressly Boyd, was getting married again. However, that is
pure speculation on my part and apparently not the case. Thomas
Pressly did remarry, and that has been a rich story passed through
succeeding generations. His second wife was Pamelia Lassiter
Baugh, born October 11, 1867; died January 13, 1944. Her son,
Arthur Baugh, was born December 9, 1888. Her husband had
died, and she and Thomas Pressly were married about 1897, exact
date unknown. They had three children:

Minnie Grover Boyd, born August 30, 1898; died in 1987. Married Sam
Easley. Lived in Mayfield, Kentucky. (Minnie was younger than Daddy,
and I remember her.)

Maggie Boyd, born April 22, 1899; died October 16, 1899. Buried in Jetton
Cemetery.

B. Knox Boyd, born August 19, 1900; died December 19, 1980, in Costa Mesa,
California. Married Hattie Newberry.

The only story I recall hearing about Thomas Pressly was that
he married a young widow who was thirty years old when he was
sixty-five. Some say he took her to Pike's Peak on their honey-

moon, while others say the trip came after their three children were born. In any event, it was the trip to Pike's Peak that is the embellished part of the story passed down through the years. This was before paved roads, and cars were very rare in the countryside. Railroads were the modern mode of travel.

Shortly after the sixth child (my grandfather) was born, in 1866, Thomas Pressly and Mary Elizabeth moved to Graves County. The land purchased was north of Boyd's Crossing near Tri City. My brother, Nelson, formerly owned a portion of the original farm owned by Thomas Pressly. My grandfather's farm was located just across the road. The farm was self-sufficient, with tobacco as a cash crop, fruit trees, cows for milk and meat, and sheep for wool.

A story recently passed to me by Margaret Howard Adams was that Lewis, my grandfather, was responsible for the sheep. Once he was holding an older ewe so she would allow the lamb to nurse. Something spooked the ewe, and Grandpa was trying to hold onto her as she ran out of the barn. The commotion roused Thomas Pressly, who saw Grandpa's gray coat through the thick fog and thought a wild animal was after his sheep. He got his gun to kill the wolf when Grandpa moved just in time for Thomas Pressly to see that it was his son in the line of fire.

A tradition attributed to Thomas Pressly was that at the first snow each winter he would make a snowball and, barefooted, carry it around the house. This was a sign of health for the winter. I remember Daddy going outside barefooted and wading around in the fresh snow. Then he would come inside to warm those red feet by the fire. This always amazed me, as I could never understand how he could endure the cold snow on his bare feet. The tradition stopped with him.

When Uncle Jeff—Thomas Jefferson—got married in December 1887, he and his bride lived with T. P. and Mary Elizabeth and their six other children. Soon after they were married, Uncle Jeff came in complaining of a fever and an itchy feeling. His mother looked at him and said, "Jeffie, you have the measles, and I will take it and it will kill me." This is indeed what happened, and Mary Elizabeth Boyd died with pneumonia on February 4, 1888.

Thomas Pressly had a big bay horse to pull his buggy, which was always neat and clean. The buggy was kept in a buggy house with a raised wood floor and special rack for the harness. T. P. and Mary Elizabeth were devout members of Beech Grove Cumberland Presbyterian Church, where he served as clerk of session for several years.

Apparently all but one of the children were married by the time Thomas Pressly married again. However, it seems that all were quite unhappy when he announced that he was marrying the young widow with a nine-year-old son. Soon after the marriage, it became evident that Walter Boyd, who was nineteen, could not get along with the new bride's son, Arthur Baugh, so Walter went to live with my grandfather and grandmother. Walter headed out west in about 1900 and did quite well in Oklahoma City in the booming oil business.

A family reunion was held at the Yarbrough residence in Lone Oak, Kentucky, in 1931, and honored Mrs. B. L. Yarbrough and Walter Boyd, brother and sister, who hadn't seen each other in thirty-one years. Among the multitudes attending were my grandparents (Mr. and Mrs. L. G. Boyd) and Mother and Daddy, as well as Nelson and me. Of course, having been three years old at the time, I do not remember this event, but I do remember going to Daddy's cousin Silas Yarbrough's house near Lone Oak with the Boyd clan about ten years later.

The will of T. P. Boyd included all of the children and his widow. In item number 1, he directed the executor to

> . . . pay my son Walter Boyd $60 and to my son Knox Boyd $600. I have heretofore made gifts to all my children except Knox Boyd, and these two gifts are made for the purpose of making all of my children share equally in the distribution of my property. Item #2—I give to my wife P. A. Boyd

all livestock, farming implements, vehicles, provisions and family supplies, and household and kitchen furniture. I also desire that she shall have for her use and occupancy so long as she shall live and remain unmarried, one-third of all real estate. It is my further desire that as long as she shall remain my widow she shall have the income from my stock in the First National Bank at Mayfield, Kentucky. Item #3—My grandson, W. V. Gregory, has assisted me in looking after my business matters and has never made any charge for his services, and in appreciation it is my desire that he shall have the old wooden clock which was once owned by my father John Boyd. Item #4—After satisfying all of the foregoing bequests, it is my desire that all of the balance of my estate shall be divided equally among 12 children, viz, Belvie Yarbrough, Azalee Gregory, W. E. Boyd, T. J. Boyd, L. G. Boyd, John B. Boyd, Pernecy Rogers, Sallie Furchess, Rachel Howard, Walter Boyd, Minnie Easley, and Knox Boyd.

A more complete record on the descendants of John Boyd and of Thomas Pressly Boyd is in an unpublished booklet entitled "The Life and Times of Maude Lee Boyd and Her Descendants," which was researched, compiled, and printed by Margaret Howard Adams (her daughter, at 65 Noonan Lane, Hickman, Kentucky, 42050). Her booklet was completed in the mid- to late 1990s. Also, a rather detailed listing of the Thomas Pressly (Preston) Boyd descendants is in a book entitled *Turnbow—Turnbough Family of U.S.A.*, compiled by Olive G. Stone. The author was Olive Louise Guymon, born July 8, 1908, in Huntington, Utah. Her mother was Mary Daisy Turnbow, born in 1887 in Troup, Texas, a daughter of John Lexington Turnbow. Olive Louise married Clifton Blackburn in 1932 and had two children. On November 23, 1938, she married Lawrence Edward Stone in Provo, Utah. They had three children born in Provo, Utah:

Kenneth Lawrence Stone, born October 10, 1939.
Elva Lucille Stone, born November 27, 1942.
David Charles Stone, born July 16, 1944.

L. G. Boyd and three of his children—Clarice, Tola,
Ethel (daughter-in-law), and Bernice.

The Turnbow book by Mrs. Olive Stone is not indexed for libraries, and neither a date of publication nor a publisher is listed. Mother is pictured in the book as one who helped materially in gathering information on the Turnbows (as her immediate ancestors) and on Mary Elizabeth Turnbow (as the Boyd ancestors). Mother worked relentlessly and accurately on these records in the 1960s after she and Daddy moved to Murray. She kept me informed and shared some of the records she'd compiled for Mrs. Stone. Mrs. Stone gave a copy of the book to Mother, and she wanted me to have the book. It is truly a special possession to me.

36

Children of Lewis Gray Boyd and Hattie Murphy

There is no official recording of the more recent ancestors and descendants of my branch of the family tree, so I am listing them numerically, commencing with my grandfather, Lewis Gray Boyd.

1.0 **Lewis Gray Boyd,** born January 19, 1866, in Calloway County (or Graves County), Kentucky; died December 31, 1948, in Graves County, Kentucky. Buried in Beech Grove Cemetery. Married Hattie Murphy March 20, 1892, in Graves County, Kentucky.
• **Hattie Murphy,** born September 26, 1869, in Calloway County, Kentucky; died January 31, 1955. Buried in Beech Grove Cemetery. Daughter of Lafayette Murphy and Rebecca Turner.

1.1 **Bernice B. Boyd,** born March 25, 1893, in Graves County, Kentucky; died November 11, 1979, in Calloway County, Kentucky. Buried at Highland Park Cemetery, Mayfield, Kentucky. Married Ethel Belle Turnbow, September 29, 1912, in Fulton, Kentucky.
• **Ethel Belle Turnbow,** born May 12, 1893, in Graves County, Kentucky; died August 26, 1976, in Calloway County, Murray, Kentucky. Buried at Higland Park Cemetery, Mayfield, Kentucky. Daughter of Isaac Jefferson Turnbow and Mary Minerva Page (see chapter 37).

1.2 **Tola Boyd**, born January 13, 1895, in Graves County, Kentucky;
died October 13, 1973. Buried at Highland Park Cemetery in
Mayfield, Kentucky. Married Jasper Stoe Wheeler, February 8,
1925, at Cuba, Kentucky.
• **Jasper Stoe Wheeler**, born December 16, 1892; died 1964.
Buried at Highlands Park Cemetery in Mayfield, Kentucky. Son of
Alvin D. Wheeler and Etta Stroup of Tri City, Kentucky.

1.3 **Clarice Boyd**, born May 26, 1897; died June 11, 1970. Buried in
Beech Grove Cemetery, Graves County, Kentucky. Married Thomas
Ray, October 14, 1932.

1.31 **Ruth Elizabeth Ray**, born July 14, 1934; died January 22, 1982.
Buried in Beech Grove Cemetery, Graves County, Kentucky.
Married William Thomas Evitts, May 24, 1952.
• **William "Tommy" Evitts**, born March 30, 1933, in Henry County,
Paris, Tennessee. Son of Charles Clyde Evitts and Irene Byars of Bell
City, Kentucky.
(William Thomas Evitts married Katherine Elaine DeHoney, May
30, 1983, at Louisville, Kentucky.
Katherine Elaine DeHoney, born April 12, 1948, in Pineville,
Kentucky. Daughter of Willian Wayne DeHoney and Lealice Bishop
of Madisonville, Kentucky, and Louisville, Kentucky.)

1.311 **Thomas Mark Evitts**, born December 23, 1961, at Mayfield,
Kentucky. Married Robin Elizabeth Weber, May 3, 1999, at Tarpon
Springs, Florida.
• **Robin Elizabeth Weber**, born September 12, 1969, at Mt.
Clemens, Michigan. Daughter of William Barrett Weber and Helen
Marie Holencik at New Port Richey, Florida.

1.3111 **Thomas Hunter Evitts**, born January 10, 1995, at Tarpon Springs,
Florida.

1.3112 **Sydney Gabrielle Evitts**, born October 27, 1996, at Nashville,
Tennessee.

1.312 **Tonya Rhnee Evitts**, born August 2, 1972, at Jeffersonville,
Indiana. Married Christopher Nolan Towles, March 23, 1996, at
Louisville, Kentucky.

> • **Christopher Nolan Towles,** born October 9, 1971, in Lexington, Kentucky. Son of Ronald Dean Towles and June Katherine Burrows of Georgetown, Kentucky.
>
> 1.32 **Jetta Sue Ray,** born June 6, 1936; died June 9, 1938. Buried in Beech Grove Cemetery, Graves County, Kentucky.
>
> 1.4 **Irene Boyd,** born March 15, 1903; died March 18, 1933. Buried in Beech Grove Cemetery, Graves County, Kentucky. Never married.

As the youngest child in the family, seven years younger than my brother and thirteen years younger than my sister, I was denied valuable information and precious memories of siblings and ancestors. I have mentioned earlier the paucity of memories about Kathleen at home (other than the day she left to get married when I was four years old). I never had the opportunity to talk meaningfully with any of my grandparents beyond my teenage years, and, of course, teenagers have little or no interest in such matters as family history.

I had wondered many times where the Lewis and Grey came from in my grandfather's name. But it took me seventy-five years to learn that his maternal grandfather was named Lewis Turnbow and that the maiden name of his maternal grandmother was Mary Gray. It is natural to assume that he was named after his grandparents, just as I was named after my grandfathers, Lewis Boyd and Jefferson Turnbow.

One mystery still remains, and that is the spelling of his name as "Lewis" versus the spelling of my name as "Louis." Moreover, for years I have seen his middle name spelled as both Gray and Grey. As customary years ago, especially in the south, young people were called by their initials, and for many this continued on into adulthood. Grandpa Boyd was known as L. G., and I was called L. J. until I was in high school. So there wasn't much occasion to be concerned about my full name nor how it was spelled.

My guess is that when Dr. C. H. Jones, the birthing doctor, filled out my birth certificate, he wrote my name as Louis, and thus it

L. G. Boyd (1866–1948).

became official without any regard to ancestral history. Mrs. Easton A. Terrell, an accomplished educator and graduate of Purdue University, was our English teacher and mother of one of our classmates. When she asked what L. J. stood for and received the answer, she said, "Oh, you have the French spelling for Louis." With our country-school lack of exposure to literature and history, I did not know what she was talking about. But from that day when she called me Louie it replaced L. J. as my name.

Some records list that Grandpa Boyd was born in Graves County, but I believe he was born in Calloway County just before T. P. and Mary Elizabeth moved to Graves County. I have no information on his younger days on the farm or of how he and my grandmother met. I don't know where Grandma Boyd (Hattie Murphy) lived, but I presume it was in Calloway County near Protemus because her ancestors are buried at Young Cemetery west of Lynn Grove, Kentucky, on Highway 94.

After I returned from the army, soon after Grandma Boyd had her stroke in 1947, I remember her telling me that her family was from Murphy, North Carolina. She was paralyzed and totally bedridden and could not speak well. But after Becky and I were married she told Becky that her (Grandma Boyd's) mother was also named Rebecca. A story that I heard in later years was that her family had moved from North Carolina and settled in west Tennessee. Her brother, while playing, had thrown a rock and killed a playmate. Apparently the public pressure was so great that the family pulled up stakes and moved to Kentucky.

When L. G. Boyd and Hattie Murphy were married, on March 20, 1892, they lived in a log cabin across the road from the T. P. Boyd home on land that was part of the T. P. Boyd farm. This land was purchased from S. B. Adair on February 19, 1881, by T. P. Boyd. Records show that 100 acres were deeded to L. G. Boyd in 1893 or 1894, and 73 acres to J. B. Boyd in 1894. Apparently these two brothers purchased the land from their father shortly after they married. L. G. Boyd purchased the J. B. Boyd land in

1900, and he purchased the remainder of the T. P. Boyd farm from the other heirs to the T. P. Boyd estate in 1925. The deed was signed by W. E. Boyd and wife, T. J. Boyd and wife, Belvie Yarbrough, Pernecia Rogers and husband, Sallie Furchess and husband, Rachel Howard and husband, John Boyd and wife, Walter Boyd and wife, Azalee Gregory, Knox Boyd, and Minnie Easley and husband. The total amount of land was approximately 240 acres owned by L. G. Boyd at his death in 1948.

Daddy (Bernice) was born in the little cabin that Grandpa built when he got married. Perhaps Aunt Tola was also born there. However, in the late 1890s the cabin was moved about 300 yards north and additional rooms were built around it. The resulting house was rebuilt and added to in 1935, and thus became the house I remember. It had two separate upstairs—which did not connect on the second floor—one for the boys and one for the girls. There was a porch around the back of the house and all across the front. This house never had electricity or indoor plumbing. No one lived in the house after the mid-1950s, so it deteriorated rapidly, but portions of the house and roof remained in 2003.

The iron fence that once surrounded Grandpa Boyd's house is now at Nelson's house, located at The Highlands Golf Course on the Cuba Highway south of Mayfield. The front door of Grandpa Boyd's house, as well as the ten-inch baseboard from one room, are in our house, built in 1988 in Bogart, Georgia.

L. G. Boyd and Hattie lived a simple, conservative life. He never owned or drove a car. He never rode a train and never traveled more than fifty miles from his birthplace. The few groceries they purchased consisted of flour, sugar, and salt in large quantities. He never had a bank account. Just a few days before Grandpa died he asked Daddy to bring in his ragged, weather-worn denim jumper (jacket), which had been hanging on the back porch for years. As directed, Daddy looked in a pocket and found a wad of hundred-dollar bills. Daddy counted them and said, "You have forty bills [$4,000]. Grandpa said, "No, there are forty-one." But there were

L. G. and Hattie Boyd, fiftieth anniversary, 1942.

only forty, so apparently one had disappeared. In those days hundred-dollar bills were very rare. It is a mystery how he accumulated that many, since he rarely traveled even to the local country stores.

It was believed to be common practice for farm families to bury money in glass fruit jars. After Grandpa's place was vacated, it was rumored that people came and dug in the garden looking for "hidden treasure." It is certain that the mantels in the house were ripped off the walls by vandals looking for money. Also the beautiful railing for a winding staircase was taken.

Despite his quiet, ultra-conservative lifestyle, Grandpa Boyd still ended up buying out his "successful" siblings and owning all the land formerly owned by his father, T. P. Boyd.

I understood he was a very hard worker, but I never saw him work. My sparse memory of him was limited to the last fifteen years of his life, when I was five to twenty years old. Almost every time I would see him he would be on the front porch in a rocking chair or sitting by the fireplace. I would go with Daddy in the wagon in the spring to plow and prepare the garden and in the fall to cut wood for the fireplace during the winter and for stove wood for cooking throughout the year. I remember once Daddy wanted me to drive the mules with the loaded wagon to take the wood to the house. I told Daddy I couldn't drive the mules through the woods. Grandpa was on the wagon with me, and he said, "I can do it," so he grabbed the reins from me and drove the mules.

Most of my contact with him was on Sundays. There was preaching only one Sunday a month at Beech Grove Cumberland Presbyterian Church, and frequently we would go and take him. Occasionally, the pastor at Beech Grove would come by on Sunday afternoon while the family was sitting on the front porch. He would visit briefly, and then he, Grandpa, and Daddy would go into the living room. It took me a while to discover that they were going in there to pray.

Grandma Boyd was a Baptist, and occasionally we would take her to the Bell City Baptist Church or she would go with Aunt Tola and Uncle Jap, who lived just down the road. Whenever we took them to church, it meant a big Sunday dinner at the huge table in the kitchen.

On other Sundays, we would go there to visit on Sunday afternoons. The routine was always the same. I would get to see the funny paper because we did not get a Sunday paper at home. This was a real treat, and in the summer when the family was gathered on the front porch I became the entertainer, standing on my head or doing other crazy, awkward antics in the front yard. I was the only one there my age, so there was no competition. A favorite place to visit was the buggy shed, which was a nice enclosed building with a wooden floor and wooden ramp into the shed. Everything was neat and orderly, with a sparkling buggy inside in my earliest years. However, I never saw anyone use the buggy and cannot recall when it disappeared from the shed. Another usual activity in the spring would be to go back to the creek and look at the fox den. Many times we would see the baby foxes playing outside the den.

I have only one faint memory of Aunt Irene, and that was seeing her in a single bed in the front room. I'm sure it was shortly before she died, but I don't remember anything about her death or a funeral. Within three or four years after Aunt Irene died, her sister Clarice got divorced, and she came back with two children to live with her parents. She was there until the sickness and death of Grandpa Boyd broke up the household. The second child of Clarice's was sickly and died at a young age. The only time I ever spent the night at my grandparents' house was the night that "Baby" Sue died.

Daddy and Mother married at nineteen years of age, but his sisters were much older when they married. Aunt Tola was thirty years old, and Clarice was thirty-five. Irene, who died of tuberculosis at thirty years, was never married. Aunt Tola's husband, Jap

Wheeler, was a neighbor living at Tri City about one mile north. His father, Alvin D. Wheeler, was killed when Uncle Jap was nineteen years old. Alvin was working in the tobacco field, and a neighbor rode up on a horse and shot him with a shotgun. He is buried at Lebanon Church of Christ Cemetery at Sedalia, Kentucky. His tombstone reads:

Alvin D. Wheeler
February 18, 1864, June 24, 1912
Assassinated by Rufus Billington, who
was given a life sentence

I do not remember when Uncle Jap's Mother, Etta Stroup Wheeler, died in 1935, but I remember an event soon afterward. He and his brother, Harvey, did not get along, and I presume there was a problem over the estate. We were visiting Uncle Jap and Aunt Tola on a Sunday afternoon when Harvey picked up Uncle Jap to go and select a tombstone for their Mother. Aunt Tola kept saying that Uncle Jap might not get back, so I was really scared.

Uncle Jap and Aunt Tola did not have any children, so I got special attention. They lived in a little house that Daddy and Mother had built on the L. G. Boyd farm when they got married in 1912. The house was located on the south edge of the farm, just across the road (what is now Kentucky Highway 97, or Mayfield-Paris Road) from Sugar Hill School. That is where all the Boyds went to school after Thomas Pressly moved there in 1866.

When the one-room schools in Graves County were consolidated in 1935, Uncle Jap bought the Sugar Hill School building at auction and used the lumber to build a house at Tri City. It was on a small plot of land that had been a part of the Wheeler farm. But they never lived in the new house. They continued to live and farm there on Grandpa Boyd's place.

I have very little recollection of Clarice's husband, Tom Ray. I remember going to their house only once, which was probably after the second child was born. It seemed to be "many" miles away near the Kentucky-Tennessee state line, and was a two-room tenant house on a farm. Within a year or so, Clarice and Tom were divorced, and she and the two girls went to live with Grandpa and Grandma Boyd. I remember Mother saying that when Clarice left, Tom told her that if anything happened to either of the children not to come to him for any help. And Baby Sue did die about a year later. Clarice graduated from high school at Sedalia at thirty-three years of age—it was common in those days for graduates to be older. She got married two years later.

My brother, Nelson, remembered more about our grandfather because he was older than me. He relates that Grandpa Boyd was the toughest man he had ever seen. Even though Grandpa was a small man—only 5' 8" and 140 pounds—those who had grown up around him and others who lived in the neighborhood told Nelson about his ruggedness. When he would go to the field to plow, he would take two mules. When one would get tired, he would switch them and keep working with the fresh, rested mule. He never took water to the field and never owned a water jug. When he came in for lunch he would drink an excessive amount of water and not drink any more until he quit work and came in for supper. That was the way the work animals were managed on the farm: they would drink water from the pond before going to the field and again at noon, when they would be fed and watered. But despite extreme heat and perspiration, they would not have any more water until the work day ended. I often wondered if this might have been the reason Grandpa did not drink water while working, so he would endure the same conditions as his mules.

Nelson cannot remember when Grandpa farmed, as he retired when he was in his early fifties. But Nelson is convinced that Grandpa shortened his life by overworking. He never owned a pair of gloves, and on cold days he would saw wood without any covering on his hands. In later years, the fireplace was converted to burn coal instead of heating with wood. Frequently, a red-hot, live coal would fall from the grate onto the hearth and he would pick it up with his bare hand and put it back in the fire.

Once, when Nelson was about eight years old, he was at Grandpa's house while Daddy was working in a field nearby. He and Grandpa walked down the road to the field and as Grandpa was crossing a fence, he waded through a thick growth of poison ivy. Nelson stopped and said that he could not go through it because he was allergic to it. Just then, Grandpa reached down, pulled several leaves of poison ivy, put them in his mouth, chewed them up, and spit them out. This left a lasting impression on an eight-year-old.

Apparently Grandpa never owned a toothbrush and never went to a dentist. Yet he had most of his teeth at his death at age eighty-three. After each meal he would go to his chair by the fireplace or the rocker on the porch, get out a piece of chicken feather, and pick his teeth.

The will of L. G. Boyd stipulated that his son Bernice (my daddy) would get the fifty acres L. G. had first purchased from him, and also the home place, consisting of about ninety acres. The balance of his property of 100 acres was given to Tola for five years after his death; then it became the property of Bernice. The house where Aunt Tola lived and a small tract of land were given to her as long as she lived, after which it became the property of Bernice. L. G. gave $300 to his daughter Clarice and $200 to her daughter, Ruth Ray. Grandma Boyd had use of the home place as long as she lived. The will was dated October 4, 1943, just six years before he died. Nelson remembered that Grandpa asked him to take him to Mayfield, but no one knew until after his death why he wanted to go or what he did there.

No one ever knew why he structured the will the way he did, either. Although we were away from Graves County (living in Lexington; Champaign, Illinois; and Knoxville, Tennessee) for the decade after Grandpa died, I know it was not a happy time for my parents or for Daddy's sisters. Grandma Boyd had been bedridden for about two years before Grandpa died. Mother had been going about eight miles every other night during that time and staying with Grandma Boyd, and also caring for Grandpa as his health declined. Soon after Grandpa died, Mother and Daddy moved Grandma to their house, and Mother took care of her day and night for about five years, when Mother's health faltered. She had to have emergency surgery, which resulted in a prolonged staph infection. Daddy had to move Grandma into a nursing home in Mayfield, where she remained until her death in January 1955.

Shortly after Grandpa died, Uncle Jap and Aunt Tola bought a house in Sedalia and moved from the farm. I presume they also sold the house they had built in Tri City. Poor Clarice had nothing and no place to go.

I am confident that Daddy was more saddened by the will than either of his sisters were. He tried desperately to be helpful to Clarice. Aunt Tola lived for nine years after Uncle Jap died. Aunt Tola had also written a will, which is another story. She named N. L. Galloway, a neighbor, as executor. However, after she died it was discovered that there had been no witnesses for the will, so it was invalidated. Clarice had died before Aunt Tola, so this left Daddy as heir to her estate. But Daddy wanted Ruth (Clarice's daughter) to have everything.

The attorney handling the will called Nelson and said, "This is highly unethical, but I want you to know what your Daddy is trying to do. He has inherited his sister's estate, but he won't take it." Nelson called me, and we quickly decided that Daddy should be allowed to do what he wanted to do, and that is exactly what he did—he gave the estate to Ruth and her husband. I feel certain that this was Daddy's effort to try to compensate for the exclusion of Clarice in Grandpa Boyd's will. In addition, he did make a contribution to the Bible College at Mayfield and to Sedalia Baptist Church from the estate.

Ruth died eight years later in 1982, at age forty-eight. With the loss of my two aunts (Tola and Clarice), my cousin Ruth, and my parents, I had lost track of Ruth's family. In November 2003 I learned that Nelson had an old address of the church in Clarksville, Indiana, where Ruth's husband, Tommy Evitts, was pastor. I looked him up on the Internet and located him in Clarksville. Following a reuniting phone call, we stopped by to visit him on the way to Beve's home in Carmel, Indiana, for Thanksgiving 2003.

I was so pleased to learn that after he and Ruth were married in 1952, he had pastored two Baptist churches in Kentucky, three in Illinois, and two in Indiana. He and Ruth had two children, and I got to meet their daughter Tonya, who was thrilled to learn more about her mother's family. Following Ruth's death, Tommy had married Kathy DeHoney, who was the daughter of Dr. Wayne DeHoney, pastor of the Walnut Street Baptist Church in Louisville, Kentucky. Tommy and Kathy then moved to Clarksville, Indiana, where he pastored the First Baptist Church until retirement. Tommy was highly complimentary of Daddy and Mother and credited Daddy as being very instrumental in his going to seminary.

Apparently the children of L. G. Boyd and Hattie Murphy had no middle names, which was unusual in those days. There is no record of a middle name for Tola, Clarice, Irene, or Daddy. His name was Bernice only, but he later added the initial B. so his initials would be B. B. B. This was probably done about the time he and Mother were married. I became aware that the full name or middle initial was important in the identity of a person when I went into service. If a soldier did not have a middle name or initial, he was assigned "NMI," meaning "no middle initial." In my case, my name would have become Louis NMI Boyd.

❧ **37** ❧

Children of
Bernice Boyd and
Ethel Belle Turnbow

1.1 **Bernice B. Boyd**, born March 25, 1893; died November 11, 1979. Married Ethel Belle Turnbow, September 29, 1912.
Ethel Belle Turnbow, born May 10, 1893; died August 28, 1976.

1.11 **Mary Kathleen Boyd**, born December 1, 1915, in Graves County, Kentucky; died April 6, 1991. Buried at Sinking Springs Cemetery, Calloway County, Kentucky. Married Sylvester Paschall, February 25, 1933, at Metropolis, Illinois.
• **Sylvester Paschall**, born April 2, 1912, Calloway County, Kentucky; died August 15, 1983. Buried at Sinking Springs Cemetery, Calloway County, Kentucky. Son of Barney Paschall and Mary Jones.

1.111 **Gedric Boyd Paschall**, born February 6, 1937, in Calloway County, Kentucky. Married Norma Lee Elkins December 22, 1962.
• **Norma Lee Elkins**, born January 14, 1942. Daughter of James Oralee Elkins and Rubie Tabors, of Almo, Kentucky.

1.1111 **Stanley Boyd Paschall**, born December 22, 1963. Married Michele Lockhart April 4, 1992.
• **Michele Lockhart**, born November 11, 1967, in Trigg County, Kentucky. Daughter of Bill G. Lockhart and Donna Anderson.

1.11111 **Heatherly Boyd Paschall**, born August 29, 1994, at Lourdes Hospital in Paducah, Kentucky.

Bernice Boyd and Ethel Turnbow, wedding portrait, 1912.

1.11112 **Abigail Lockhart Paschall**, born September 30, 1997, at Murray–
Calloway County Hospital in Murray, Kentucky.

1.1112 **Stacy Lee Paschall**, born August 21, 1970, in Calloway County,
Kentucky. Married Brian Thomas Mills January 16, 1993.
• **Brian Thomas Mills**, born May 2, 1968, in Hopkins County,

Kentucky. Son of Thomas Mills and LaJean Robinson, of Madisonville, Kentucky.

1.11121 **Bryce Thomas Mills**, born October 24, 1994, in Nashville, Tennessee.

 1.112 **Martha Deane Paschall**, born June 7, 1946, in Calloway County, Kentucky. Died July 29, 2004. Buried at Puryear City Cemetery in Puryear, TN. Married Bonnie Joe (B. J.) Nance, August 8, 1968, at Sinking Springs Baptist Church in Calloway County, Kentucky.
 • **Bonnie Joe (B. J.) Nance**, born December 7, 1946, in Henry County, Tennessee. Son of Thomas Franklin Nance and Sarah Murphy Darnell. Died August 30, 2002. Buried at Puryear City Cemetery in Puryear, Tennessee.

1.1121 **Stephen Keith Nance**, born March 26, 1971, at Murray–Calloway County Hospital in Murray, Kentucky. Married Maria Kathleen Hoover, December 30, 1991, at Murray–Calloway County Courthouse in Murray, Kentucky.
 • **Maria Kathleen Hoover**, born January 20, 1969, in South Ricelip, England. Daughter of John Lamar Hoover and Doris June Whitaker, of Clarkson, Kentucky.

1.11211 **Riley Kathleen Nance**, born July 21, 1992, at Murray–Calloway County Hospital in Murray, Kentucky.

1.11212 **Austin Evan Nance**, born December 22, 1996, at the Medical Center in Bowling Green, Kentucky.

1.1122 **Anthony Eric Nance**, born March 25, 1975, at Murray–Calloway County Hospital, in Murray, Kentucky. Married Ginger Rae Hoofman December 16, 2000, at the Greystone in Paris, Tennessee.
 • **Ginger Rae Hoofman**, born June 26, 1979, at Murray–Calloway Hospital in Murray, Kentucky. Daughter of Carl Ray Hoofman and Pamela Rose Melton of Mansfield, Henry County, Tennessee.

1.11221 **Bonnie Elizabeth Nance**, born February 13, 2004, at Henry County Medical Center in Paris, Tennessee.

 1.113 **Mary Belle Paschall**, born July 13, 1947, in Calloway County, Kentucky. Married Jerry Dan Boyd August 30, 1969.

• **Jerry Dan Boyd**, born February 21, 1948, in Henry County, Tennessee. Son of Carnol and Pauline Boyd of Puryear, Tennessee. Divorced January 1977.
Married Richard (Dick) N. Armstrong IV, January 2, 1978, in Clinton, Kentucky.
• **Richard (Dick) N. Armstrong IV**, born June 29, 1939, in New York, New York. Son of Richard Noble Armstrong III and Charlotte Klitz. Died January 17, 2001, at Mayfield, Kentucky. Buried at Murray City Cemetery, Murray, Kentucky.

1.1131 **Jeremy Damon Boyd**, born December 9, 1975, at Murray–Calloway County Hospital in Murray, Kentucky. Married Julie Ann Matheny, August 23, 2003, in Murray, Kentucky.
• **Julie Ann Matheny** is the daughter of Charles L. Matheny and Jean Wilson of Paducah, Kentucky.

1.1132 **Lynn Marie Armstrong**, born February 12, 1963, in Fulton, Kentucky. Daughter of Richard N. Armstrong and Sidney Anne Adams, who was born July 12, 1937, in Vicksburg, Mississippi. Married David Ladd Kelley, December 31, 1982, at First Methodist Church in Fulton, Kentucky.
• **David Ladd Kelley**, born May 25, 1959, in Fulton, Kentucky. Son of Larry Glen Kelley and Anita Sue Dedmon of Fulton, Kentucky.

1.11321 **Lindsey Marie Kelley**, born March 4, 1987, in Murray, Kentucky.

1.11322 **David Ladd (Lake) Kelley II**, born November 10, 1993, in Greenwood, South Carolina.

1.1133 **John Noble Armstrong**, born June 11, 1965, in Fulton, Kentucky. Son of Richard N. Armstrong and Sidney Anne Adams, who was born July 12, 1937, in Vicksburg, Mississippi. Married Tammy Althea Stringer, January 18, 1997, in Union City, Tennessee.
• **Tammy Althea Stringer** is the daughter of Emery Mayo Stringer and Althea Fisher of Columbia, Louisiana.

1.11331 **Anthony Dylan Noble Armstrong**, born October 15, 1991, in Salisbury, North Carolina. Adopted at age 10.

1.114 **Kindred Mark Paschall**, born August 30, 1957, in Calloway County, Kentucky. Married Tammy Ann Albritton, December 5,

1980, at Sinking Springs Baptist Church, Calloway County, Kentucky.

• **Tammy Ann Albritton,** born November 29, 1961, at Murray–Calloway County Hospital, Murray, Kentucky. Daughter of Sarah Ann Outland of Murray, Kentucky, and Dr. James Franklin Albritton of Memphis, Tennessee.

1.1141   **Amberly Kathryn Paschall,** born July 14, 1984, at Murray–Calloway County Hospital, Murray, Kentucky.

1.1142   **LeAnna Kaye Paschall,** born March 23, 1990, at Murray–Calloway County Hospital, Murray, Kentucky.

 1.115   **Karen Paige Paschall,** born March 13, 1952, in Calloway County, Kentucky. Married Calvin Mason Milby, January 11, 1969, at Cherry Corner Baptist Church, Calloway County, Kentucky.

• **Calvin Mason Milby,** born January 9, 1949, in Calloway County, Kentucky. Son of Baxter Calvin Milby and Martha Agnes Tarman, of Calloway County, Kentucky.

1.1151   **Michael Dale Milby,** born November 22, 1969, in Calloway County, Kentucky. Married Cara Lee Nickell, July 17, 1999, at Sinking Springs Baptist Church, Calloway County, Kentucky.

• **Cara Lee Nickell,** born March 8, 1973, in Fayette County, Kentucky. Daughter of Robert Winston Nickell and Margaret Lee Conrad, of West Liberty, Kentucky.

1.11511   **Alexandrea Nicole Milby,** born January 1, 1995, in Fayette County, Kentucky.

1.11512   **Reece Conner Milby,** born June 12, 2001, in McCracken County, Kentucky.

1.1152   **Christa Gayle Milby,** born July 16, 1973, in Calloway County, Kentucky. Married James Robert Cole II, September 28, 1996, at Sinking Springs Baptist Church, Calloway County, Kentucky.

• **James Robert Cole II,** born June 9, 1970, in Calloway County, Kentucky. Son of James Robert Cole and June Kay McKeel, of Murray, Kentucky.

1.11521   **Talon Gabriel Cole,** born December 8, 1999, in Calloway County, Kentucky.

1.12 **Bernice Nelson Boyd**, born June 11, 1921, in Graves County, Kentucky. Married Sue Mae Wilson, May 13, 1944, in Starkville, Mississippi.

• **Sue Mae Wilson**, born September 10, 1922, in Graves County, Kentucky. Daughter of Joseph Benjamin Wilson and Lillie Swann, of South Graves County, Kentucky.

1.121 **Gregory Nelson Boyd**, born January 14, 1950, in Mayfield, Kentucky. Married Martha Layne Whitlow, October 16, 1970, in Clinton, Kentucky.

• **Martha Layne Whitlow**, born January 11, 1952, in Graves County, Kentucky. Daughter of Ralph Cletus Whitlow and Pansy Murdock, of South Graves County, Kentucky.

1.1211 **Lora Elayne Boyd**, born December 10, 1971, in Murray, Kentucky. Married Anthony Wayne Searcy, December 2, 1998.

• **Anthony Wayne Searcy**, born in Carrollton, Kentucky. Son of Herbert Daniel Searcy and Sondra Jo Harmon.

1.12111 **Alayna Danielle Searcy**, born March 22, 2005, at Baptist Northeast Hospital in LaGrange, Kentucky.

1.1212 **Leslie Lynn Boyd**, born December 22, 1975, in Graves County, Kentucky. Married Dylan Williams, August 31, 2001, at Sedalia Baptist Church in Sedalia, Kentucky.

• **Dylan Brent Williams**, born September 27, 1972, in Paducah, Kentucky. Son of Gloria Key, of Mayfield, Kentucky.

1.122 **John Benjamin Boyd**, born January 22, 1955, in Mayfield, Kentucky. Married Elizabeth Anne Culpepper, December 12, 1996, in Farmington, Kentucky.

• **Elizabeth Anne Culpepper**, born May 18, 1958, in Mayfield, Kentucky. Daughter of Leon Culpepper and Suzette Jordan, of Mayfield, Kentucky.

1.1221 **Brian Leon Schuster**, born May 8, 1978, in Mayfield, Kentucky. Son of Elizabeth Anne Culpepper and John M. Schuster (married August 22, 1976). Married Melissa Siza, June 4, 2000, in Mayfield, Kentucky.

• **Melissa Siza**, born November 30, 1978, in Rio de Janerio, Brazil.

Daughter of Jamal Siza and Jeannie Balew, of Rio de Janerio, Brazil.

1.1222 **Benjamin Jordan Boyd**, born July 9, 1998, in Jackson Purchase Medical Center, Mayfield, Kentucky.

1.1223 **Lillie Anne Boyd**, born December 18, 2000, in Jackson Purchase Medical Center, Mayfield, Kentucky.

1.13 **Louis Jefferson Boyd**, born March 14, 1928, in Graves County, Kentucky (see chapter 38).

Bernice and Ethel Boyd, fiftieth anniversary, with three children and spouses.

B. B. Boyd home, built in 1937 on same site where
Ethel Turnbow and Louie Boyd were born (photo 1962).

Eleven grandchildren and great-grandson (bottom right)
of Bernice and Ethel Boyd (photo about 1965).

Ethel and Bernice Boyd and children Nelson, Kathleen, and Louie
at sixtieth wedding anniversary, 1972.

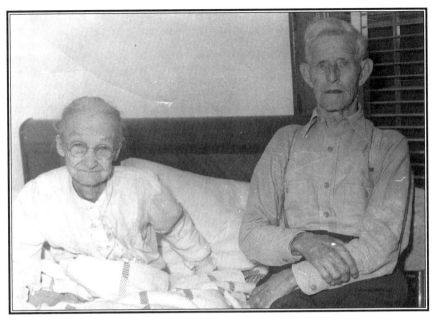

Grandma and Grandpa Bazzell, Ethel Turnbow's mother and stepfather, photographed in 1950, shortly before they died.

Louie, Aunt Nona (Ethel Turnbow Boyd's sister), Kathleen, and Nelson.

38

Children of
Louis Jefferson Boyd and
Rebecca Charlotte Conner

1.13 **Louis Jefferson Boyd**, born March 14, 1928, in Graves County,
Kentucky. Married Rebecca Charlotte Conner, June 12, 1948, at
Lebanon Church of Christ, Sedalia, Kentucky.
• **Rebecca Charlotte Conner**, born May 10, 1928, in Graves
County, Kentucky. Daughter of Walter Henry Conner and Gladys
Christine Byrd, of Cuba Road, Mayfield, Kentucky.

1.131 **Beverly Charlotte Boyd**, born September 11, 1951, in Good
Samaritan Hospital, Lexington, Kentucky. Married Timothy T.
Gallagher, June 17, 1972, in Okemos, Michigan.
• **Timothy Thomas Gallagher**, born May 7, 1951, in Carrington,
North Dakota. Son of James A. Gallagher and Charlotte Fern
Kohler of Okemos, Michigan.

1.1311 **Meghan Boyd Gallagher**, born December 13, 1977, in Elkhart, In-
diana. Married Tom Lentz, November 4, 2001, in Fischers, Indiana.
• **Thomas Joseph Lentz**, born April 30, 1976, in Indianapolis,
Indiana. Son of Robert Lentz and Patricia Hannon of Indianapolis,
Indiana.

1.13111 **Makenna Marie Lentz**, born March 24, 2004, at Sherman
Hospital, Elgin, Illinois.

1.13112 **Delaney Elizabeth Lentz**, born January 19, 2006, at Good
Shepherd Hospital, Barrington, Illinois.

Becky and Louie's parents: Walter and Gladys Conner
and Ethel and Bernice Boyd, 1971.

1.1312 **Caitlin Elizabeth Gallagher**, born June 9, 1981, in Elkhart, Indiana.

1.1313 **Travis Scott Gallagher**, born May 10, 1983, in Kalamazoo,
Michigan.

 1.132 **Beda Janine Boyd**, born October 7, 1954, in Burnham City
Hospital, Champaign, Illinois. Married Steven Francis Smith, March
22, 1975, in Athens, Georgia.
• **Steven Francis Smith**, born September 2, 1949, in Jesup,
Georgia; died November 1, 1993. Buried at Jesup, Georgia. Son of
Wendell Smith and Betty Anne (Queenie) Richardson, of Jesup,
Georgia. Divorced August 1984.
Married William Andrew Cain, April 12, 1985, in Athens, Georgia.
• **William Andrew Cain**, born September 6, 1952, at Kennesaw
Hospital, Marietta, Georgia. Son of Larry Nevin Cain and Adelaide
Elizabeth Osborne. "Addie" was adopted by Edmond and Sarah
Osborne as a young girl. Later she found her birth mother, Dolly
Hill, in California.

1.1321　**Jeremiah Francis Smith**, born November 3, 1977, at St. Mary's Hospital, Athens, Georgia. Married Kimberly Ann Bennett, June 16, 2001, at Tuckston Methodist Church, Athens, Georgia.
• **Kimberly Ann Bennett**, born February 8, 1979, in Athens, Georgia. Daughter of Gary Keith Bennett and Patricia Ann Lloyd, of Athens, Georgia.

1.1322　**David Alan Cain**, born December 25, 1977, at Kennesaw Hospital, Marietta, Georgia. Son of William Andrew Cain and Kimberly Ann Loeffler, of Marietta, Georgia.

1.1323　**Brandon Andrew Cain**, born May 16, 1980, at St. Mary's Hospital, Athens, Georgia. Son of William Andrew Cain and Kimberly Ann Loeffler. Married Jessica Amy Gongi, July 18, 2003, at Onslow County Courthouse, Jacksonville, North Carolina.
• **Jessica Amy Gongi**, born March 13, 1981, in St. Paul, Minnesota. Daughter of Louis Joseph Gongi and Jaquelin Ann Hemmesch, of St. Paul, Minnesota.

1.13231　**Kinleigh McKenna Cain**, born January 22, 2006, at Camp LeJune Naval Hospital, Jacksonville, North Carolina.

1.133　**Garth Winston Boyd**, born August 15, 1957, at East Tennessee Baptist Hospital in Knoxville, Tennessee. Married Mary Lynette Latchaw July 21, 1979, at the Y Camp of the Rockies, Fraser, Colorado.
• **Mary Lynette Latchaw**, born June 11, 1957, in Durango, Colorado. Daughter of James Lloyd Latchaw and Ruby Viola Amyx, of Fountain, Colorado.

1.1331　**Levi Latchaw Boyd**, born July 30, 1981, at St. Mary's Hospital, Athens, Georgia.

1.1332　**Kristin Charlotte Boyd**, born June 28, 1984, in Forsythe Hospital, Winston-Salem, North Carolina.

1.1333　**Cody Garth Boyd**, born December 14, 1986, in Manhattan, Kansas.

1.1334　**Garrett Winston Boyd**, born May 3, 1989, in Fort Collins, Colorado.

1.134　**Bettina Gayle Boyd**, born November 6, 1958, at University

The Boyd children—Garth, Beda, Beve, and Tina—
at Walter and Gladys Conner's sixty-fifth anniversary, 1986.

Hospital, Knoxville, Tennessee. Married Curtis Gerald Mize, July 29, 1978.

• **Curtis Gerald Mize**, born May 4, 1958, in Athens, Georgia. Son of Curtis Wofford Mize and Frances Marie Anglin, of Gainesville, Georgia.

Divorced March 1995.

1.1341 **Joshua Kelley Mize**, born November 29, 1978, at Athens General Hospital, Athens, Georgia.

1.1342 **Cameren Nichole Mize**, born August 9, 1980, in Stuttgart, Germany. Married Larry Scott Wilson, June 19, 1999, at New Haven Congregational Church, Gainesville, Georgia.

• **Larry Scott Wilson**, born October 2, 1978, in Albany, Georgia. Son of Donna Marie Whitley Merck, of Gainesville, Georgia, and Lonnie Larry Wilson, of Lula, Georgia.

1.13421 **Loganne Marie Wilson**, born June 29, 2002, in Northeast Georgia Medical Center, Gainesville, Georgia.

Again, as the youngest child, I have no information on Daddy's early years—about his growing up or what he did. And I don't know how he and mother met.

Mother and Daddy married on September 29, 1912, when they were nineteen years old. They built a two-room cabin on Grandpa Boyd's farm, where Uncle Jap and Aunt Tola lived, after they were married in 1925. Daddy farmed with Grandpa Boyd, and he bought fifty acres of land from his grandfather, T. P. Boyd, in 1917. Their first child, Kathleen, was born in that little house in 1915.

As mentioned earlier, when mother was twelve, her daddy (Jeff Turnbow), two sisters, and a brother all died within two months of each other in 1905. Six years before, an older sister had died. This left a thirty-five-year-old widow with two young daughters, Mother and Aunt Nona, who was six years old. Mother's mother later married Matthis Bazzell, whose wife had died, leaving him with two sons and three daughters. With a new stepfather and five stepsiblings, I presume it didn't take long for Mother to determine that she was ready for a new life.

After nine years in the two-room cabin on the L. G. Boyd farm, Mother and Daddy moved to her home place just before their second child, Nelson, was born. My guess is that the timing of their move had to do with Aunt Nona's coming of age (twenty-one years), at which time she and Mother could get half the farm as their father's heirs. Daddy sold his fifty acres to L. G. Boyd, and then he and Mother bought the half-interest in the farm from my grandmother, Mary Minerva Turnbow Bazzell, and the other one-fourth interest from Aunt Nona. So Mother was going back to the farm where her father and she had been born—in the same house. A new house had been built about 1900 by her father, and that is the house where I was born. The perils of paying for this farm during the droughts and economic depression of the late 1920s and early 1930s were recounted previously.

Daddy and Mother lived there for forty-one years, then sold the farm and moved to Murray shortly after their 50th wedding anniversary, which was celebrated on the farm. Daddy spent some of his "retirement" time managing Grandpa Boyd's farm, which he had inherited. After ten years, Mother and Daddy wanted to give the inherited farm to us—Kathleen, Nelson, and me. This was arranged in December 1972, just a few days before Mother had a stroke. In the division of the farm into three equal parcels, I was the last one to draw, but the home place with the buildings is what I got. I kept the farm for about twenty-five years and then sold it to John Boyd, Nelson's son. I wanted it to stay in the Boyd family—and it has now been owned by five generations of Boyds.

When Daddy died in 1979, we three children inherited the home (duplex and two lots) in Murray. After a couple of years, Becky and I bought it from Kathleen and Nelson. Handling rentals long distance was not satisfactory so we eventually gave the property to Murray State University as a Charitable Remainder Unitrust. Later, the Bernice and Ethel Boyd Scholarships will be awarded to students at that fine institution—where Becky attended in 1946–47.

When Kathleen, Nelson, and I cleared out the "old home" in 1979, Becky and I took some old pictures hanging on the wall. About fifteen years later, Becky reframed some of the pictures that had been stored in our attic and found Mother and Daddy's wedding certificate dated September 12, 1912. It was a usual practice on the farm to preserve important documents inside a framed picture. I had the certificate framed separately, perhaps for the first time, as a treasure.

I never knew where Daddy's name, Bernice, came from. And I never heard of anyone else with that name. As I was growing up and would mention my Daddy's name, people would say, "Oh, it's Berniece," which was a rather common girl's name. So I began to avoid telling people his name because I didn't want everybody to think it was feminine.

39

The Paternal Line of Louis J. Boyd

Louis Jefferson Boyd was born at Route One, Lynn Grove, Graves County, Kentucky, on March 14, 1928. He is the son of Bernice B. Boyd, who was born at Tri City, Graves County, Kentucky, on March 25, 1893, and died at Murray, Kentucky, on November 11, 1979; and Ethel Belle Turnbow, who was born at Route One, Lynn Grove, Graves County, Kentucky, on May 12, 1893, and died in Murray, Kentucky, on August 26, 1976. Bernice and Ethel were married in Fulton, Kentucky, on September 29, 1912.

Bernice B. Boyd was the son of Lewis Gray Boyd, who was born in Tri City, Graves County, Kentucky, on January 19, 1866, and died in Tri City, Graves County, Kentucky, on December 31, 1948; and Hattie Murphy, who was born in Graves County, Kentucky, on September 26, 1869, and died in Mayfield, Kentucky on January 31, 1955. Lewis and Hattie were married in Graves County, Kentucky, on March 20, 1892.

Lewis Gray Boyd was the son of Thomas Pressly Boyd, who was born in Protemus, Calloway County, Kentucky, on June 27, 1832, and died in Tri City, Graves County, Kentucky, on January 9, 1921; and Mary Elizabeth Turnbow, who was born in Kentucky on September 12, 1837, and died in Tri City, Graves County, Kentucky, on February 4, 1888. Their marriage date is unknown.

Jasper "Uncle Jap" Wheeler and Aunt Tola Boyd, wedding day.

Thomas Pressly Boyd was the son of John Boyd, who was born in South Carolina on December 25, 1807, and died in Protemus, Calloway County, Kentucky, on March 24, 1891; and Jane Montgomery, who was born in South Carolina on January 10, 1807, and died in Protemus, Calloway County, Kentucky, on August 11, 1895. John and Jane were married in South Carolina in February 1827. No information is available on the ancestors of John Boyd.

40

The Maternal Line of Louis J. Boyd

Louis Jefferson Boyd was born on March 14, 1928. He is the son of Ethel Belle Turnbow, who was born at Route One, Lynn Grove, Graves County, Kentucky, on May 12, 1893, and died at Murray, Kentucky, on August 28, 1976.

Ethel Belle Turnbow was the daughter of Isaac Jefferson Turnbow, who was born in Farmington, Graves County, Kentucky, on October 8, 1863, and died in Farmington, Graves County, Kentucky, on August 27, 1905 (buried at Antioch Cemetery); and Mary Minerva Page, who was born on December 27, 1869, and died on December 31, 1952 (buried at Antioch Church of Christ Cemetery).

Isaac Jefferson Turnbow was the son of John Turnbow, who was born in South Carolina about 1799 and died in Graves County, Kentucky, on September 24, 1892 (buried at Antioch Cemetery); and Minerva Elizabeth Goodrum, who was born in Tennessee on December 23, 1825, and died in Graves County, Kentucky, on June 30, 1900 (buried at Antioch Cemetery).

John Turnbow was the son of Isaac Turnbow (date and place of birth unknown), who died in Perry County, Alabama, on June

11, 1829; and Margaret Talkington (date and place of birth unknown), who died in Perry County, Alabama, on August 5, 1835.

Isaac Turnbow was the son of Andrew Turnbow. No additional
information is available on him or his ancestors.

41

The Ending

"May you be alive as long as you live."

—J. W. FANNING

The first draft of what this document has become was begun on a cold, rainy, wintry night in 1957 at a motel in Dickson, Tennessee. I was returning to Knoxville from the experiment station in Jackson, Tennessee. Actually, I was so proud of all that had happened to me that I just had to record it. I had been in service, just received my Ph.D., and established our first home; I was happily married, with two children and another on the way, and was just beginning my first real position. I was bubbling over!

Almost five decades later, I still want to shout from the mountain top! With Becky's apparent good health following three bouts with cancer, I tell all who will listen (and many who won't listen) just how fortunate and blessed I am.

As I did in the preface, I wish to salute my ancestors, who made it possible for my being here. Early immigrant families flocked to these shores for a distinct purpose—taking flight from famine and adversity, and seeking freedom. As prosperous descendents who have reaped the benefits of their sacrifices, we should certainly pay homage to them.

During the last six or eight decades, we in the United States have lived through (what I hope were) the worst of times but perhaps also the best of times in our country. It is doubtful whether future generations will enjoy the freedoms and world prominence that we have relished as citizens of this wonderful country. In the near future, residents of countries such as China and India may well have many of the frills we have enjoyed, and many people in our country may well encounter some of the perils and hardships they have endured during the past century.

But only you can determine how you respond to whatever confronts you in the future. As an individual you may look in the mirror one day or find yourself doing something and have that "ah-ha!" moment—"Goodness, I'm just like Mama (or just like Daddy)." And then you discover or soothe yourself by saying, "Well, that's not too bad."

At that point you look back with fond memories and greater appreciation for those who have gone before you. Actually, it's a good feeling. That's why I take great pride in being a Kentucky boy.

❧ Appendix I ❧

From ADAM to ATOM

I am confident there is an inverse relationship between the length of the introduction and the importance of the individual. The shorter the introduction, the more important the person. This holds true, as the chief official of this country is always introduced simply as "The President of the United States." Mr. Wiggins took three and a half minutes for his most generous introduction. So, you really can't expect very much from me!

While sitting here just now I overheard a feeble, but most meaningful, conversation. One of my knees said, "I ain't never held this feller up to give no speech before in front of his high school English teacher, and I'm scairt he'll really goof it up." The other knee replied, "I ain't never done that neither, so let's shake."

I wish to greet you, graduates, platform party, parents, dedicated faculty, acquaintances whom I consider dear friends, and unknown friends. The lapse of more than a quarter of a century since I felt that I knew everyone in the community brings in new faces and people I don't remember or don't know—but, really, wherever you go there are never any strangers—just friends you

By Louis J. Boyd. Presented as the 1974 commencement address at Sedalia High School, Sedalia, Kentucky.

haven't met. One thing I have noticed this evening is that the parents are much younger today than they were when I graduated. It must be the Geritol advertised on TV, and I want some of it!

As graduating seniors, this is certainly a red-letter day in your lives. And I hope you will have many more during your lifetime. I learned the meaning of "a red-letter day" here in this high school, and I am sure you are aware of what it means. If not, I hope you will take the time to look it up in the dictionary.

I especially want to salute Sandy and Carla and all those who pushed you to achieve your high distinction. That 100% is just about perfect—don't know how you improve on that very much. It is indeed admirable for any class this size in which forty-three win honorable mention. The teachers here must have learned a lot in the last twenty-five years.

I would venture a guess that in five years or less, none of you will remember who spoke at your high school commencement, and in less than a decade you will not remember a single word that was said. I am certain that this is the way it should be, because it is your graduation that is the highlighting event tonight. However, since a speaker has become accepted procedure at commencement exercises, I am distinctly honored to share this memorable occasion with you.

I dislike intensely long speeches on history, and I know you are not particularly interested in that,

or in a glowing description of the great successes of preceding generations,

or in a blistering attack on the evils of our governmental system,

or in someone trying to paint a cheerful picture of the glorious opportunities awaiting you now that you are ready to charge out into the world.

However, if I may be so bold as to solicit your attention for nineteen minutes only, I may do a little of all of these things as we consider some important issues of the past, present, and future. Frequently, we must look at the history of the past to help us chart our course for the future. If my comments deserved a title, it would be—"From A-D-A-M to A-T-O-M."

For tens of thousands of years, man's greatest need was well-developed muscles; now man's greatest need is well-developed minds. Thinking has become important! For thousands of years most people had little need and little time for thinking. They were needed to push, to shove, to lift, to haul, to carry, to till, to plow, to dig and do the multitude of hard physical jobs for which machines had not yet been invented.

Despite this massive, dawn-to-dusk drudgery by masses of human beings, people at best eked out a precarious living. Survival demanded endless physical toil and strong muscles. Education was a luxury that few could afford, and for most people, "thinking" was pointless! Today we live in a different world, where, in most instances, machines, not men, do the jobs that involve drudgery.

Let's attempt to gain a better perspective of the age in which we now live. Historians contend that man has been on earth for about 50,000 years. None of us, not even your parents, can visualize a span of 50,000 years. So, let's pretend that all man's history has been condensed into fifty years. On this basis, man's history would read like this:

1. Ten years ago, man stopped being a caveman.
2. Two years ago, Christianity was born.
3. Twenty days ago, electricity came into use.
4. Ten days ago, radio came into being.
5. Yesterday—one day ago—jet airliner service began.

The whole world as we know it would be about twenty days old.

Notice the concentration of progress in the last twenty days of a fifty-year period. For about 98% of the time man has been on earth, nothing much happened. Most of the world's scientific and technological progress happened in the lifetime of your parents. There has been more change during their lifetimes than there was in all the previous history of man, all the way back to Adam. In fact, a tremendous percentage of the world's technological and scientific progress has happened in *your* own lifetime.

It has been estimated that the volume of man's knowledge doubled in each of the following time spans:

From the time of Christ to 1750 (1700 years)
Between 1750 and 1900 (150 years)
Between 1900 and 1950 (50 years)
Between 1950 and 1960 (10 years)
Between 1960 and 1967 (7 years)

And it has the potential today to double every five years into the foreseeable future. If we are 20 months behind the time, it's like your father being 20 years behind his time, or your grandfather being 200 years behind his times.

This phenomenal progress can be illustrated in terms of the speed of travel. Originally, a caveman could travel as fast as he could run—then somewhere, sometime in antiquity, he learned to ride a horse. Despite the opinions of a lot of race fans, the speed of a horse is about 35 miles per hour. In fact, the average speed for Cannonade in his Run for the Roses earlier this month was 36.5 miles per hour.

We can review thousands of years from the caveman to Paul Revere, but during all that time the speed at which man could travel remained unchanged. More than ten centuries separated King Solomon from George Washington, yet they both lived in the same technological era. During all that time there had been no significant improvement in heating, lighting, plumbing, communications, or the speed of travel.

In 1830 a tremendous event happened that revolutionized the world. In England, a steam locomotive beat a horse in a race. The barrier was broken, and machinery started to replace muscles. Brains started to replace brawn. From 1830 to 1945 man progressed from 35 miles per hour to 470 miles per hour. But, during *your* lifetime, man leapfrogged from about 600 miles per hour to better than 18,000 miles per hour.

I cannot resist the impulse to identify one of the greatest successes ever achieved, and one that made it possible for all of this progress to be made. This is *agriculture,* which I salute with great admiration!

In the midst of the Civil War, only 110 years ago, this country took a gigantic step forward by creating the land-grant colleges, designed to make higher education available to the sons and daughters of farmers and the industrial classes of people. This is a beautiful story, but I dare not take the time to tell it—only to say this act of Congress was signed by Lincoln. Before that time, college education in this country was patterned after that of the aristocratic society in England. Only the rich kids went to college, and it was possible to prepare for only four professions   law, medicine, theology, and teaching. The phenomenal progress in agriculture fostered by the land-grant universities is truly a miracle story and has been a most significant factor in making the United States the most efficient producer of food and other agricultural products of all nations in the world. And it has given this nation the highest standard of living of all nations in the world.

In 1800, 95 percent of our people in the United States lived on farms—only 5 percent lived in cities. In 1968 these figures were reversed. Today, it takes only about 4 percent of us to produce more than enough food for our 212 million people in the United States. My point is, if 95 percent of our people had had to dig out their own food supply, as is true in many of the underdeveloped countries, we would not have had these fantastic developments in engineering, electronics, and space technology. Our existence would still be one of drudgery and muscle-power, with little or no time for exercising brain-power.

Well, what does all this mean, when man now routinely makes more scientific progress in a month than he used to make in a century? One important factor is that man's economic, political, and social patterns have not kept pace with the scientific progress in a world that has changed drastically. They are leftovers from the age of muscles. We have not kept pace with the technological age in our ability to get along with our neighbor, in our honesty and integrity in government, or in our Christian commitment or moral character.

Man now has the know-how to create a world of sufficiency. We can produce enough food to feed the world. The problems are who would pay for it and how to distribute it. The limiting factor to adequate food is not science and technology—but social, economic, and political concepts that have changed little since the day of sailing ships. These are barriers that challenge your generation—but barriers are not new!

Throughout history, man's resistance to change, in a constantly changing world, has frequently made stumbling blocks out of scientific advancements that should have been stepping stones. For example, steam was first used to fire cannons, before it was used to propel locomotives; just as atomic bombs preceded atomic medicine. For this reason, some people deplore scientific achievements and label them as works of the devil. Such labels are untrue. Science itself is neither evil nor good. Science and technology have no morals or patriotism. They will work for good or evil, for friend or foe; they will wipe out polio or people, and do it with equal effectiveness. Just like a knife—it can be a murder weapon or it can save lives in the hand of a skilled surgeon.

Man must decide what to do with what has been created by God and Man. He will decide whether we will have a paradise or a hell on earth. Our future depends upon these decisions.

We are just one generation away from the twenty-first century. You in this graduating class make up the last generation for this century! You are the ones who will be firmly in charge when we reach the year 2000—in only twenty-six more years. By then you will be seated where your parents are this evening. When that time arrives, what will you be able to say that you have done to make your world, country, and community better places to live?

Your job—the job of the last generation of this century—is to preserve the peace and pioneer a better world. Neither can be done by good intentions or wishful thinking.

Down through history, Utopian dreamers have naively dreamed that it would be paradise if everyone possessed equal wealth. This has never been true, and I doubt if it ever will be. But, I submit to you that there is something of much greater value than money—you and everyone else receive exactly the same amount every day. This precious, very scarce commodity is called *time.* Every day, you, I, and every other living creature receive an allotment of 1,440 minutes. No one gets more—no one gets less.

This "time" cannot be stockpiled, loaned, or borrowed; it cannot be sold or purchased. The only thing you can do with time is use it. At the end of each day, all 1,440 minutes are gone, whether you used them foolishly or invested them wisely. Not one of those 1,440 minutes can ever be reused or relived. They are gone forever!

Yet, each day of your lives you will get a new allotment of 1,440 minutes. Use your time wisely, it is irreplaceable. A favorite saying of mine is, "Today is the first day of the rest of my life." It is never too late to make a fresh start or resolve to make self-improvement.

In speaking of time, I wish to illustrate just how precious it is. You have only 4,200 days to make your contribution through your career. That is just about twelve years. Many of you will say that you plan to be around much longer, and we hope that is true; but, let's look at the total picture.

A person who lives to be seventy years old will live 25,550 days. At eighteen years of age, 6,570 of your days will have already been deducted, leaving 18,980. You will sleep 6,327 of those days, leaving 12,653. By working eight hours per day, recreation and work will take about 4,216 days. These will be your working days to make your mark in the world. Now there are still 8,437 days left, but when you deduct time to eat, dress, bathe, and so on, you have only 4,200 days left—or the same amount of "free time" as you have worked. How you spend these twelve years will largely determine your contribution to society. You can waste the time, or you can do something to promote your work or to help your fellow man. You can let your brain run idle and become useless, or you can use it for positive, constructive thinking. For the most part, it will be your choice.

No matter what careers you choose, always have an objective; work with a purpose. Whatever work you do, it is you who will make it "exciting" or "dull." There are no dull jobs—just some dull people. If you want to associate with interesting people, start by becoming an interesting person. Regardless of your background or your ranking in class, when it comes to living your individual lives, you are always like a man who owns his own business. You are the manager; you make the decisions that will make you!

We can be grateful to God we live in a country where our vocation or position in life is not determined automatically for us. Certainly some of you will become intelligent, thinking people, who also possess the intangible but rare ability to "get things done" or "cause things to happen." No doubt others will be less constructive and less successful. But, regardless of whatever happens to you, the happening itself is of less importance than how you react to it. Events, whether seemingly good or bad, are merely rungs in the ladder of life; some people use them to climb up—others use them to go down. *Today is the first day of the rest of your life.* You should never stop striving for greater achievements. I like your motto—"The Class of '74 Has Its Dreams. Never stop dreaming and worrying to put those dreams into action."

In final, I wish to issue a strong appeal to you on behalf of an old man or an old woman. The appeal is to use your time wisely in accomplishing a meaningful mission in life. Depending on how you use your time, you can be a public benefactor or a public bum, a doctor or a drunkard, a statesman or a shoplifter, a wizard or a weakling.

That old man or old woman so vitally interested in your welfare is not your father or mother, nor your grandfather or grandmother—it is *you* in the year 2024, fifty years from now. What you do with your daily allotment of time will greatly influence what life does with you and most assuredly will have a profound effect on your happiness and contentment as a senior citizen in the improved society you built. Commencement is not an ending—the word itself means *beginning.* I wish for each of you the richest blessings in your new beginning!

❧ Appendix II ❧

The Miracle Club

As we begin a new year of 1973, some of us become more aware of the years fleeting by, and that we are moving rapidly toward a new century. In fact, we are just one generation away from the twenty-first century. The babies born today will make up the last generation of this century. So, these people plus the young people of today (those under twenty or thirty years of age) are the ones who will be in charge when we reach the year 2000.

Let's take a quick glimpse at the responsibility we are going to hand over to them in another twenty-eight years. It has been estimated that the world population will double during the last thirty years of this century. This means there will be about 7 billion people on earth in 2000, compared to 3.5 billion in 1970.

These are big figures, but what do they mean in terms of food? Stated simply, they mean that for every plate of food we have today, we will need *two* plates of food by 2000. And this staggering need would feed us only at the present level, which is not satisfactory, because there is malnutrition and rampant starvation existing in many parts of the world. Thus, to feed our population adequately

By Louis J. Boyd. Presented January 19, 1973, at the Agricultural Alumni Association Area Meeting in Statesboro, Georgia.

and provide proper nutrition in 2000, we will need *three* plates of food for every plate we have today.

Let's look at it another way. It has taken us 1,972 years to come this far in food production—that is, to produce enough food to feed us at our present level. But we must make as much progress in food production in the next 28 years as our forefathers accomplished in 1,972 years. And that will still keep us in the presence of malnutrition and starvation! If we hope to achieve proper nutrition for all people on earth, we have only 28 years to make *twice* as much progress as that made previously.

Closer to home, it is expected that we will have about 100 million more people in the United States by 2000. Still closer, it has been estimated that there will be almost 2 million more people in Georgia by the turn of the century. These figures represent a 50 percent increase over 1970 figures. So, our exploding human population will greatly expand the demand for food.

I wish to point out, however, that measures may be taken to curb the projected population increase. A definite slowing of the population increase has already been evidenced in this country. In fact, last year (1972), we had the lowest birth *rate* in the history of the United States. Three weeks ago, our U.S. population was 210 million people. During 1972 there was an increase of 1.6 million, and one-fourth of this increase was by immigration. Other countries are joining in this move to decrease population, so the increases projected in the late 1960s may not come about. It appears rather certain that there will be a sizeable net increase in population by 2000, but the magnitude may not be as great as was estimated only two years ago.

Regardless of the number of extra mouths we have to feed in twenty-eight more years, I am confident we can meet the challenge! I do *not* subscribe to the Malthusian theory, developed about 150 years ago by an Englishman named Malthus, who came up with an idea on population growth and food production. In essence, the theory states that the population will increase much more rapidly than the capability to produce food. Thus, he predicted eventual and complete famine.

In 1920, an American scientist at Johns Hopkins University stated that the United States would have a population of 197 million people, the maximum that the country could support, by 2100. The United States passed the 197 million mark in 1966. And as a result of American agriculture's advancing more in the last fifty years than in all previous years of history, we have no problem in feeding that number.

Let's take a look at what has happened in this country during the past century to foster this enviable position. One development stands out well above all others as being responsible for the tremendous progress we have made in food production. And that is the establishment of the land-grant universities. You are alumni members of the most successful club in the world—that of the land-grant university. In fact, we could rightly refer to it as the "Miracle Club."

Few people outside the academic profession really appreciate the origin of the land-grant universities. So, I would like to relate some highlights in this development.

Today's colleges of agriculture were developed as a result of the federal Land-Grant College Act (Morrill Act) in 1862, but land-grant institutions have not been solely for agriculture. From the beginning, these institutions have also developed liberal arts, engineering, home economics, business administration, and so on. The term "land-grant" is part of the description that explains the history-making procedure used by the federal government to create these institutions.

We can better understand *why* if we look back at the situation in 1850s. College education was patterned largely after that of the aristocratic society of England, composed mainly of languages and math. Only the rich kids went to college, and it was possible to prepare for four professions only—law, medicine, theology, and teaching.

In short, this did not serve the needs of a young democracy. Our country was bent on unprecedented development in engineering, business, and agriculture, and in having a well-balanced culture.

The big question was how this education could be financed. In the 1850s the nation was not wealthy, except in terms of people and land. The area west of the Mississippi River was largely unoccupied. So, the idea was to put part of this wealth of land to the service of education so that learning could be brought to the working class of people. Thus, open up college doors to the sons and daughters of the common people.

A grant of federal land was made to each state—30,000 acres for each member of Congress for each state. The land was sold (at $1.25/acre) and the money used to endow and support at least one college in each state.

Justin Morrill (Vermont) was author of the legislation. A bill was passed in 1859 but vetoed by President Buchanan (who had misgivings about its cost and constitutionality). The second measure passed in 1862 and was signed by Lincoln that year.

Thus, in the midst of the Civil War, this nation took a forward step to promote the practical education of industrial classes of people. States were to support these colleges from taxes. The University of Georgia was established in 1785 and was the first state-supported college—being established seventy-seven years before the Land Grant Act was passed.

The act of 1862 established teaching of agriculture. Research followed in 1887, and extension in 1914.

These developments have meant the difference between our country and other nations. Our tremendous progress in food production has been unequaled. And, of course, when agriculture flourishes, other developments follow. If 50 to 80 percent of the people in this country had to work directly on the farm for their food supply, then we would not have atomic scientists, space engineers, electronics, or the many luxuries we enjoy.

In 1800, 95 percent of the people in the United States lived on farms—only 5 percent lived in cities. In 1968 these figures were reversed, because the achievements in agriculture had freed so many people from the land.

We certainly don't know what will confront us at the turn of the next century. But I honestly don't believe that food will be our limiting factor. It is much more likely that other natural resources and social services might be of greater concern. Can we provide jobs, housing, services, and so on for all the people on earth in 2000?

The prime objective of the College of Agriculture today is to pursue the same goals established more than 100 years ago, and to continue the progress that has marked the last three decades. In animal science we are attempting to look at the future in an effort to assess what needs to be done.

We are conducting a long-range study of the beef, dairy, swine, and horse industries to try to describe what we think they might look like in 1985. We are looking at population projections and trends in consumption patterns, and basing our forecasts on what has happened during the past twenty years. We are convinced that these studies will help us tool up to meet the country's needs during the next ten to fifteen years.

Once these studies are completed, we want to talk to people in industry about them. If the leaders in the swine industry agree with the projections, then we can gear our programs to cause things to happen. If they don't like what is projected, then we will have time to plan and channel our animal industries in the direction in which we think they ought to be going.

We are grateful for your support of your Alma Mater, and we solicit your continued support and encouragement as we try to continue the long-standing tradition of service to people.

❧ Appendix III ❧

Letter to
Charles Butterworth

May 1998

Dear Charles,

Since there may not be anyone else who has known you longer nor
been more closely associated for the past fifty-eight or sixty years,
it must be time for reminiscing.

I have just returned from the outside privy. Boy, the Sears catalog has some fancy-looking girdles this year! I didn't stop by the
cistern to wash my hands but they didn't look dirty. So I lit the
kerosene lamp and picked up my quill pen.

I could start with wheat threshings, suckering tobacco, making
cider, hard work, dusty roads, and watching John Tracy trying to
start his tractor, but no one else would understand nor believe it.

The first modern convenience was that sparkling yellow bicycle with all the frills on it. Compared to my plain black-and-
white bicycle, it was real mod, with the makeshift mirrors and
whistles. Those four wheels carried us lots of miles on rainy days
and Saturday afternoons. We could spend an entire afternoon at

On Charles' fiftieth wedding anniversary, May 6, 1998. (He and I grew up on adjoining
farms and married sisters.)

Brown's Grove, Howard's Store, or Darnell's Store for ten cents nursing a Double Cola with a bag of peanuts in it. Or for the same cost we could have an RC Cola and a Moon Pie—a really special treat. One Sunday afternoon stands out in my memory. I had stayed up all night Saturday night with my old great-uncle, who was a night watchman at a car lot in Mayfield next door to a hamburger drive-in. The latter was the main enticement. My folks were to pick me up on Sunday morning to go to my grandparents' house in Hickory. My uncle went to bed and I waited and waited and waited. At 11:00 A.M. I became impatient and started walking and hitchhiking home—fourteen miles. I got home alone about 4:00 P.M. on a hot summer day, put my swimming trunks on, and went to sleep on a cot out in the yard. Soon my uncle and aunt from Tri City came and woke me up. I was very sleepy, hot, tired, hungry, and quite angry and rude at being awakened. The point of that long story is that just as I woke up I saw you riding up on your yellow bicycle. So I ran in the house and changed clothes and we rode off on our bikes, leaving my uncle and aunt there in the yard. When my folks got home they still didn't know where I was but since the bike was gone no alarms were sounded.

One Saturday I went with you to Murray, where we got our first introduction to tips. We were uptown!—going into the Bluebird Café to order a Coke. The people in the booth before us had left some money on the table so we (I'm sure it was you) picked it up and kept it. We drooled over our Cokes for a long time, then left. The only trouble was—we went back about two hours later and the first thing the waitress said was that she knew we took her money from the table earlier. Great introduction to tipping—something we didn't know about at Brown's Grove or Howard's Store.

Then there were basketball games and the annual rivalry between Lynn Grove and Sedalia—also, the discovery that there were girls at both Lynn Grove and Sedalia. And then that fateful trip to Sedalia that you made with Jimmy and me. Little did I know what we were getting into—what a strange twist from all of that!

Fast-forward to August 1947, when I returned from the army and was helping you cut tobacco. We heard some tall tales from Mason Holsapple and I learned that you were going to UK in Lexington in September. I didn't have anything to do so, I decided to go to Lexington with you to look around. In late August we went outside your house early one morning with two suitcases and started hitchhiking to Lexington. About 10:00 that night we got to downtown Louisville and walked into the exclusive Brown Hotel. No rooms were available, but they finally rented us the bridal suite for $5.00—a good deal. The next day we used the secret method of eating cheaply at Walgreens, and then moved on to Lexington.

Well, much to my surprise I decided to go to UK, so I got admitted and we started looking for a house. What rat holes we looked at, and finally rented one—a single room all the way across town from the university, but only one block from Limestone where we got a bus directly to UK. What an experience at the McAfees' where we shared a bathroom with the mother and two grown children—Ann and Tommy. To get to the cold bathroom we had to go through Tommy's bedroom—every night after he went to bed and every morning before he got up. That one small room with one bed and a small table wasn't very conducive to studying.

But before we moved to Lexington we went to Nashville over Labor Day with two girls. That was a revealing trip, on the Southeastern Stages bus. We took an airplane ride and rode around in the girls' great-uncle's pickup truck to see the sights of Music City.

That fall in Lexington you gained some practice in quitting smoking. Once, you bet $5.00 that you would quit smoking and I took the bet. Two days later I met you on the sidewalk on campus and you were puffing. When I called attention to the cigarette you took off and got a job as a waiter in a Greek Restaurant to pay off the debt (but I don't remember you ever paying me!). Bear Bryant had a winning football season that fall and UK got a bowl bid. We went down one night to a pep rally at the train depot to see the team off on the special train. While there you decided to go and climbed on the train—no suitcase, no toothbrush. When you got back four days later your feet smelled even worse than usual—bad.

Our good friend Glynn Sims had a car—the little Willys—and that's how we moved to Lexington that fall. We rode lots of miles in that little car—back to Murray a few times. One rainy night when you were driving it just ran off the road near Horse Cave.

One weekend your folks and Linda came to Lexington. "Miss Palmer" and Linda stayed in the hotel while your dad shared our luxurious room. While you were out on a date your dad and I had a splendid evening at the Zebra Lounge. Buses had stopped running, so we had to walk from downtown out to Rand Avenue.

One semester was enough at the McAfees'. So after Christmas we moved to Forest Park in the house where Glynn lived—much nearer the university. Again, only a single room with one bed, and sharing the bathroom with Glynn and an older couple as the owners. It was in that house fifty years ago when you had a sudden revelation one night. It was—hey, I've got a mobile home that can be set up anytime in Mr. Palmer's trailer court, so why don't we go ahead and get married and not wait until the semester is over. After two minutes you were on the phone to the Conner residence and it was suppertime. As you popped the question with this new proposal to Linda she started crying and said "You gotta talk to my daddy." He must have agreed, because May 6, 1948, was a mighty big day—Linda's graduation at Sedalia followed by the wedding in Mayfield!

Congratulations and best wishes for many healthy, happy anniversary celebrations beyond the fiftieth!

Louie

🍂